# SPIRITUALITY
# FOR OUR
# GLOBAL
# COMMUNITY

# SPIRITUALITY FOR OUR GLOBAL COMMUNITY

## BEYOND TRADITIONAL RELIGION TO A WORLD AT PEACE

DANIEL A. HELMINIAK

ROWMAN & LITTLEFIELD PUBLISHERS, INC.
Lanham • Boulder • New York • Toronto • Plymouth, UK

ROWMAN & LITTLEFIELD PUBLISHERS, INC.

Published in the United States of America
by Rowman & Littlefield Publishers, Inc.
A wholly owned subsidary of The Rowman & Littlefield Publishing Group, Inc.
4501 Forbes Boulevard, Suite 200, Lanham, Maryland 20706
www.rowmanlittlefield.com

Estover Road
Plymouth PL6 7PY
United Kingdom

British Library Cataloguing in Publication Information Available

**Library of Congress Cataloging-in-Publication Data:**

Helminiak, Daniel A.
  Spirituality for our global community : beyond traditional religion to a
world at peace / Daniel A. Helminiak.
     p. cm.
  ISBN-13: 978-0-7425-5917-2 (cloth : alk. paper)
  ISBN-10: 0-7425-5917-3 (cloth : alk. paper)
  ISBN-13: 978-0-7425-5918-9 (pbk. : alk. paper)
  ISBN-10: 0-7425-5918-1 (pbk. : alk. paper)
  1. Spirituality. 2. Globalization—Religious aspects. I. Title.
  BL624.H3865 2008
  204—dc22                                                2007037759

Printed in the United States of America

To

Bernard J. F. Lonergan, SJ
(1904–1984)

Whose life's commitment was the understanding of
understanding itself—a topic most obscure but germane to
all human pursuit. As his graduate assistant, I was awed by
his reputation and too callow to realize his depths. Now I am
inspired as I read his words in print or catch the nuance of
his voice on audio recordings. Would that I had been mature
and wise enough back then to appreciate the beautiful and
genuine human being he was as well as

Genius for our times,
Person of striking common sense,
Ardent lover of God, Church, and Humanity, and
Unrelenting seeker of truth.

*Om Sahanā vavatu, saha-nau bhunaktu*
*Saha vīryam karvāvhai*
*Tejasvi-nā-vadhī-tamastu*
*mā vid-visāva-hai*

*Om Sāntih. Om Sāntih, Om Sāntih*


*May That One protect us and nourish us together.*
*May we work together with enhanced vigor.*
*May our learning be enlightening and fruitful.*
*My we not dislike each other.*

*Peace, Peace, Peace*

A peace invocation that appears in several of the older
Upanishads and dates back to some 5000 years. It is
traditionally recited at the start of any learning.

# Contents

# Preface

This book has been long in the making. I have files of a completed draft dated as early as 2003. Originally, this offering was to be a popular presentation of the psychology of spirituality that I had been publishing since 1981 in professional journals and technical books.* As written, this book does serve its purpose as a popularization while anyone intent on the technical details can find them in those cited volumes. But my starting this new book with a description of my childhood neighborhood quickly inclined me to focus the book on a specific problem, global community. Thus, the end result is not only a popularization of a technical theory but also a suggested solution to the most pressing challenge of our day.

The uniqueness of my suggestion is that I seriously believe I am proposing a coherent scientific explanation of spirituality and, if so, an approach relevant to every human being, every various religion, and, indeed, every secular institution and agency on the planet. Building on the breakthrough analyses of human consciousness, or spirit, that Bernard J. F. Lonergan achieved, I present spirituality first and foremost as a natural expression of our dynamic human minds and their open-ended wonder, curiosity, and love. I see spirituality—including the search for and worship of God, the pursuit of transcendent experiences, and belief in otherworldly realms and

---

*Spiritual Development: An Interdisciplinary Study* (Loyola University Press, 1987), *The Human Core of Spirituality: Mind as Psyche and Spirit* (State University of New York Press, 1996), and *Religion and the Human Sciences: An Approach via Spirituality* (State University of New York Press, 1998). Regarding community, see *One in Christ: An Exercise in Systematic Theology* (unpublished doctoral dissertation, Boston College and Andover Newton Theological School, 1979) and "Human Solidarity and Collective Union in Christ," *Anglican Theological Review*, 1988, 70, 34–59.

spiritual entities—as the expression and product of our wondrous human make-up. This is not to say such otherworldly concerns are necessarily false, mere fictions of our creative minds, but to say that the principles of correct knowing enjoy veto power over all beliefs and efforts, however sacred.

I am aware that at first blush this approach to spirituality is unappealing to many people. It seems to fall under the Bible Fundamentalists' extreme damning category of *secular humanism.* Nonetheless, although I do propose a humanism, it is unique: at its core lies the spiritual. Whether so spiritually infused a humanism could truly be merely secular is debatable. So despite the fact that most religionists might want to make their belief in God—or claimed revelation or sacred texts—the center of their spiritual world, faced with a pluralism of religions, I point out that any beliefs and claims come from our own mouths; like assertions about anything else, they enjoy no guaranteed accuracy simply because they regard religion and are made in good faith. In the competing diversity of a globalizing society, every human assertion must be subject to the scrutiny of open-mindedness, insight, honesty, and goodwill, which characterize the healthy human mind. Otherwise, fantasy and superstition reign. Even in the case of spiritual realities, the rigor of insightful and coherent thinking must prevail. Welcome or not, an unrelenting historical trend forces this novel approach upon us. Not claimed knowledge of God, but our own spiritual nature must be the beginning point for current discussion of spirituality.

From a scientific stance, as well, others would likewise protest such a this-worldly emphasis. By nature, they aver, spirituality and religion are suggestive and merely inspirational and cannot and should not become the object of scientific investigation. But again, the times force me to argue otherwise. With the advance of modern psychology and the breakthrough of Lonergan, not only are we already able to explain spirituality to a large extent, but we also realize that the personal pieties and imaginative spiritualities inherited from former eras betray us in the third millennium. Unless we can move beyond merely inspirational religion, consoling personal beliefs, cherished metaphysical claims, and self-righteous religious tactics—all the while preserving their legitimate benefits—we will never develop the consensus needed to hold our globe together. In this endeavor, science seems our best human hope.

We are in a new era. The old solutions no longer work. To a large extent, the traditional religions have become the problem. Today, even the supposed eternal verities need to be boldly re-encountered, creatively reconsidered, accurately reformulated, and responsibly re-presented. I have conscientiously intended these goals in this book. I hope that you, my fair-minded reader, will recognize this effort in these pages. Inspired by this popular presentation while trusting the technical competence behind it, may you find a new spiritual orientation in this, oh, so topsy-turvy and dangerously misguided postmodern world. May you be empowered to make your own lasting contribution to our burgeoning global community in the third millennium.

I am grateful to Anthony J. Marsella and Elena Mustakova-Possardt for their generous endorsements of this book. I am well aware that no one is likely to agree with every opinion I express on this touchy topic, so I am all the more encouraged that they would publicly stand by my work. I am also grateful to Erik Hanson, Ross Miller, John Loudon, Sarah Stanton, Nancy Driver, and the unknown others at Rowman & Littlefield who helped this book come to light after so many years of gestation. Finally, family, friends, colleagues, and even virtual strangers provided encouragement, support, input, and criticism as I worked on this book. My heart warms as I thank them, also: Luiz Amaral, Doug Bradford, Barnet Feingold, Tommy Gallick, Karen Greene, Roy Hardin, Allan Helminiak, Paul Drew Johnson, Peggy Kleinplatz, Jennifer Lemly, Raymond Machesney, Cecilia McHirella, Anne Richards, Subhas R. Tiwari, and Kevin Winters. May the goodwill behind this collective project diffuse and inform the whole planet. May there be peace on earth and rejoicing hope among whatever spiritual entities also share this universe with us.

# Introduction

## The Search for a Middle Ground

Religion used to hold communities together. In traditional societies it still does. But on a wider scale, religious diversity is fragmenting our world. The "melting pot" of the United States of America was the original experiment in secular pluralism. In it, we have a microcosm of the burgeoning world of the third millennium. What we see in it is not reassuring. Religious differences splinter this nation, and, likewise, our world is literally blowing up because of them.

An article in the April 9, 2007 issue of *Newsweek* was titled "The God Debate." It featured atheist Sam Harris—author of the best sellers *The End of Faith* and *Letter to a Christian Nation*, and the Bible-believing pastor Rich Warren—author of the international best seller *The Purpose-Driven Life*. This reported exchange revealed the intensity of those religious differences.

The topic was God, and specifically, His/Her/Its existence. A narrowness of perspective is already obvious: belief in God is just one of today's burning religious issues. Of course, "God" functions as a symbol for a package of religious beliefs, and in practice adherence to religion includes belief in God. But this identification is mistaken. Nontheist religions exist—Buddhism, Taoism, Confucianism, Shinto—and their adherents probably outnumber the world's theists. Besides, in their own way, without God the nontheists are as ethical or moral as others.

Religion, morality, and belief in God—and also life after death—are quite commonly linked, but they do not necessarily go hand in hand. Nonetheless, for most of us, they do. We collapse them all into one. To be fair, then, despite its narrow focus, that discussion about the existence of God did involve other religious topics.

The intricacies do not end there. According to the best of theology in all religious traditions, God is the Great Unknown. So any coherent debate about God must first agree on what *God* means. The *Newsweek* debate glossed over this point. Were the atheist and the theist, then, talking at cross-purposes?

Both parties did agree that God's existence cannot be proved. But now the question becomes "what would count as proof?" The atheist spoke in the name of science and a reliance on reason, but contemporary science never claims to prove anything. Rather, scientists stand by supporting evidence for "the best available opinion of the day," and they completely expect that that opinion will change or, better, be refined. No one has ever seen or could ever see the subatomic particle, the quark, but science confidently affirms that quarks exist. On the other hand, relying on personal experience and a broadly flung net of reasoning, human longing, and hope, the theist expressed firm conviction but without claiming proof.

If one probes deeply, perhaps honest theism and reasonable atheism are not so different, after all. But the very structure of this debate seemed to preclude any consensus: does God exist, yes or no? The two sides were bound to disagree.

Unfortunately, that doomed setup accurately reflects our social reality. A similar state of affairs controls our discussions at large. The times are unsettling. People are scared. Nerves are frayed. It gets hard to just hold on. We want answers. We have to act. We have no more patience for subtleties.

The accusations hurled from either side are egregious, and they call for redress. The secularists allege, "Religion is dictating curricula in our schools. Religion is undermining science and critical thinking. Religion is taking over our courts and government. Religion is fueling explosive world conflicts. Religion is spawning terrorism and violence." On the other hand, according to the religionists, "Science has undermined the dignity of 'man.' Science is destroying religion and all that we hold dear. Science supports evolution, abortion, homosexuality, stem-cell research, and divorce. Science leaves no room for the morality of our traditional way of life."

From one side or the other, it is obvious that the root of our current problems is either religion or science, unthinking fundamentalism or godless secularism, narrow-minded conservatism or wishy-washy liberalism. Yes, the setup of the *Newsweek* debate might have determined its outcome from the beginning, but that setup fairly represents the situation in which we actually live.

We are a badly divided nation: no longer the blue against the gray but now the red states and the blue. Moreover, as the world's only superpower, the United States—or history itself—is exporting secular pluralism around the globe, which is also badly divided.

Our world needs some middle ground, a common terrain on which all could stand comfortably. But when religion, God, and morality are at stake, middle ground is hard to find.

Letters to *Newsweek* in response to the debate did call for a middle ground: "spiritual but not religious." This emphasis on spirituality in our day is no accident. In the 1950s or '60s, the distinction between *religion* and *spirituality* was virtually unheard-of. But the very historical forces that are splintering our societies have also fed the mushrooming of spiritual interests. Historians know that a tumultuous age provokes intense spiritual concern, a rethinking of the basic issues, a new mining of the religious sources. Indeed, if anything will, it is spirituality that will open onto a middle ground—if only we could ever get some handle on spirituality.

But approaches to spirituality tend to succumb to the familiar either/or treatment: religion or science. A truly new approach is a rarity. We in the West are uncomfortable conceiving of spirituality apart from God. To bracket religion is easy enough; to remove God from our equation is nigh impossible. So most appeals to nonreligious spirituality still rest on some belief in God—or the Goddess, a Higher Power, the Sacred, the All, or some other vaguely conceived otherworldly entity. Spirituality in this guise is but a watered-down version of Western religion.

On the other hand, some innovative approaches to spirituality rely on contemporary science, usually quantum physics, plus a good dose of esoteric Eastern philosophy, which introduces the notion of an all-pervasive power, force, or "energy" that might or might not, again, qualify as the Western God. But quantum physics remains riddled with questions even for true scientists; naturally, lay people hardly understand its complexities at all. Thus, the imponderables of quantum physics provide the perfect playing field for creative imagination and spiritual fantasy, and our media abound with offerings of "science-based spirituality"—for example, *What the #$\*! Do We Know!?*—that rest on misunderstandings, misapplications, and scientific half-truths. Spirituality in this guise is but a fictionalized version of science.

Ah, alas, there they are again—two forces competing for allegiance in our day, science and theism, both offering spiritual visions that amount to more of the same. In place of church and weekly services, collections, and doctrines, we have spiritual circles and book clubs, high-priced boutiques, costly lectures, and New Age affirmations. In place of the mystery of the Trinity, we have dark matter, wormholes, and ubiquitous presence via travel at the speed of light. In place of Bibles, revelation, and infallible popes, we have intuitions, psychics, channeled readings, and privileged access to libraries in the sky. In place of angels, saints, and reincarnated bodhisattvas, we have the reassuring presence of extraterrestrials, who covertly watch over and guide us, waiting till our world comes to its senses. Still unable to face squarely the realities of the human condition—limitation, disappointment, illness, aging, uncertainty, death—we find new creeds to take away the challenge of life and guarantee this-worldly fulfillment and eternal bliss hereafter.

Be that as it may, attention to the spiritual does hold our best hope for a middle ground. The key to finding it is to direct our search toward what truly lies in the middle. Between science and theism, stretched in both directions as in the *Newsweek* debate—there in the middle we find . . . ourselves, us human beings, spiritual in our very makeup. We humans mark ground zero.

It is the very longing of our souls that leads us to discover and affirm the Divine. It is the very outreach of our minds that urges us to understand our reality through scientific method. The very same self-transcending dynamism that makes us persons—the wonder, the awe, the question, the outreach, the longing, the desire, the love—is itself the ground of our spirituality and the basis of both religion and science. Delineate the human spirit and remain open to its unfolding, and you have a cross-cultural, universally valid, human basis for a "generic spirituality" that opens onto an array of religious expressions and powers our secular pursuits.

A spirituality grounded in the human spirit

- Meets the empirical criteria of science because it appeals to a facet of reality that is available to everyday-ordinary human experience.
- Opens onto belief in God because the spirit's infinitely open capacity points ultimately toward some ideal fulfillment.
- Provides the guidelines for genuine morality because the spirit's very inclination is toward positive and secure growth.
- Relates to all the religions of the world because it explicitly focuses on that which lies at the heart of religion.
- Applies equally to secular agencies because it springs from the very people who constitute them and the people whom the agencies serve.
- Engages nonreligious and even antireligious folk because it rests on this-worldly humanity, not on a proposed otherworldly being.
- Embraces every human being because, carefully and conservatively developed, it includes only what is common to all humanity, only what any person of goodwill could abide in good conscience.

This is the vision of *spirituality for our global community* that I propose in this book. I not only propose it but also concretely sketch its implementation. Humbly but boldly, I share what I think is an original perspective on globalization. I base my offering and my optimism on the incisive analyses of consciousness of the late Canadian philosopher/theologian Bernard Lonergan

(1904–1984), whom *Newsweek* (April 29, 1970, p. 75) portrayed as the Saint Thomas Aquinas of the twentieth century and for whom I was a teaching assistant at Boston College.

This vision represents a middle path that weaves between the screeching preaching of hardcore, self-validated religion and the dead-end materialism of rationalistic, reductionistic secularism. At issue is not the oppositional question, "Does God exist, yes or no?" set up such that any hope of consensus is doomed from the start. Nor is the issue the simplistic dichotomy of religion versus science, or the spiritual versus the material, or faith versus reason, or this world versus some world to come. Emanating directly from the epicenter of human spiritual capacity, by its very nature this vision pertains to every person, religion, culture, community, institution, and nation in the human family. Presuming, of course, open-mindedness, honesty, and good will—what hope have we otherwise?—this vision truly offers a unique prospect for peace.

Share this vision with me, dear reader, to the extent that you are able. This vision means only to express the very best in ourselves. Let our meeting of minds begin a new era for planet Earth.

# 1

## The Current Cultural Crisis

"The best of times" and "the worst of times"—with these words Charles Dickens described the French Revolution. These words describe our era, too, but a new brand of social upheaval.

Unstoppable historical trends are breaking down national boundaries. Near-instantaneous electronic communication, fast and easy travel, multinational economic ventures, and globally marketed entertainment draw in all peoples toward that ever longed-for "one human race." We are becoming a global community.

Yet the onrush is overwhelming. It sweeps away the variety that is the spice of life: the variegated beauty of fascinating peoples and intriguing nations. The changes come too fast. The loss of inherited cultures and the uprooting from land and home frighten the human heart and stun the collective psyche. Responding in kind, crazed terrorism threatens to blow our world apart. Religions that used to bond individual peoples now breed hateful hostility. The very gods of the different nations all lose credibility; science and comparative studies reduce them all to the same level and grant them the dubious status of "myth," if not fantasy.

In this wrenching status quo, what overarching vision could inspire global harmony? The visions followed thus far—the beliefs of traditional religions—now breed competition and fuel conflicting agendas. In itself, each shrinks to pettiness in light of global realities. Alas, the hope for world unity could devolve into a Star Wars nightmare.

This state of affairs weighs heavy on me. I gave my life to religion. I had a dream. I sang of "peace on earth, goodwill toward men." Now my religion-inspired dream tempers my vows to religion. Now I pull back from religious institutions and dutiful, pious practice. These, I used to think, had

1

the answer. Now, I search out the one life source that must flow through all the religions. Head aswirl, I plumb uncharted depths—the depths of religion, yes, but more so, the depths of the human heart and mind.

If only we could discern a faith-and-love code that any person of goodwill could embrace by dint simply of being a human being! Then—only then, it seems—would we have a rock-bottom foundation, our common humanity, on which to build a global community. If this foundation was spiritually genuine, it would support, as well, any religion that is truly worthy of the name. On this foundation, peoples, cultures, religions, governments, corporations, secular agencies, all could support and work toward global harmony.

I believe such a foundation exists, and in this book, I propose it. I believe that there exists a viable basis for global community. Community is real. I have tasted it. I know community. It is inconceivable to me that so basic a human longing and need would be impossible to attain.

Therefore, dear reader, I share my conviction optimistically. Please, do not write me off as a dreamer, an idealist, a congenial fool. I ask only your open-mindedness, your honesty, and goodwill. Follow along with me. See if you might not agree. Even as hard-nosed, pragmatic, and somewhat jaded adults, we can—somehow we must—"get back to the garden."

## THE LOST PARADISE

I grew up in a world that was safe and secure. There, in my neighborhood and city, we all knew who we were and how we fit. We belonged. Life's meaning was clear; its values were strong. Religion guided the way. Our religion did what religion is meant to do—*re + ligare*, from the Latin, to tie back, to restrain: religion held us in place; it held us together; it gave us a common vision and purpose. Our perspective was broad; it reached around the globe and beyond, all the way to heaven and life hereafter. Our goals were lofty. People were good. Life was simple, if not always easy. Our neighborhood was truly a community.

That was South Side Pittsburgh in the 1940s and '50s, home of Jones and Laughlin Steel. People made a good, honest living in the mills. No one I knew—except the priests and the nuns—had ever been to college. No one in my family had ever finished high school. But the people were intelligent, thoughtful, and shrewd. They knew how to make life work.

People were proud of their homes and their neighborhood. They took care of them. On Saturday mornings in summertime, they washed down their front steps and swept their sidewalks. They helped one another, especially the elderly, shovel snow, and the men organized crews to clear hilly Pittsburgh streets in the wintertime.

Almost everybody in that Polish community was Catholic, and life revolved around the local parish. The church bells rang the Angelus as a call to prayer at six a.m., noon, and six p.m. every day. The bells tolled at funerals. On Sundays, the bells sang out a symphony of sounds, summoning people to Mass. Neighbors met and talked as they walked to church, and later they congregated in front of the church before going their separate ways after Mass, the women near the church steps, the men across the street in front of the war memorial.

Everyone knew everyone else. They all had strange sounding names—Szymkowiak, Barszczowski, Wesolowski, Ruszala, Pokora, Balmunczek, Janiak—which we took for granted although I was never able to connect the names with the faces as accurately as the grownups did. We kids had adults watching out for us, and watching over us, everywhere in the neighborhood. They would call us on misbehavior, and, although we grumbled, we listened to them; and our parents would always find out about the incidents.

We all attended the parish school. We walked in church processions, brought flowers for the classroom altar, and contributed nickels and dimes for missionary efforts to "ransom pagan babies." Each Sunday of the month was assigned as "Communion Sunday" for a particular group—the Women's Sodality, the Men's Holy Name Society, the Choir and Ushers Club. To prepare for Communion, people had to go to confession at least once a month: there was subtle but firm social pressure to stick with the program.

When we kids hit adolescence, we began to go our separate ways, and our world broadened a bit. My family exemplified the narrow range of our diversity: my sister went to St. Casmir's High School, I went to St. Michael's, and my brother, to South Vocational High. Even so, we were all part of the same neighborhood mix that made up the "Sa-side." Petty ethnic rivalries and interschool competitions were ripples on a pond in comparison to the monolithic worldview and consistent values that were sunk deep in that world of yesteryears.

## THE BREAKDOWN OF COMMUNITY

Sometimes I think that I was caught up in a time warp, that my community was mysteriously preserved from the shifting sands of time, which now blow like biting desert storms. I feel as if I grew up in a small European village, not in a major American city. I find it hard to identify with acquaintances who take television, cars, and shopping malls for granted. I came from the "old world." I came from a different world. Sometimes I feel like Robert Heinlein's *Stranger in a Strange Land*.

It is hard for me to understand the world in which we now live—not simply because today's world is different nor simply because today's world is so complex, but more so, I fear, because today's world just does not make sense. This world's cynicism and despair have even given up caring about making sense. This world trashes the environment and risks long-term survival for the sake of immediate gratifications; its recreations are more often self-destructive than not; its speed is assaultive; its mobility prevents rooting; its pace precludes thought or musings; its mechanization eliminates wonder; its insistence on procedures produces automatons; its pseudo-sophistication prevents bonding; its urgency instills anxiety; its unrealistic expectations induce depression. And its ultimate purpose promises only more of the same.

In contrast to the community of my youth, our world has no grand vision. It offers nothing lasting for which to work, nothing honestly worth dying for. I am left to wonder, "What do we really believe? What do we think is important? What meaning is life supposed to have in this 'postmodern' society? What common commitments do we share? Do we believe in anything of grandeur? Do we actually hold to noble values?" I fear we are adrift. Without unity of mind and heart, how can we ever experience community—in a neighborhood, across a nation, and, indeed, around the globe?

Oh, to be sure, our lives entail many a wondrous and beautiful experience—above all, precious moments with dear friends, family, and lovers. Besides, there is still music, art, science, and poetry, and television extravaganzas and big-screen movies with mesmerizing scenes, and stars, sky, seas, and mountains, and skylines, grand hotels, Bohemian neighborhoods, and jewel-chained cities viewed from night-flying planes.

Still, these moments are few. They are precious for that very reason. The pace of our daily living snuffs them out or truncates them. We have structured a society, at least it seems so to me, that substitutes the mechanics of comfortable living for the richness of human experience. This setup simply makes no sense. The human psyche is not designed to survive it. Quite literally, it is crazy-making. Those who are well-adjusted to it might as well be deranged. No truly healthy person could adjust to it for long. It is living that does not give life.

Maybe, I sometimes think, maybe my childhood experience was just like everybody else's. Maybe childhood cradles us all in safe and secure spaces. Maybe, as adults, we all move into a competitive and fragmented world, and life inevitably becomes a challenging struggle for survival. Maybe nostalgically we all long for a world that still makes sense, where all of life holds together, where you feel as if you belong to something bigger than yourself and you know that everybody else is also part of the whole.

Maybe . . . but I don't think so. More likely, something unprecedented is unfolding in today's world.

The adults whom I knew as a child had a sense of community that I seldom see any more—warm greetings on the street, respect for property and privacy, willingness to help in a pinch. They retained that outlook even to their deaths, just recent years ago. Likewise, my contemporaries who never moved from Pittsburgh still know that community feeling. They can name it, and they lament its passing—especially when they see the old neighborhoods break down as the senior generation dies off and transient strangers, committed to schooling or jobs, move in to rent the renovated homes.

On the other end of the spectrum, the young people I meet today or teach in college, many of them, simply don't grok the communal togetherness that I just described. When pressed, they'll recall a childhood friend with whom they were close, a grandmother who made them feel special, or a church group to which they belonged. They remember isolated experiences of camaraderie, but they knew no whole world to which they belonged. They had no overarching purpose for living, no inspiring connection to a shared vision. Their lives seem to be but bits and pieces that happenstance holds together. Their experiences make up their lives only because these experiences happen to be part of their biography. There is no coherence, no meaning, no unifying storyline.

They come from broken families and at age twenty already know broken dreams. They had friends who suicided in high school or died in auto crashes. They are divorced or unmarried parents. Some struggle with addictions or have already been through rehab. Others live for weekends of "partying"—a euphemism for drinking and drugging. Their goals, if they have any, are small: to land a lucrative job, own a nice car, get good sex, maybe someday settle down and raise a family but, in any case, have fun and "enjoy life."

The ones who have some inkling of belonging to a bigger world usually grew up with a strong religious background, but many of these are fundamentalists, smiling mechanically on the outside but secretly close-minded and self-protective inside, holding on for dear life to whatever beliefs they have left. Or else, now open-eyed and disillusioned, they are totally turned off by the religion of their upbringing, and without a spiritual compass, they dabble in whatever esoteric faith systems they come across. Or else they outrightly profess to be agnostic, certain already at age twenty-two that nothing can be known for certain—and oblivious or indifferent to the self-contradiction in their position.

My graduate students inevitably protest when I make such sweeping statements. I must admit I am perhaps exaggerating or projecting unfair

generalizations. Yet often at the end of a semester, having felt the remarkable community in our MA program, those students privately confess that
they begin to think I'm right. Then it is I who am left wondering. "Well, yes,
I believe so," I think. But then again . . . how could they really know? How
could they understand my point about what they never experienced, or
miss from their lives what they never had? Then I recall that the longing for
belonging is natural to the human soul. Without ever tasting its fulfillment,
one could still feel and identify the hunger. Our world does neglect the
soul—no question there!

We no longer live in the world I once knew. It no longer exists. We have
no shared vision and virtues. Things have changed.

## POLITICAL AND SOCIAL SIGNS OF THE BREAKDOWN

We can chronicle that change or, at least, point to some of its markers. The
World Wars, for example, were a watershed. The social changes they
brought on prepared the ground for more upheavals to come. The uprooting and military mobilization of countless citizens, the mixing of classes,
genders, and races, the soldiers' experiences of other countries—"How ya
gonna keep 'em down on the farm/After they've seen Pa-ree?"—the employment of women outside the home, the mushrooming of industry, the
ensuing American sense of power and intoxicating invulnerability—all
these effects of war transformed the underlying social base of our society.
The conservatism of the 1950s, the "McCarthy era," attempted to put the lid
back on that Pandora's box, but there is no holding back social change once
it is triggered. So the sexual revolution of the 1960s and '70s erupted, and
the civil rights movements emerged in force—black, feminist, Native American, gay and lesbian, handicapped, transsexual, intersex.

The Vietnam War played a key role in the changes that were happening. Not
only were Americans unsure about what we were fighting for in Vietnam—and
now, again, in Iraq—people also easily saw through the official rhetoric of
"preserving democracy" and "defending freedom." As always, there were
cruder motives at stake: oil, money, and political power. People and their
freedoms seemed not really to matter unless they were our people or, more
accurately, certain moneyed segments of our people. These realities were becoming painfully clear, so, when the United States lost the war, patriotism—
belief in our country—suffered a double blow. Not only did we lose, but we
also recognized that much of what we stood for was a sham. In some way,
in the minds of many people, we were on the wrong side: we were on the
side that was wrong. As a result, many people, including disdained veterans,
found it hard to believe any more.

The crass economic values that control America were surfacing for all to see. The financial bottom line was turning out always to be "the bottom line," and the value of money and power was in conflict with deeper American values such as equality before the law, "certain inalienable rights," equal opportunity, and "government of the people, by the people, and for the people." That the wealthiest nation ever to exist on the face of the earth has infants suffering from malnutrition, children unable to read or write, people sleeping on the streets, and elderly persons dying from lack of medical attention is a scandal beyond proportions. Our inability to guarantee workers' earned pensions, to secure Social Security, to respond effectively to natural disasters, or to provide quality education and universal health care—and the transparent financial focus of HMOs, as mythologized in the movie *John Q* and documented in the movie *Sicko*—demonstrate that, despite all private efforts and rhetoric to the contrary, as a nation we care more for profits than for people. After the boom of the '90s, the financial debacles of the fledgling twenty-first century—Enron, Arthur Anderson, MCI WorldCom, Martha Stewart, Hewlett-Packard—raised a disturbing question: do we lack the basic honesty and minimal goodwill required to keep even a capitalist society functioning effectively?

The court-appointed presidency of George W. Bush further weakened faith in our public system. No matter which candidate a person supported in the 2000 presidential election, the fact remains that the American people—those who still thought it worth voting—were split down the middle in hostile disagreement over the candidates and the election's outcome. The intensity, negativity, and animosity of the subsequent presidential campaign in 2004 showed that the differences remained as deep as ever or had grown deeper. The Democratic sweep of the Congress in the 2006 mid-term elections might be just another sign of disillusionment, the reluctant realization of a betrayal of hope against hope that we could be secure again, that tough talk and military might could keep us safe. We live with opposing views about the conflicts in the Middle East, religious differences over sexual and medical practices, the now taken-for-granted division among states as "red" or "blue," unprecedented deficit spending linked with diminished services and benefit cuts for the needy, conflict over personal privacy and civil rights versus the need for national security, and the escalating stridency of wearying debates between conservatives and liberals. These facts suggest that America is profoundly fragmented. We seem no longer to be one people, if we ever were, but a collection of groups who are managing somehow to coexist under one tottering system.

That point came home to me when I recently served on a jury. The case was in traffic court, and the jury was hung. We split cleanly along racial lines. The differences were not of opinion and judgment, but of perception itself. It was as if we were not talking about the same case. What was clear evidence to one group was dubious testimony to the other. At first baffled by the situation, I later came to think that the blacks, with their history of social oppression, were cautiously reluctant about trusting the "justice" system while the privileged whites were willing to give the system the benefit of the doubt.

Because of my jury experience, I also understand better why blacks and whites were so divided over the O. J. Simpson trials. Moreover, the more I live in the South, the more I am sympathetic to my black fellow jurors. I now know, for example, about the "D.W.B." infraction—Driving While Black—and I have personally experienced its force. I have learned to come to a full stop at every stop sign and to drive strictly within the speed limit when a black friend is following behind. I can afford to bend the rules, but, if he tries to keep up with me, he will be stopped and ticketed, no questions asked.

We live in different worlds, white and black, and brown, yellow, and red. This division is only one example of the splintering of our society. There are also differences between women and men, between rednecks and white collar workers, between gays and straights, between skinheads with their paramilitary groups and the standard forces of law and order, between "bag" women and men milling on the streets and the "productive citizens" driving those streets or holed up in high-rises along those streets. The prejudices that thrive in our society are not just personal matters. In many ways, they are built into the system: inequalities of race, class, region, employment, educational opportunity, and medical care. The whole world witnessed this American disgrace in televised reports of Hurricane Katrina: for the most part, the neglected were African American. The inequities sustain the different worlds for different people. In this regard, I have pondered the words of Madonna's song: "Do you know how it feels for a girl in this world?" And I realized that I do not know. Nor do I know how it feels for so many others.

Our very being urges us to make sense of things; we cannot live facing sheer absurdity. So we find meaning. We concoct meaning, if necessary. With different experiences, different groups of people must develop different visions and hold to different values in order to survive. The priorities of the street people are a far cry from those of the business executive. Likewise, life for me and mine does not mean what it does for those others. When the differences become grave, community breaks down. Then we may be living at the same time and in roughly the same place, but we no longer share the same life. We do not live for the same reasons.

Historian Arnold Toynbee produced a multivolume study of the rise and fall of civilizations. One sign of decline, he wrote, is that the society's leaders cease being creative and function with worn-out ideas while a growing majority of the population quietly withdraws its allegiance from the society and its decaying leadership. Part of the withdrawn majority consoles itself by turning to ardent religion and esoteric spiritual pursuits. Others effectively break off from society. As Toynbee phrased it, these latter revert to "barbarian tactics." They live on the fringes of society, they support it only to the extent that it still benefits them, they disregard laws and conventions, and they bide their time, waiting for the collapse. Then they will take what is left of value and secure for themselves what life they can. They have no real investment in the society.

I see forebodings of such decline in the happenings of our everyday lives. There is the surge of interest in religion—unthinking fundamentalism, mistrust of scientific reasoning, exploration of mysticism, an explosion of spiritual writings, the attraction of promising gurus, the multiplication of religious movies and TV shows, and the decline of mainline faiths. On the other hand, there are hordes of homeless people roaming the streets of our cities, paramilitary groups practicing resistance to federal control, a majority of American citizens who do not bother to vote, and waves of disenchanted youth, often privileged and educated, for whom selective anarchy is a virtue.

## THE CHALLENGE OF UNITY IN A PLURALISTIC SOCIETY

I am speaking of politics, economics, and social change, not of religion at all. Yet religion and spirituality is supposed to be my topic. Have I lost focus? Should I not mix religion and politics? Am I off the point? No way! My point is precisely that all social cohesion depends on the same mechanism— whether people are members of a secular nation, a globalizing world, or only a religious neighborhood like South Side Pittsburgh.

Most fundamentally, the beliefs and values that people share are what holds them together. But beliefs and values come in many guises. The beliefs and values of the jet-setters, of street gangs, financial planners, or sports enthusiasts, whether explicit or assumed, whether compatible with religion or not, are beliefs and values, nonetheless. They give meaning to people's lives, and they hold communities together—just as surely as a shared religion does. A challenge to societal beliefs shakes a people as much as losing one's religious faith might. Indeed, in earlier societies, religion and society were coterminous. The duties of religion and the duties of citizenship were one and the same. For this reason, for example, refusing to reverence the Roman gods, the early Christians faced execution for treason; their crime was subverting the state. The current phrase "for God and country" still captures this homogenous perspective.

In a pluralistic society, however, religions are many, and the state is religiously neutral. Religion cannot be the glue of society. No one's religious practice can bond him or her with all others—of course not: Muslims, Jews, and Christians keep Friday, Saturday, or Sunday holy, and they do penance during Ramadan, Yom Kippur, or Lent, respectively. In such a situation, only the rituals of public holidays and the sharing of civil responsibilities can foster overarching social cohesion. Secular beliefs and national values, common understandings and commitments, must form the societal bonds, and patriotism can even function as religious zealotry: "My country, love it or leave it!" Whether secular or religious, beliefs and values function in the same way.

Recently, the diversity in society seems to have overwhelmed our communalities, and maintaining unity becomes increasingly difficult. Although we live in the same country and work under the same public system, on the deepest level we might not hold the same beliefs or cherish the same values. What is law and order to some is oppression and injustice to others. What is the requirement of prosperity to some is the loss of quality of life to others. What is clever entrepreneurship to some is environmental insanity to others. What is prescribed by God's very word to some is prejudice and small-mindedness to others. What are despicable lies or deliberate misinformation to some is simply "spin" or expected "politics as usual" to others. As the visiting French diplomat Alexis de Tocqueville argued in 1835, such deep-seated conflict might well be the inevitable consequence of "the American experiment." Yet the experiment of pluralism is now social reality on a global scale. Can we actually maintain social coherence in the face of ethnic, cultural, and religious pluralism? Tocqueville was not optimistic.

The verdict of history is still out. Nonetheless, in recent decades, the unity of mind and heart that had held the United States together as a people has begun to fragment. This same trend is occurring in other nations, as well, in both the older, established countries and the newly emerging states. All are experiencing the centrifugal forces of pluralism—as is, indeed, also the "global community" as a whole. What is happening on a smaller scale within individual nations now applies on a worldwide scale among the nations. On a shrinking planet, the challenge is no longer merely to keep a neighborhood together, or even a nation, but to structure a community of the whole human race.

Maintaining social unity calls for a shared system of beliefs and values, and in a pluralistic society these must be nonreligious—something that Tocqueville was unable to imagine and that we have yet to develop. With this book, I intend to propose such a system. I have realized that the beliefs and values of any society are parallels to religion's beliefs and values, and I have recognized the essential role that shared beliefs and values, of whatever kind, play in holding people together. It seems to me, therefore, that what our nation and world need is a set of beliefs and values that any person of goodwill could embrace. I propose this generic solution, but not only it. I also suggest specifically what these common beliefs and values must likely include, and I explain why. My ambitious project is to supply a viable spiritual basis for a genuine global community in a secular and pluralistic world.

## THE BLESSING AND CURSE OF TECHNOLOGY

The recent rise of technology is another key feature of the social changes I am chronicling. Surfing the Internet can bring home what I mean. There are so many different sites for people of so many different interests that no one person can possibly be familiar with them all. No one can bridge the cultural divides. Some of the sites portray valuable and accurate information; some solicit adherents to their particular worldviews; some are downright frightening in their purposes; some are unbelievably narrow and misinformed in their outlooks; and many are out simply to make a buck. People can "hang out" on those sites and spend all their leisure time in those virtual worlds. Those worlds become the real world for those who live in them, but what connection those worlds or their inhabitants have with others is hard to know.

The blessing of this technological marvel is that the Internet caters to a virtually unlimited variety of interests and tastes—just as do the hundreds of channels available on television, the thousands of musical recordings for sale and DVDs for rental, and the millions of books on the shelves of libraries and bookstores or in the listings of Internet sites. The Internet offers something for everyone, and awesomely it links people of common interests in cyber communities that cut across boundaries of culture, politics, and geography. Cell phones also serve the purpose of linking together people who are physically far apart. To some extent, technology offers a solution to the problems that technology itself creates. In its own way, it allows the communication, builds the community, and provides the person-to-person contact that this postmodern world otherwise prevents.

Yet there is the curse of our technological world. Following their individual proclivities, mentally people live farther and farther from one another, and, although they might be next-door neighbors, they grow ever more intellectually and emotionally distant. They all inhabit different worlds—which may be nothing new, because neighbors today, even those on the same street or in the same building or complex, are as likely as not to even know one another. Besides, there is a serious question whether virtual communities meet the human need for togetherness. Mammals are built for physical closeness; the very regulation of our brain function depends on it. A greeting over the phone or an animated birthday card via e-mail is a poor substitute for a warm embrace or the skin-to-skin contact of a sleep companion. Intellect and language may be among the greatest of human gifts, but intellectual sharing at a distance through mere words is no substitute for emotional and physical togetherness.

## THE ONGOING CHALLENGE OF REGROUPING

We profess the United States to be "one nation, under God." More realistically, the unity of the nation—as far as beliefs and values go, the things that "God" stands for—is oftentimes only a veneer over a hodgepodge of diversity and festering oppositions. Of late, the actual religious character of our differences has come blatantly into view. Even belief in God is an explicit part of the debate—over abortion, evolution, homosexuality, comatose patients, stem cell research, the Pledge of Allegiance, and the location of Ten Commandments monuments. But no one ever asks "whose God?" or "which version of 'God'?" We maintain the illusion that we all believe, or, at least, *should* believe, in God.

Of course, America did pull together after the terrorist attacks on September 11, 2001. Traditional American communal values surfaced again. People of all classes, races, and religions had suffered in the attacks, so all were respected, and all were publicly defended. Besides, all were needed for the "war effort," so all—except, perhaps, Muslims and gay Arabic specialists in the military—were again deemed worthy. The surest way to unite any people is to confront them with a common enemy: give them a shared vision and purpose.

However, the national unity that resulted from the terrorist attacks did not last. Its waning only intensified the poignancy of fragmentation that burdens the national psyche. Within months after the attacks, the same differences in values that existed before 9/11 began to resurface. After the hymns were sung, the poetry read, and the dead publicly grieved, the de facto American values reigned again: the solution to the terrorist problem was to be increased shopping and military might. Our knee-jerk reaction was true to form. We would counter terrorism with militarism and economic influence. Ironically, the terrorists attacked symbols of these very values on 9/11: the Pentagon and the World Trade Center. Although the solution of the terrorists holds no promise of global peace, with keen insight they pinpointed as problematic the crass materialism and moral bankruptcy of the United States. Falling back on these would likewise hardly offer a promising solution.

There is no doubt that the United States has been exporting corrosive consumerism internationally and, in the process, subverting the traditional way of life of many peoples. Perhaps this trend is just the unavoidable outworking of historical forces. Still, rain forests, ancient cultures, and political regimes tragically continue to fall, all in the service of "economic progress" and under the name of "freedom" and "democracy." Truth be told, traditional values worldwide collapse in the wake of greed and materialism. Multinational corporations more and more govern the world, so the commitment of people to one another in close-knit communities or even in nations withers away. The breakdown of community that has occurred in this country is becoming the norm around the world.

## A CRISIS OF MEANING AND VALUES

I am not placing responsibility for these happenings on any one person, group, or factor in particular. The phenomenon I am sketching is complex and far-reaching—historical, cultural, economic, political, technological, psychological. In many ways in the long run, it represents an inevitable and hope-filled human tendency toward a truly global community; it moves toward the unity of the human race. In the short run, however, and until we come to grips with the historical process in which we are caught up, the practical effect is the disruption of people's ways of life and the offering of trivialities in return—like trinkets given to Native Americans in exchange for their sacred homelands. No wonder some people are reacting with desperate and insane retaliation. No wonder terrorism has become a worldwide threat. Caught in the path of a heartless political and economic juggernaut, the poor and disenfranchised peoples have no other recourse. They panic because their worlds are falling apart—just as my childhood world has slipped irrevocably toward oblivion.

The culture shift that I discern in my own life story, the loss of shared meaning and values, is now not only a national but also an international phenomenon. Also on a global scale, the forces that have traditionally bound people in community are dissolving.

Whether or not you agree with my analyses, dear reader, whether you share my understandings and commitments, my point remains. You may not agree, but others do agree—and sometimes adamantly so on either side. The upshot is that, as a society, we lack consensus on fundamental issues.

This state of affairs constitutes a crisis. A nation and world that share no bedrock consensus cannot long endure.

## INADEQUATE OPTIONS:
## TOLERANCE, DICTATORSHIP, BANALITY

Of late, we have appealed to tolerance to hold society together. We cry "Tolerance!" to maintain peace when unresolved differences begin to emerge. But tolerance alone is not an adequate basis for community. Tolerance is only as powerful as the higher values to which it appeals—like peace. Yet

peace at all costs can become intolerable and especially when being tolerant of others means approving of, or at least allowing, what you hold to be
profoundly wrong. The current struggle over abortion offers a clear case in
point. When abortion is the topic, tolerance breaks down, and in the name
of goodness and virtue, clinics get bombed, people get murdered, or letters
containing what appears to be anthrax arrive in the mail. The attack on the
World Trade Center is another case in point. Threatened, people go to outrageous extremes to defend their beliefs and commitments. Tolerance is a
flimsy shield for protecting community.

A common vision and shared values are needed for community. People
bond because they have a collective understanding about life and hold similar commitments. Such sharing unites people as they work toward common goals and maintain mutually inspiring dreams. Apart from these, only
a totalitarian regime could secure the "peace." Apart from shared vision,
dictatorship becomes the most viable option. Case in point: it may well
have been the wiser choice to have left Saddam Hussein in power; at least
he held volatile, sectarian Iraq together.

I do see one other option in the current dilemma. To preserve peace and
tolerance without a common vision and without dictatorship, a society
could turn to banality. Refraining from raising serious questions or from pursuing issues of any real substance, a society could extend its life by remain-
ing utterly superficial. The ready availability of drugs—on the street, over the
counter, or by prescription—and an abundance of frivolous entertainment—
sports, TV sitcoms, reality shows, blockbuster movies, concerts, and festivals
as well as clothes, cars, cuisine, and travel—would facilitate such a culture of
banality. The strategy is to keep the populace distracted and unthinking, burdened by the mere need to make a living or preoccupied with a whirlwind
of activities, so that serious questions about life and its meaning never get a
chance to arise. This strategy was that of the decaying Roman Empire: give
the people more circuses. This strategy also seems to describe much of contemporary American life as decreasing educational standards and increasing
entertainment options now define "the good life."

However, again it is doubtful that such a strategy could be successful in
the end. People inevitably think, boredom sets in, the heart aches for fulfillment. Then conspiracies form, uprisings occur, and the banal is seasoned
with blood. Then a military or police force must step in to restore "the
peace," and totalitarian dictatorship rounds the corner.

In the end, the options seem to be two: dictatorship or societal consensus. Sometimes it seems that the United States, as bully of the world, is opting for dictatorship. But only consensus has a promising future, so the possibility of such consensus is the focus of this book. Yet, for the present, we
have no consensus, we think and act in diversity, and our diverse visions
and virtues often conflict. Thus, we are at a crisis.

## A SPIRITUAL CRISIS

This crisis is spiritual. It is a crisis of *meanings and values*—or, said otherwise, a crisis of

- credos and commitments, or
- beliefs and ethics/morality, or
- understandings and evaluations, or
- ideas and ideals, or
- visions and virtues, or
- dreams and promises.

With this list of paired nouns, I am stretching to express the same idea. In one way or another, more or less, all these pairs are synonyms. They also parallel another well-known pair,

- knowledge and love,

which relates to still another familiar pair,

- intellect and will.

The ancient and medieval philosophers of the Western tradition saw the intellect and will as the highest faculties of the human mind or soul. They would even say that these dimensions of the mind are *spiritual*, that they constitute the *human spirit*. As products of the human spirit, the other items in that list would also be spiritual: knowledge and love, ideas and ideals. These transcend space and time, and they are impalpable, yet they are real, powerful, and active. They are nonphysical realities. Nonetheless, we may not readily recognize them as strictly spiritual. We may not because we tend to associate spirituality with religion and God, not with the human mind. Besides, our topic has been secular society and global politics, not religion at all.

Hopefully, however, at least these realities—meanings and values or ideas and ideals or visions and virtues—now do seem to apply to what I wrote about my religious childhood community as well as about our secular nation and world. The sharing of meanings and values is a thread that runs throughout, whether the discussion is about my Catholic neighborhood or our pluralistic world. Something similar winds through both cases. Moreover, terms such as *credos, beliefs, ideals, ethics, morality,* and *virtues* call up religious associations. My legitimate use of these terms in a nonreligious context suggests that something of religion operates even there. That "something," I suggest, is the essential aspect of religion, namely, the spiritual. To some extent, it is also detachable from religion. I would go further and say that it is also detachable from belief in God or any supernatural entities. Thus understood, spirituality, not religion per se, is the crux of the matter.

All well and good, but what is spirituality?

Let me be completely up front. I am asking you to see meanings and values, and all the rest of my list, as spiritual realities, yet my use of the term *spiritual* is peculiar. It is neither strictly related to religion nor even to belief in God, as most people would suppose it should be. I will treat the crucial topic of belief in God in chapters 2 and 5. In the meantime, realize that one goal of this book is precisely to explain this term, to say exactly what *spiritual* means. In the process, another goal is to suggest a solution to the crisis we face. These two goals go hand in hand. A proper understanding of spirituality entails a solution to our world's crisis of meanings and values. Take the obscurities of God and religion out of the discussion, at least temporarily, and the problem before us becomes significantly less daunting. Following this strategy, as hope for our fragmented world, I am proposing a universally valid spirituality, a "generic" spirituality, applicable to all religions and to secular society as well.

Simply put, by *spirituality* I mean deliberately lived concern for the transcendent dimension of life. Said another way, spirituality is explicit dedication to the meanings and values, the ideas and ideals, the beliefs and ethics, that a person holds. Spirituality is primarily about the ongoing enhancement of the spiritual potential that is ours as human beings. The human spirit is the key to spirituality, not, in the first place, God or the divine Holy Spirit. A "spiritual person" is one who actively strives to refine, enhance, and live out his or her own beliefs and ethics, whether or not these are expressed in terms of God and religion at all. At the same time, the word *spirituality* also refers to the actual set of beliefs and ethics that a person might hold. Accordingly, in this book I propose a spirituality that people could adopt to inform their own spirituality: That is, I propose a set of beliefs and ethics (spirituality) with which individuals could deliberately structure their lives (personal, lived spirituality) and on which our secular world could securely rest (spirituality for our global community). My meaning will become clear as this book unfolds.

## SPIRITUALITY OR RELIGION?

In the meantime, grant me, please, dear reader, at least for the sake of argument, that the crisis at hand is spiritual. Doesn't it have to do with the meaning and purpose of life and with our differences of opinion on this crucial matter? Aren't these spiritual issues?

"Well, perhaps," you might concur. But not so fast, please! Might the crisis actually be, rather, religious? Isn't the breakdown of religion precisely the root of our problem?

Many people insist as much, and to some extent, I do agree. This suggestion about religion is on target. However, the sword of religion has its second edge. To push religion in a pluralistic world raises problems of its own. Which religion? What tradition? Whose God? Aren't religious differences often the very cause of our conflicts?

These questions illustrate how profound is the crisis we face. They also help focus the solution I propose: to take religion—and with it, even belief in God—temporarily out of the equation even while our concern remains spiritual. In the end, I cannot agree that more religion will be our salvation. Rather, I seek a middle ground between conflicting sectarian religions and a "value-neutral" secular society. I find this middle ground in the spiritual inclinations of our human nature. I posit human-based spiritual commitment as the common ground between secular society and traditional religion.

In the following chapter, therefore, I examine the problem of religion in a pluralistic society. Subsequent chapters unfold my vision of a nonreligious, secular, spirituality that applies, nonetheless, to a range of different religions. Might such a spirituality be able to unite our world? In my final chapter, still cherishing the memory of the secure community of my upbringing, I suggest how a world united around a common spirituality might actually look.

# 2

## The Relevance and Irrelevance of Religion

I grew up in a community that enjoyed an unusual coherence. Literally and figuratively, the community centered on the local Catholic Church. Religious celebrations were community celebrations and vice versa; there was no real difference. The two overlapped almost completely. The alderman would speak at the blessing of a church monument; the priest would pray at the installation of the alderman. While you were in South Side Pittsburgh, regardless of what you were doing—shopping at the stores, studying at the parochial or public schools, swimming at the public pool, repairing the sewers or sidewalks, voting at the polls, or petitioning a politician— religion inevitably carried the day. Virtually everyone was Catholic, so you were always dealing with a fellow believer. Religion colored everything, and religion mattered more than anything else: people still believed in God, heaven, and hell.

To all appearances, religion held the community together. In fact, as things were then, it did. However, deeper analysis suggests that, not religion per se, but the shared beliefs and values that are a part of religion are what actually held the community together. Even without the religious connections, the effect could have been the same as along as everyone still bowed to the same values and held the same beliefs.

As it was, the Catholic faith of that day encapsulated the values of almost everyone in that community. Undoubtedly, the very same effect occurred in other communities, and they might not be Catholic or even Christian. The important thing for social cohesion is that people believe alike. What they believe, the specific religion they follow, is secondary.

The point I make is rather straightforward. Logically, it is easy enough to grasp. However, more than logic plays into religion. My suggestion is that it

19

doesn't really matter what religion a group holds, as long as people all hold the same religion. But who would accept such a claim? The implication is that differences in religion are irrelevant, that one religion is as good as another. No faithful adherent of any religion would agree. None could agree without betraying his or her own religion. And in a pluralistic society, there's the rub.

An essential feature of religion, if it is to work, is that people believe it. Suggesting that any other religion would be as good destroys the very power of the religion—the power not only to disclose reality in the heavenly realm but also to hold a community together in the earthly realm. Only things taken as true hold people together; shared beliefs and values are the basis of human community. Level all beliefs or question their validity, and social cohesion weakens and fails. If people cannot believe their religion is true, the religion does not work. Most of us are already aware of this disconcerting state of affairs because, unlike people in former ages, we know too much about other religions and at some level we cannot help but question our own.

## THE EMERGENCE OF POSTMODERNITY

That point came home to me as I sat in on a support group for gay and lesbian teenagers. My question for them was "What kind of problems does religion create for people who are struggling with their sexual orientation?" For that select group, the answer was simple and, to me, surprising: no problem at all. I wondered how they had dealt with the opposition that religion often presents. These young people pointed out that there are many religions, which tend to have different teaching, and that even translations and interpretations of the Bible differ widely. Why, then, they concluded, should they listen to any religious teaching? They knew who they were and that they were good people. As they say in the meetings of twelve-step groups, these teenagers had decided to take what was helpful and leave the rest. Religion had no firm hold over them. They represent a new order.

That new order is characteristic of a new historical era. We are outgrowing modernity and entering what scholars have called *postmodernity*. The certainty of modern science characterizes modernity, and that certainty is gone.

Isaac Newton epitomized modern certainty. He achieved a stunning mathematical breakthrough. The ancients believed that the heavens were a sacred realm with laws different from those of the earth. Supposedly, movement of the heavenly bodies was eternal and perfect: their orbs described circles. In contrast, the natural path of mere physical bodies was downward, toward the center of the earth: mere physical objects fall. But under one set of equations, Newton united the heavens and the earth. The fall of an apple to the earth and the orbit of the moon around the earth or of the planets around the sun all exemplify the same forces. Like the apple, the moon is also falling, but distant from the earth and moving quite fast, the moon in its fall never hits the earth but ever shoots beyond it in a perpetual fall called an orbit.

Newton's world was precise, mechanical, and predictable. With exact equations, he could calculate the fall of any body, earthly or heavenly, and explain why the path of the fall had to be what it was. His synthesis entranced the seventeenth century. Further breakthroughs regarding electromagnetism, chemistry, and even biology held the promise of completely explaining the universe. Further progress was to entail mere refinements in the scientific theories. The apparent certainty of these achievements dominated the age. Modernity was synonymous with exact science.

But the early twentieth century challenged that modern scientific certainty. Albert Einstein's theory of relativity—now hardly just a theory, but a scientific law as sure as any other—made time and space themselves variable factors. Even worse, Max Planck, Erwin Schrödinger, and Werner Heisenberg's quantum theory introduced probabilities into the laws of physics. In dealing with subatomic particles, every predictability was gone. As in predicting the weather, likelihood is the best we can have. Even Einstein was uncomfortable with this outcome and protested, "God does not play dice with the universe." However, if things must be phrased in theological terms, all evidence suggests that, as far as we can know, God does. The realities about which modern physics was so certain were turning out to be more complicated than expected.

At the same time, similar conclusions were emerging in the humanities and in religious studies. Historical research had become precise enough to detect important shifts in religious teaching over the centuries. It was no longer possible to credibly argue that, for example, Christianity has *always* held such-and-such. The fact is that doctrines shifted, developed, and even changed, and their changes can be linked to social trends and political needs.

For example, it took 325 years for Christianity to proclaim that Jesus is literally God, and the realization that the Scriptures could be read either way was the reason for this proclamation. Western and Eastern Catholics are still not in agreement on issues of the Trinity and the nature(s) of Christ. Standard Protestant belief that Christ "paid the price of our sins" turns out to have no basis in the Scriptures but stems from the Reformation theologians Martin Luther and John Calvin. Until the sixteenth and even eighteenth centuries, taking interest on money was a grievous sin throughout Christian Europe; today even clerics keep their money in interest-bearing accounts and invest in retirement plans. Only head-in-the-sand believers could go on ignoring such documented facts—and they do.

In addition, social studies showed similar results. The beliefs of various societies and cultures turn out to differ in significant ways. Whereas Western religion insists that, as creatures, human beings cannot possibly be God, Eastern religion insists that our deepest nature is the Ultimate of the Universe: atman is Brahman (rendered in Western terms: the human soul is God). In a similar but not identical way, Western believers, being more Hindu than Christian, sometimes also speak of the soul as a "spark of divinity" within us. As is obvious, it is simply not true that "all religions teach basically the same thing." Of course, you could make such an argument, and in certain important regards that argument would be correct—as I will carefully suggest in subsequent chapters. Still, it would be hard to find consensus on the matter. Nowadays, people wonder if there can be consensus on anything.

Indeed, the more common opinion among contemporary intellectuals is this: since people differ so much from culture to culture, we do not even share a common human nature! Moreover, it is impossible to ever know objective "truth" since there is no such thing! What's more, the notion of universally valid ethics is an illusion since all values are culture-bound!

Supposedly, common human nature, truth, and goodness are all passé fictions. To me, this extreme opinion is absurd, and in this book I will argue precisely against so radical a conclusion. Still, the point remains: we now live with considerable lack of consensus on absolutely fundamental matters. And whole schools of thought argue seriously that such consensus is impossible because there is no way of ever knowing the truth. These schools of thought are also nonplused by the fact that their own claim—that there is no truth—is itself a truth claim. Their response is that logical consistency is also the small-minded preoccupation of a former age.

I have been making my point by appeal to scientific and highly scholarly pursuits. But the point is the same as the one I made in chapter 1 regarding everyday life. Ideas do have power. They structure everyday living. What only scholars may have surmised decades or centuries earlier eventually colors the thinking of the woman and man on the street. The world of ideas eventually shapes the world of everyday living. So today, we all know and use the word *pluralism*. We live with its reality and struggle with its consequences. We live in a world of widespread diversity and intense differences of opinion.

By the early twenty-first century, you don't need to be an intellectual to be aware of these realities. Anyone who watches television, reads the newspaper, surfs the web, listens to the news, or holds a serious discussion with someone other than a bosom buddy knows that our world is very complicated and that there is very little agreement of opinion, even the most basic. How different from other times and places! Compare South Side Pittsburgh in the 1940s and '50s. Compare any nation in the nineteenth century. Compare any tribe or village in any nonindustrialized country. We are in a new age, and it is not the much touted New Age of optimism and widespread good will, the Age of Aquarius. It is an age of unavoidable pluralism, dizzying confusion, and disconcerting uncertainty, and sometimes it is an age of cut-throat competition, petty defensiveness, and—as we all know too well—outright hostility and terrorism. We no longer live with the sense of certainty and security that characterized the modern era. We have entered an era characterized by awareness of the complexity of reality, the pluralism of peoples and cultures, the diversity of beliefs and ethical systems. We live in an era of uncertainty: postmodernism.

## THE POSTMODERN RELIGIOUS DILEMMA

The uncertainty of postmodernism invades the sacred precincts of our very souls. Diametrically opposed to the heart of religion, postmodern uncertainty provokes a disturbing dilemma. That dilemma is this: only committed adherence to a religion allows it to do its needed work, yet with growing awareness of religious differences, it becomes harder and harder for any believer to maintain committed adherence, so no religion can function effectively any more. The important social work of religion now goes undone, and as a result, society comes undone. Religion that once served society can no longer be what it was, and to the extent it remains what it was, it no longer serves the best interests of society. What used to be the solution has become the problem. Whereas shared firm beliefs and assured values used to hold society together, today they inspire divisions. Yet, for a people not to share beliefs and values with assured confidence is also a problem. It also results in the fragmentation of society. On all fronts, human community is under fire.

I see a way out of this dilemma, and I am proposing it with this book. The way out is to discern a common spirituality at the core of all religions and all societies. If truly common, that spirituality would provide a protean set of beliefs and values to ground a global community.

However, mine is not the strategy that we have seen before. I am not suggesting that we sift through the religions and find what they have in common. We have, for example, seen lists of "the Golden Rule" as found in a wide range of religions. This widespread Golden Rule is supposed to stake out our common ground.

I do not think that appeal to religion as such will solve our problem. What is taken from religion still remains entangled with religion. If so, what does the Golden Rule mean? It means whatever the various religions take it to mean.

For example, Biblical Fundamentalists have accosted me on street corners, preaching their version of Jesus. Their demeaning religious billboards along public highways, their television spots, newspaper ads, and propaganda over pop music stations insult my intelligence and impugn my personal integrity regularly. In their minds they are doing for me—helping me be "saved"—what they would certainly wish someone would do for them. They are only thinking of my good, only wanting to save me from hell. Their particular brand of "doing unto others" fits hand in glove with their guilt-filled beliefs about God, redemption, and the afterlife. In more serious forms, the murder of doctors, the bombing of clinics, the battering of wives, the abuse of children, the bashing of gays and lesbians, all result from this same "true Christian love."

But for my part, I just wish they would leave me alone—and all of us! And I am quite willing to leave them alone—as long as neither of us is causing real harm . . . in this present world.

Depending on people's worldviews, the Golden Rule means different things. Appearing in many different religions, what seems to be common is not really so. To seek a basis for common beliefs and values in religion is self-defeating. Besides, if our common ground derives from the religions, how fair is it to expect nonreligious people to stand with us? And how could we ever expect the cooperation of the secular governments, the secular businesses, and the secular agencies that orchestrate our world? Without these secular forces, could we ever forge a global community?

To be effective, that common spiritual core must derive from something that we all have absolutely in common. The only thing I know that meets this requirement is our very humanity—not a shared culture, not a common history, not any particular religion, not revelation, not even "God." The way out of the postmodern dilemma is to find and build on the human core of spirituality.

Many might reject my proposal—either because on principle radical postmodern thinking just does not allow an alternative, or else because some might conclude that this specific proposal is mistaken, or, most likely of all, because that same bugaboo is still at work in many arenas: this proposal offends people's sense of religion. Being good people, being deeply committed to "the things of God" as they understand them, they will find it impossible to trust anything except their own religion. To them it would be blasphemous to seek a solution to a serious problem apart from their religious beliefs. So my first task here is to show that the old religious solution is useless.

But, please, patient and fair-minded reader, be attentive to what I am actually saying. I am voicing serious reservations about religion and belief in God, but I am not suggesting that we just throw them out. We humans cannot live without religion or something that functions as religion. Only a fool would think we could banish all religion.

This is what I am suggesting: traditional religions do not meet our current needs, so we need something new. In later chapters, I will, of course, specify that something new. I believe that the human basis for that something new is actually the source of all religion and already lies buried in every religion. I present a humanistic or naturalistic spirituality that, as would be expected, opens onto wholesome religion and genuine belief in God. But in large part, traditional self-assured religion has served its purpose; new forms must emerge.

In my hope for world unity, religion remains for those who are religious, but more importantly at this point in history, my emphasis on humanity provides common ground also with those who are not religious. The core spirituality that I envisage, grounded in humanity, involves equally the religious and the secular. It offers a hope for truly universal fellowship.

As for today's religions, their challenge is to discern within themselves the human core of all spirituality and, on this basis, to recognize the commonalities across religions, rather than to emphasize the differences among them. As Jesus put it, "every scribe who is trained in the kingdom of heaven is like the master of a household who brings out of his treasures what is new and what is old" (Matthew 13:52). I am attempting to be like that household master. I bring out a new version of something as old as the human race.

## THE DANGER IN AN ALL-OUT RETURN TO RELIGION

At this point in history, it should be obvious that insistence on any one specific religion will not bring the human family together. It should be obvious, but it is not.

The religions still mount massive missionary efforts to make converts, and some missionaries actually believe that they will eventually convert the entire world and have it proclaim the name of their God. After all, they believe that their religion is the true one and that God really supports their efforts. Such missionary zeal is not a subversive, totalitarian campaign. For the most part, these missionaries act in good will. They truly want to be of help. They sincerely want what is best for others. But the only way they know to help is to share with others the religion that helped them. So they go out to make converts. And that effort has become the problem.

In the United States, Biblical Fundamentalism provides the most obvious example. I speak of Biblical Fundamentalism or Biblicism or Bible Religion, not Christianity, because the Bible movement has departed from defining essentials of the Christian tradition and become a new religion with its own proper name. In its (selective) insistence on a literal reading of biblical texts, the Bible movement ignores the emphasis on history that is essential to Judaism and Christianity.

These faiths believe that God spoke through specific historical personages in particular historical situations: Abraham, Isaac, Jacob, Moses, Jesus, Peter, Paul, John. Accordingly, to understand God's message, one must be able to juggle an array of information: the facts about those varied historical situations, the ancient Hebrew and Greek languages and their nuances, the worldview of those times, the literary forms of those texts, the purpose in the mind of the authors, the audience to which the texts were directed. In short, one must know all that makes up contemporary biblical scholarship and its "historical-critical" method.

This method presumes that, first and foremost, a text means what it meant to those who originally wrote it, as best we can determine. But Biblicism would ignore these historical complexities and claim to understand God's word simply by reading the Bible in the English of King James. Just as Buddhism emerged from Hinduism, Christianity branched off from Judaism, and Islam developed out of Judaism, Christianity, and indigenous Arabic religions, so, it seems, Biblical Fundamentalism has branched off from Christianity to form a new religion. Deliberately ignoring history, it cannot be Christian at all. It is a new religion.

The "witnessing" efforts of Biblical Fundamentalists are everywhere: street corners, television networks, radio stations, billboards, stadiums, rock concerts, church schools, high school and college campuses, real estate agencies, auto dealerships. The strategy of this movement is to set up a segregated and self-sufficient world in which the Biblicists' worldview dominates. Understandably, the intent is to recreate the kind of community in which I grew up. However, the Biblicists' version of such community is harder, narrower, and more suffocating. Whereas what I knew was a natural outgrowth of given circumstances, the Biblicist campaign represents a deliberate activism, an attempt to gain hegemony and impose control over a shifting society.

Biblicism is an all-out missionary effort, so one gets the impression that more than devout religion drives the proselytizing effort. The need to persuade others seems to serve the believers' own faith. Insistent preaching to others keeps personal doubts at bay. What is telling is this: the doubts are there, and they require an aggressive response. Biblical Fundamentalism is a reaction to the uncertainty of the postmodern era, for the uncertainty of the age has crept into the souls even of the true believers. This turn of events explains why the Biblicists portray themselves as the caring, loving, charitable salt of the earth even while others often experience them as intrusive, arrogant, and offensive spokespersons for an alien cause. The Biblicists need their beliefs so much that they are blind to what everyone else sees: the simple message of literal biblical faith just cannot work anymore.

In fact, that simple, literalist message never was the biblical faith; it is not Christianity. Fundamentalism is actually a modern-science version of a much softer, traditional faith. It is no accident that Fundamentalism arose in the early twentieth century. Fundamentalism is a modern response to emerging postmodernism. Biblicism is the religious version of classical physics' reaction against quantum mechanics, like Einstein's forbidding God to play dice.

Fundamentalism represents the modern mentality of absolute certainty applied to religion: Bible texts are treated as sure, literal, scientific laws from which other principles of living flow by deductive logic. Promising clarity and certainty, the whole Biblicist system operates with mechanical precision. No wonder I've encountered so many lawyers, engineers, and computer scientists among the lay leaders of Biblical Fundamentalism! Their religious and professional mentalities go hand in hand. Unwittingly, they turn religion into a modern science, the very force they claim to be repelling, although contemporary postmodern science has already moved on. As so often happens in social conflict, the Fundamentalists have taken on the mindset of their opponent as they try to meet it on its own ground.

In *The Battle for God*, Karen Armstrong studies the emergence of fundamentalism in Judaism, Christianity, and Islam. I spoke of Biblical Fundamentalism in the United States, but this twentieth-century phenomenon is consistent across religious traditions. Fundamentalism is the mechanization of religion in the face of the breakdown of traditional societies. It is a defensive maneuver that would stave off the dizzying changes of modernization and, now, postmodern globalization. Its goal is to turn back the clock and restore the simple life of a former age. Its strategy is to impose the religion that, it believes, structured that former age. Its concern is the same as mine, but its strategy is very different.

Three different fundamentalisms—Jewish, Christian, and Islamic— claim to be the solution to the world's problems. These fundamentalisms could not possibly be: they all differ, and they oppose one another. Their screeching preaching escalates to the point of physical violence. In the United States, the bombing of abortion clinics, the murder of physicians, the oppression of women, the physical abuse of "disobedient" children, the bashing and murders of gays and lesbians, opposition to the defenders of civil liberties as "activist judges," insinuation of private religious beliefs into public life, all go on in the name of the Biblical Fundamentalists' "Lord Jesus." Israeli occupation of Palestinian territory and repeated military assaults express an orthodox belief in the Torah and its story of a "promised land." Finally, there is the Islamic Fundamentalist destruction of the World Trade Center. If this religious act does not demonstrate the insanity of infallibilist religion, nothing will—yet this act is of a kind with others that have gone on for centuries in the West and East. A return to hardcore religion is not a viable option in the postmodern world. We need some other approach.

## THE FAILURE OF APPEALS TO REVELATION

One facet of fundamentalist religion and of even the moderate faiths is reliance on "revelation." It is the supposed transmission of privileged knowledge directly from God. There is some claim that the ancient Vedas of Hinduism were revealed. Supposedly, too, God spoke to Abraham, Isaac, Jacob, Moses, and the prophets, and the received message is in part recorded in the Torah. Then, God not only supposedly spoke through the Christian apostles and evangelists but also actually became human in Jesus Christ, who supposedly continues to inspire his followers, the Christian Church, and consummately through the Bible or the self-proclaimed infallible Bishop of Rome. For a second time—Jesus being the first—the final revelation of God supposedly came through the Prophet Mohamed, whose writings form the Koran, the holy book of Islam. Then for a third final time, Joseph Smith supposedly received a message from God through the Angel Moroni and a set of golden tablets, now unfortunately lost, although the intended information is preserved in the Book of Mormon, the holy text of the Latter Day Saints, who periodically receive further revelations from God through the president of their church. Many other, lesser-known religious groups, such a Bahá'í, Aumism, and Aum Shinrikyo, also claim divine revelation.

Former ages relied on words come from the gods to direct human behavior on matters sublime and mundane. Today, we rely on more methodical means to answer our questions—research, study, analysis, discussion, debate, and, generally, honest and goodwilled human intelligence and imagination. If solutions to problems sometimes emerge in a flash of insight, which would seem to come from beyond, we hardly call that insight "revelation" except in a metaphorical sense. Revelation is a problematic notion today. Not only do we have a better understanding of the creative human mind as a source of ideas, mysterious though the process remains. And not only can we partially explain the "revelations" of the great religions by appeal to social situations, political conditions, geographical configurations, psychological processes, and personal propensities: it is no accident that the Vedas, Torah, Bible, Koran, and Book of Mormon belong not only to specific religions but also to different societies, cultures, and even civilizations. But our knowledge of multiple and differing revelations also necessarily raises doubts about all of them as infallible, divine knowledge.

As with the fundamentalist religions, so also with their moderate counterparts, they cannot all be right: their revelations contradict one another. Revelation from God simply cannot be our much-needed basis for social cohesion. Some other approach is needed.

## THE DIFFERENCE BETWEEN GOD AND
## BELIEFS ABOUT GOD

Of course, most religions believe in God in one form or another, so it might appear that belief in God offers a basis for unity among all peoples. Were it truly God that people believed in, this possible basis might be realistic. But God is one thing, and people's beliefs about God are another.

When people speak of God, they mean that in which they believe, and once again the supposed common basis becomes an array of opinions. The problem is that, granted God really does exist, nobody actually knows what God is. The best of theological opinion consistently insists on this fact. If God is supposed to be the ultimate cause, end, and explanation of all things, well, no human mind is capable of comprehending God, so all human talk of God is but talk.

Whenever God comes up in discussion, one must quickly distinguish between God and people's opinions about, or images of, God. Is God the Ground of the Universe, the Brahman of Hinduism that is supposedly identical with the human soul, thus, making us all God? Or is God the One, Creator God of Israel who stands in inviolable contrast to other things, creatures all? Or is God a Trinity of Persons, one of whom incarnated in Jesus Christ? Or, in contrast to the Trinity and to the Holy One of Israel, is God the One and Unique Allah of Islam, whose prophet is Mohamed and whose demand is absolute allegiance? Or is God the Mormon reality that all faithful saints are destined to join, they themselves also having become individual Gods? There is no consensus when people speak of God. Undoubtedly, the discussion is about opinions and images of God, not about God per se. I would certainly hold that God exists, but equally so, I would insist that we do not know or understand God. For all practical purposes in human discussion, God is just an idea—my idea, your idea, someone else's idea. So appeal to God lends no weight whatsoever to people's assertions.

One wonders, then, what all the fuss was—and why it continued in congressional debate during the 2004 presidential campaign—when in 2002 the San Francisco federal court ruled unconstitutional the Pledge of Allegiance to include one nation "under God." The reference to God is indisputably religious, and insistence on it means requiring that all Americans be religious in a particular, officially approved way. Why are political leaders, at the highest level, so adamant about this national profession of faith in God? Are they ignorant of the ambiguity of the notion "under God"? What advantage do they gain by insisting on this official union of "God and country"?

This incident makes clear that belief in God often has more to do with earthly politics than with any heavenly entity. "God" is a symbol for whatever people want to make it mean. Having such a nationally approved blank screen onto which people can project their varied beliefs expediently blurs the religious diversity of a pluralistic society.

This assertion applies blatantly in the case of Chief Justice Roy Moore of Alabama. He set up a two-and-a-half ton monument of the Ten Commandments in the rotunda of the state judicial building . In the summer of 2003, the other eight justices of the Alabama Supreme Court decreed this action a violation of the separation of government and religion. But Moore refused to remove the monument. Supported by religious folk from around the nation, he claimed to be standing for "our constitutional right to acknowledge God."

How blinding religious faith can be! This chief justice seemed unaware that he was acknowledging his own particular belief in God, that not all citizens hold the same belief, and that he and his followers had no right to privilege their religious beliefs over those of others. As surprising as it might be to some people, not everyone believes in the divine status of the Ten Commandments, not everyone is Jewish or Christian. Indeed, even the religions that reverence the Ten Commandments actually have different formulations and numberings of them.

Besides, there are people who do not believe in God at all. If some have the right "to acknowledge God," don't others also have the right to pass on such acknowledgement?

Even to state that some people do not believe in God leaves one wondering what they actually do believe. Once, presenting a religious retreat to a group of teenagers, I spoke with a young man who had come along just to be with his friends for the weekend. He said that he did not believe in God and was not religious. Talking with him, I realized that what he did believe was closer to the theology of Saint Thomas Aquinas than what most of the other people on that retreat, including the adults, held. This boy had thought the matter through and rightly concluded that what people generally say about God is nonsense, so he "no longer believed in God." What he had done was to reject some very childish ideas about God in exchange for a very sophisticated understanding. But since nobody around him treated the matter with equal sophistication, he was forced to conclude that God does not exist. Then, did he believe in God or not?

As Saint Thomas Aquinas said repeatedly in his *Summa Theologica*, nobody knows what God is, and there is no way ever to adjudicate the matter. God is beyond human comprehension. To be sure, some opinions are arguably better than others. I will address this matter in detail in chapter 5. Nonetheless, every statement about God is a hypothesis, an opinion, a supposition. Appeal to God is appeal to one's own pet theory. When someone denies the existence of God, one needs to wonder what exactly is being denied—just as one needs to wonder what is being affirmed when someone insists on the existence of God.

I am not naively suggesting—as supposedly in foxholes under fire—that there are no atheists or that atheists are merely sophisticated crypto-believers. Some may be like that boy, yet others may truly be nonbelievers. The nonbelievers also have a right to their opinion, and, as persons, they are to be respected. Nor am I naively suggesting that we chuck belief in God.

There is no way to prove or to disprove the existence of God. Absolute insistence on either the existence or the nonexistence of God is equally misguided. A loose and gentle leaning to one side or the other is the more reasonable posture. Argument over the matter is entirely unproductive. What needs discussion are the issues for which "God" stands, the meanings and values, the ideas and ideals, for which "belief in God" is shorthand. These spiritual concerns, common to all humanity—and not theology—should be the focus of analysis and the basis of longed-for consensus.

Believer or nonbeliever, all people are part of our world. Any attempt to forge a global community must include them all. We are a far cry from South Side Pittsburgh. Belief in God is not a workable basis for unity. Indeed, the religions have been warring over their beliefs in God for centuries, and there is no indication that the wars are abating. Acknowledge these facts and belief in God goes the way of revelation and fundamentalist religions. In a pluralistic world and secular society, belief in God is no solution to our problems. Something else is needed.

## RELIGION'S SPAN OF HEAVEN AND EARTH

As we seek a sense of community in our neighborhoods, nations, and world, the old approach no longer works. Current religion cannot provide the basis of unity in a pluralistic society or a global village. A concerted return to religion in the fundamentalist mode, appeals to revelations from God, and even reliance on belief in God—these traditional approaches, far from being a solution, have become the contemporary problem. The more firmly people hold to their religious beliefs, the more they are part of this problem.

Yet religions did used to hold societies together. How did they do so?

Religion is a mixed bag. It contains a swath of issues: traditions, customs, dietary laws, clothing requirements, holy days, festivals, rituals, hallowed places, anointed leaders, administrative policies, treasuries, sacred texts, revelations, beliefs, ethical or moral teachings, claims about God, and even prescriptions for achieving union with God. Among these issues are not only "things of God," matters of the heavens: preexistence, after-life, spiritual beings. Among these religious issues are also "things of the earth." There are prescriptions for everyday living, specific to particular cultures—such as dress and eating regulations, religious calendars, desig-nated holy places, required roles for men and women. Moreover, among the things of the earth are also general principles for good living—such as honesty, respect, compassion, love, justice.

These two are very different kinds of things. The things of God are meta-physical; they pertain to some supposed other world; they depend on reve-lation or some other supposed communication with nonhuman entities; and they have to do with some life-to-come. On the other hand, the things of the earth are this-worldly; they pertain to everyday living, and they have everything to do with humanity and our survival and thriving on planet Earth.

All human beings, we are able to deal with the this-worldly aspects of re-ligion even though they differ from one religion to another. They are con-crete matters, down-to-earth affairs. We can test them against experience. We are fully capable of sorting them out. But as mere human beings, we are not capable of sorting out the otherworldly aspects of religion, the meta-physical claims. Over these, all we can do is argue. This difference is a ma-jor clue to resolving the dilemma of religious pluralism in the postmodern world.

## THE METAPHYSICAL SUPERSTRUCTURES OF RELIGIONS

The metaphysical aspects of religion are beyond testing. They are bald as-sertions. They are just beliefs. They are mere claims. There is no way to know if they are actually true or just fanciful; nor is there any way to prove that they are false. Like talk of intelligent life in other galaxies, these beliefs are plausible; they are even inspiring and desirable; but in no way are they proved or even provable. In these matters, there is no way to determine the case one way or the other. These are what in *The Transcended Christian* I called the *indeterminables* of religion.

Does God exist? What exactly is "God"? Did God create the universe, or has it always existed? Is "God" the sum of all that exists? Or is God some-thing in addition to the rest of the universe? Where were we before we were born? Have we always existed? Have we actually lived prior lives in this world? What happens to us when we die? Will we go to heaven? Is heaven eternal and blissful union with God? Or is heaven merely a paradise of sen-suous delight? Or is the afterlife an absorption into an impersonal All?

Does wrongdoing really matter once we are dead? Will our sins doom us to eternal misery? Is there a hell? Will we need to pass through a purifying process called purgatory? Or will we return to live this life again and again until we get it right? Do our karma-filled deeds in former lives continue to affect us in this present life? Or do we perhaps just cease to exist when we die?

There is no way to answer these questions except by expressing opinions, hopes, or beliefs. These supposed otherworldly realities are beyond human experience. They are what I am calling "metaphysical." Barring revelation, a direct pipeline to that other world—which has its own problems, as we have seen—there is no way of sorting out these beliefs.

Otherworldly beliefs make up the "metaphysical superstructure" of religion. This superstructure arises because our minds are naturally inquisitive. We have questions about everything. We are also insightful, so we come up with creative answers. We want everything to hold together in one grand scheme. When questions arise to which we could not possibly have definitive answers—like those otherworldly queries—we come up with answers, nonetheless; we cover all the bases. And, as best we can, we make the answers hold together with the rest of what we believe to be true.

Catholic faith, for example, used to include limbo. It was only a hypothesis, never a doctrine of faith, but it was generally accepted, nonetheless. It was to be a place of natural happiness for children who were not baptized but who could also not yet have sinned. A good God would certainly not condemn such innocents to hell, but unbaptized, they could not qualify for supernatural happiness in heaven, either. So limbo seemed a reasonable compromise. More recently, with increased humility before the mysteries of God's goodness, Catholicism has dropped belief in limbo for a more optimistic solution to the "problem" of unbaptized babies: God's ways surpass our feeble understanding, even of revealed mysteries such as baptism, so we should allow that in God's own way even the unbaptized could go to heaven. Sometimes with shifting explanations, but always aiming for coherence, religion proposes an explanation of everything.

Thus, we have beliefs not only about life in this world but also about things beyond this world. In fact, we don't usually work out all these answers for ourselves. Usually we get our answers from people who worked through this exercise before us. Unawares, we buy into the worldview in which we were raised. We take on the vision of our family, culture, society. To some extent or other, even if we are nonreligious, religion has shaped each of us—because religion shaped the societies in which we live. And every religion includes a metaphysical superstructure.

The metaphysical superstructures of religion present the biggest problem in a pluralistic world. They suggest the answers to the hardest and most disturbing human questions—such as life after death. As if under a protective tent, our worlds spread out beneath the cover of these metaphysical super-structures. They hold our worlds secure. They set the pale of agreed-upon reality, beyond which we should not venture. So, naturally, we tend to hold onto these otherworldly answers for dear life. We have high stakes in our metaphysical beliefs about the existence and goodness of God, life after death, or just reward and punishment. We humans shun uncertainty; we abhor ambiguity—especially on crucial matters of life and death.

But the beliefs of the various religions differ from one another. Worst of all, there exists no way of knowing which, if any, of them are actually true. Yet it is certain they cannot all be true. We might, for example, agree that we could not face God or enjoy ultimate perfection unless we are duly purified. But is purgatory or reincarnation the actual means of this purification? Beyond the differences between the God of the West and the Absolute All of the East, how could one ever discuss this question with someone who does not even believe in an afterlife?

To sort out the differences is impossible because, for every truly committed believer, his or her metaphysical beliefs are the starting point of any discussion. They are beyond question. They are the touchstone against which she or he tests everything else. It matters not that these beliefs might be absolutely irrational—that texts written centuries or millennia ago, for example, could tell us verbatim how to live in the postmodern world. Metaphysical beliefs are immune to reason. Hence, they are a problem. Like the delusions of a paranoid schizophrenic, there is no arguing them away. As important as otherworldly beliefs are to us, they are the indeterminables of life and religion. By their very nature, there can be no certainty about them; yet, because of their importance, we want them to be most certain of all.

Peoples wage wars over religious assertions that could never be known for certain. Of course, I am well aware that religion is seldom the sole, hardly ever the only, reason for "religious wars." Politicians appeal to religion to further their own campaigns: "for God and country," "one nation under God," "endowed by their Creator with certain inalienable rights." Yet religion has played significantly into wars throughout the centuries: the Roman destruction of Jerusalem, the crusades against Islam and Constantinople, the Protestant and Catholic wars of the sixteenth century, the ongoing "troubles" in Ireland, the massacres in Bosnia, the Israeli-Palestinian conflict, the dispute between India and Pakistan, radical Islam's war of terror against "the godless West," Shiite Iran's insurgency against the heretofore Sunni Muslim majority, the dissolution of Iraq's Shiite, Sunni, and Kurd populations, and the American-led "war against terrorism" in the name of all that is godly and right.

People war over religion, yet each of those peoples with their own sets of beliefs get along fine among themselves. Their various beliefs serve their various societies perfectly well. As long as the different groups are separated, the differences in their beliefs do not even matter. The conclusion must be that the specifics of these beliefs make little difference. Take them or leave them, hold this set of metaphysical beliefs or that set or even none at all, and the sun rises and sets each day, nonetheless.

There are many different ways to slice the cake of life. In themselves, metaphysical beliefs make little absolute difference in the down-to-earth world. Why should they? They pertain to some other realm! Thus, the metaphysical superstructures of religion turn out to be irrelevant—except that they create problems when we insist on them unbudgingly, when we deduce from them iron-clad, this-worldly policies, and when we fight over them.

In the postmodern world, the metaphysical superstructures of religion are a major source of trouble. We no longer have the luxury to insist on them, to hold them as absolute truths. We must recognize that they are our own creative theories, hold to them only lightly, be respectful of differing opinions, and even be open to others' choice to hold none of them. In the face of life's big questions—about our ultimate origins and our ultimate fate and the ultimate causes governing them—we need to learn to live with honest uncertainty and with the anxiety that uncertainty brings. We need to recognize the indeterminables of religion as truly indeterminable, never to be known in this world as surely true or surely false.

Perhaps with more concern for one another, the angst of fully open-eyed living would be completely tolerable. Perhaps with deeper and truer community, the beauties and small joys of life would make our existence, ever precarious, a welcome and satisfying experience, nonetheless. Perhaps we could learn to live in the here and now, grateful for the experience, and, as for the future, to trust that it will somehow take care of itself—even as our gracious coming to be in the first place resulted on its own. Perhaps, in other words, we could actually achieve the profound spiritual fulfillment toward which the metaphysical claims of religion point: humble trust in the graciousness of the universe (or the goodness of God). However, in our current situation, in the postmodern world, we will have to achieve this fulfillment via a strictly down-to-earth spirituality, free from reassuring reliance on speculative metaphysical claims.

However we might choose to make sense of life, if we are to live in peace on a shrinking planet, we must forego our desperate clinging to our preferred metaphysical beliefs. As for any rigid and unqualified adherence to otherworldly claims, religion seems to have served its day.

## RELIGION'S CONCERN ABOUT THE THINGS OF THE EARTH

Of course, there remains that other facet of religion: the concerns about things of the earth, religion's teachings about human living in this world. These this-worldly teachings are a source of hope in a pluralistic, postmodern world—simply because they are not indeterminable. From this world, of this world, and about this world, they are subject to the criteria of life in this world. They are amenable to human adjudication. Attention to them would put religious emphasis on building community on earth and deemphasize the influence of religious claims about heaven. Religion focused on this-worldly concerns would become more humanistic and, perforce, less theological, less metaphysical. Herein lies our hope.

The this-worldly aspects of religion are of two kinds. These two differ in an important way. There are the specific prescriptions for everyday life, and there are the general principles for good living. With all due respect for devotion and pious sentiment, for religious tradition and comforting custom, I nonetheless dare to call the first the *inconsequentials* of religion. On the other hand, the second pertain to the heart of the matter; they are the *indispensables* of religion.

## RELIGION'S EARTHLY CONCERNS: CUSTOMS AND TABOOS

Just as religion's metaphysical superstructures are in some way arbitrary and optional, so, too, religion's specific requirements for daily life are accidental. Is Friday, Saturday, Sunday, or no particular day at all to be held holy? Are meats to be eaten or all except pork or except cows or except dogs and cats or, rather, are only vegetables to be eaten? Is white to be the color of celebration and black, that of mourning, or vice versa? Are women to cover their bodies and veil their faces in public or to go about in comfortable exposure, and if the latter, how much exposure? Are men to be exempt from such restrictive regulations? Are only women to dance together or only men or only men and women and never just men? The wide and conflicting variety of practices in different religions and cultures makes clear that such specific requirements are accidents of history.

To be sure, cultures and religions rationalize their customs, connect their traditions with their histories, and even link their practices to metaphysical claims about the gods, revelations, and consequences in an afterlife. That Christians worship on Sunday, "the day of the Lord's resurrection," is a blatant case in point, yet, in earlier times, the Sabbath—Saturday—was the day of Christian worship.

If truth be told, such requirements are as they are because that is just how they happened to develop in this or that particular society, in one culture or another. These religious requirements vary freely from one place to another and from one time to another. In fact, they are merely customs, traditions, conventions, social taboos. They carry no weight in themselves—like driving on the right, rather than the left, side of the road or like preferring vanilla to chocolate ice cream. They could be changed, and no great harm would ensue—just as the clocks are advanced in the spring and turned back in the fall to capitalize on natural light. Just as the calendar and time are what they are simply because we have all agreed to treat them so, likewise, these facets of religion also depend on somewhat arbitrary consensus. To be sure, long-standing custom and religiously grounded traditions grow dear to every believer's heart. They become emotionally powerful, so to change them is no light matter. I am moved to tears when I hear Polish Christmas carols although I never did know what the words mean. A whole world of ardor, significance, and grandeur opens to me when I hear Latin texts sung in Gregorian chant. I understand the power of sentiment well. Yet I know equally well that my childhood Christmases and the day of the Latin Mass—*pace* Pope Benedict XVI—are forever gone. The customs of religion and the trappings of tradition have no ultimate validity in themselves, and they can be changed. For this reason, they are ultimately *inconsequential*.

## RELIGION'S EARTHLY CONCERNS: GENERAL PRINCIPLES FOR LIVING

In contrast, the general principles for living—that other set of this-worldly aspects of religion—are essential. These principles include matters such as open-mindedness, mutual respect, honesty, compassion, forgiveness, love, justice, and goodwill. These requirements pertain to the very nature of individual and social life. These are the matters covered, for example, in the latter part of the Ten Commandments, about disrespect, murder, lewdness, theft, dishonesty, and covetousness. These prohibitions are hardly optional; they are hardly accidents of history; they are hardly particular only to this or that culture. In some way, these general principles express absolute requirements for effective and successful living. Hence, they are the *indispensables* of religion. No society can survive where honesty and goodwill are absent. Not surprisingly, then, although their practical applications may differ, these requirements are similar across cultures and across religions. Versions of the Golden Rule, for example, occur in religion after religion, and their truest intent is to support the honesty, justice, and fairness that are required for any society to hold together and thrive.

Here, then, is something that is both common to religions and typical of human societies. Here is something that might become the basis of a global community. Derived from the individual and social nature of humanity itself, this basis would pertain to all peoples. Without compromising personal conscience or betraying one's own intelligence, everyone could comfortably stand on such a basis. If this basis is truly an essential of human nature, it would entail no outside impositions on a person. Standing on it, all would affirm their humanity, enhance their own beings, grow as persons, and uniquely contribute to the common good. Individually and collectively, the human race would be on a path of positive advance. We would have embraced the beginnings of a common spirituality, and it would be unthinkable that "God" stands for anything else.

## FOCUSING THE SPIRITUAL

Exemplified by the Golden Rule and the Ten Commandments, that common basis is a facet—an essential facet—of all religion. Accordingly, it could surely be called "spiritual." After all, it entails visions and virtues, ideas and ideals. This common facet of religion is also common to all humanity. It resides in the human heart, mind, or soul, and it expresses itself in spiritual sensitivity, religious affiliation, belief in God. It is the human, this-worldly root of spiritual awareness and religious concern. It is the human basis of spirituality. In the face of the inevitable collapse of religions as we now know them, this basis could support a universal spirituality in a pluralistic and secular world.

Our source of hope these days is not a fundamentalist return to an inherited religion, not an imagined projection of another world, not appeal to revelation, and not even belief in God. If our community is to include all humanity, we need something more accessible than religion, something more specific and more universal—something such as the built-in, positive, open-ended inclinations of the human heart and soul. Not religion, but the common spirituality that expresses itself in the religions and even in secular societies, will be the salvation of our postmodern world. Our collective hope is to emphasize the *indispensables* of religion and life, the this-worldly requirements that all religions and all humans have in common, and to downplay the *inconsequentials* of religion and hold only lightly to the *indeterminables*.

Such is the vision that I propose with this book. Such is the hope that I cherish. I would recover in a global community the security, cohesion, and lofty commitment that I knew in the neighborhood of my childhood and youth and that many of us knew in other times and places. My early experience and my later learning convince me that such an outcome is possible. We need not live—I doubt we can very long—with the fragmentation, confusion, competition, and hostility that have thus far characterized the twenty-first century.

In former ages, religion responded to our most basic longings. In this new age, the heart of religion, released from its husks—spirituality—must serve that purpose, if anything will. Centered in that heart, different religions could express the spiritual through an array of cultures and traditions, all the while honoring a commonality. Then generic spirituality would reign, and particularist religion would be its servant.

We make a mistake in thinking that our society can do without religion and the function it used to serve. Our society has become pluralist and, as a result, necessarily secular in its official structure. But every society, secular or religious, requires a set of shared meanings and values for its cohesion. Not only through their association with religion but also by their very nature, meanings and values are spiritual. Still, their source is not God or some other supposed metaphysical entity. Their source is the human constitution itself. Precisely because the source of meanings and values is both human and spiritual, even a secular society necessarily has a spiritual—though not a religious—dimension. Therefore, by discerning, highlighting, and embracing some common spiritual core, we can hope, even as a secular society, to hold our world together. Such is my argument in this book.

How is the common ground I point out truly something spiritual? How does it ground spirituality? If even secular society has a spiritual dimension, what is the difference between passively being spiritual and actively pursuing spirituality? How could one have true spirituality if God is taken out of the picture? Without God, what would provide the norms to distinguish true from false and good from evil? How does this proposed common spirituality relate to inevitable cultural diversity and religious pluralism? What room does this humanistic spirituality leave for God and belief in God? Indeed, what possibility does this spirituality provide for relationship with God and mystical union with God?

I begin to address these questions in the next chapter. There I will elaborate that common, human basis for spirituality. There I will begin to spell out a middle-of-the-road alternative to the doomed option between totalitarian religion and spiritually dead secularity.

# 3

## The Spirit of Humanity

When I grew up in South Side Pittsburgh, there was little religious diversity. At best, we had heard that certain people living up the hill were Protestant. I knew none of them personally. They were just an idea.

Nowadays, we all know people of other religions—Jewish, Muslim, Hindu, Buddhist, Native American, Mormon, Wiccan, Bahá'í—and of no religion. Knowing them person to person, we realize we can get along. We recognize a basic human goodness in them. Our prejudices fall away as we admit, "Wow, they really are good people."

What our hearts perceive and what our minds conclude is that, despite the differences in outlook, we have something in common. "Basic goodness" is no monopoly of any one religion, culture, or people. This chapter explores the basis of common, human goodness.

### SIMILARITIES AMONG RELIGIONS

Across cultures and religions, the same moral requirements recur: Honor your elders. Do not lie. Do not steal. Be sexually responsible. Love one another. Be compassionate. Welcome the stranger. Forgive offenses. Do no harm. Live and let live. What goes around comes around. Do unto others as you would have them do unto you.

These requirements are said to be religious because they occur in religious teaching. But the fact that they occur across religions suggests that they are not peculiar to religion but are common to humanity. They surface in all the religions because the religions are made by and for people. Something in our common humanity is the source of these requirements.

41

Of course, some would assert that God inspires those requirements in everyone or that they come from the divinity within us. These assertions may or may not be true. How would one ever know—and especially since there are also basically good people who do not believe in God? Some of my best friends fall into this category, and, if truth be told, I would never want as friends some people who loudly proclaim their belief in God or insist that only "Christians" can be truly good before God. Besides, Buddhism is a nontheist religion, and its moral standards are as high as any. So even if God is ultimately the source of morality—well, ultimately, God is the source of everything!—one need not know or believe in God to be a good person. From wherever it comes, a sense of goodness resides in the human heart. On this score, the question about God becomes moot. As ever, attention to metaphysical indeterminables distracts from the pressing issues of collective life on planet Earth. Attention to the movement of life itself offers a more promising perspective.

## THE SPIRITUAL WITHIN US

We are alive, and we know something of life. By its very nature, life pushes toward further life: grass will grow up through concrete. In animals, life becomes sensate. Animals see, hear, and feel; the higher animals have emotions: fear, rage, and affection. In humans, sensate life moves a step further and becomes self-conscious. The same force that ever pushes toward further life expresses itself in consciousness. That force is geared toward survival. It wants to advance. It wants to open up a secure future. Thus, the very awareness that makes us human—consciousness—inclines us toward positive growth. This inclination determines the indispensables that are our urgent concern.

Ever shooting for the stars, something within us recognizes when we are on track, and it is also sensitive to our being off course. Our very being wants to thrive, so it urges us to deliberately get with the program. A penchant for self-transcendence, for going ever beyond ourselves, is built into us. Familiar words apply to this inclination toward fuller experience: hunch, intuition, insight, good sense, conscience—and, covering them all, I would add "the human spirit."

Our self-awareness and drive toward expansion are not something physical. Space and time does not limit them. Our very aching for richer and fuller experience pushes beyond the here and now into distant and future realms. We are not prisoners of the here and now. We are not merely living physical bodies.

Neither are our self-awareness and expansiveness mere emotions. Of course, we get excited when we imagine a happy future, or we may feel sad when we finally recognize a mistake we made. We do not experience self-awareness and expansiveness without also feeling emotion, but in themselves self-awareness and expansiveness transcend emotion. Recognition of a mistake is something positive, a useful insight into our behavior, whereas the sadness over the mistake is a negative experience. The positive and negative cannot be the same thing. The insight is not the emotion. Likewise, the excitement over an imagined future is something present, whereas that future that excites us does not yet exist. The two are different. The feeling is not the idea.

Thus, in the first place, we live beyond space and time; we are not mere bodies. In the second place, our rich, inner life is also more than emotions. We have inner experiences of a peculiar quality: awareness, understanding, knowledge, love, planning. These are spiritual. They express a self-transcendence built into us. They make us naturally self-transcending beings. We are ever moving beyond ourselves, ever growing. Our very nature is to be open-endedly outgoing. If we are physical bodies and if we are also emotional animals, we are, in addition, spiritual beings. Part of us is cosmic. We are open to all reality. Our innermost core is geared to embracing the universe.

In making these statements, I am suggesting what the words *spiritual* and *spirit* mean. I am saying that the self-transcending dimension of our minds is spiritual; it is the expression of our human spirit. In contrast, other notions of the spiritual are more common. We often imagine spirits to be gossamer beings that float about, invisible realities that belong to some other world and sometimes haunt our own, faceless Halloween-like ghosts in flowing white sheets, angels with names and identities but without physical bodies.

I do not think that the spiritual is mysterious or elusive or ghost-like. I think the spiritual is a part of our everyday lives—not come from another world, not God within us, but a dimension of our own minds. Because of this dimension, we are naturally open to a "beyond" in our everyday experience. Our very nature is to be beyond ourselves. We are actually more than we can name.

Of course, that "beyond" is hard to get hold of. We tend to express it in vague notions and fanciful images. These sometimes come out looking like fuzzy entities that haunt our daily lives. How else could we portray that peculiar dimension of our experience? After all, these ghostly images do suggest something of another dimension. Imaginatively, they do express a transcendent and nonphysical realm.

I am suggesting, however, that ghosts, goblins, angels, and even God are not our fundamental meaning of *spiritual*. The fundamental meaning relates to our own human spirits. The naturally self-transcending dimension of our human minds is the primary meaning of *spirit*. We name other things *spiritual* because of their similarity to this primary spiritual reality. We speak of those entities as spiritual because we conceive them to be nonphysical, free from the limitations of space and time, like our own self-transcending minds. Neither those entities nor their otherworldly realms, but our own human spirits, are what the word *spiritual* refers to first and foremost.

This is the jarring point that I am trying to make here. I want to disentangle the notion of *spirit* from its usual associations with otherworldly realms and to anchor it in something as close to us as our own minds. In making my point, I am neither affirming nor denying the existence of otherworldly entities. Chapter 6 addresses that question. I am merely proposing a baseline meaning for the words *spirit* and *spiritual*, and I fill out that meaning by appeal to ordinary human experience, the experience of the functioning of our own minds.

In this chapter I introduce the notion of the human spirit, that "otherworldly" dimension of our minds. I do so suggestively. I use examples, metaphors, images, and stories. In the following chapter I present more detail. There I offer a more technical accounting of the human spirit. There I venture to actually delineate the structure of the human spirit and to describe its functioning.

In both these chapters, I am developing a particular understanding of spirit. This understanding may not square with what you think *spirit* and *spiritual* mean, but stay with me, please. See if what I propose doesn't make sense of much of what you already think. See if my presentation doesn't allow you in the end to hold onto much of what you already believe but with a new depth, clarity, and security.

In fact, the understanding that I am presenting is nothing new. It has been part of the Western philosophical tradition since Plato. It lies at the heart of the Hindu and Buddhist meditation traditions. It is at stake in any discussion of spirituality, mysticism, or enlightenment. It is the focus of recent research into the nature and basis of human "consciousness." But to most people in our contemporary world, this idea is, indeed, new—because we have come to take *spirit* to refer to otherworldly and ghostly entities; we have linked the spiritual with religion and theology; and we have lost awareness of the transcendent dimension of our own minds.

I want to bring the notion of *spirit* back down to earth, as it were. I want to open up the possibility of talking coherently about spirit, of determining what it actually is, of knowing how it functions, of understanding its openendedness. In the process I want to lay the foundation for an understanding of spirituality that might fit every human being, every culture, every religion—simply because this spirituality is grounded in the human spirit common to us all, not in mysterious, otherworldly, fuzzy, esoteric, or ghostly suppositions that freely vary from person to person.

## "FROM THE MOUTHS OF BABES"

Once while visiting Washington, D.C. for the Fourth of July, I went with a friend to watch the fireworks on the Mall. Street by street, block by block, we worked our way as close as we could to the Washington Monument, the epicenter of the display. We finally stopped at a cross street where the crowd was dense and some parked cars stood hopelessly stranded until the celebration was over. Next to us was a young family: father, mother, and a small girl and her younger brother. The girl was perhaps five or six years old.

The parents had set the children on the roof of a parked car. Worried about damaging the paint, paranoid-like, the mother repeatedly rebuked the children—dressed in soft flannels and sneakers—for moving about. Also concerned about disturbing other people, inconceivably, the parents would not let the children make any noise as the fireworks shot off. "Shut up! Be quiet!" they continued to command although other people naturally oohed and aahed. "Don't be making noise!" (Some people should never be parents.)

But the little girl would not be suppressed. She was gleeful at the spectacle. As one enormous firework exploded splendorous high overhead, she shrieked at the top of her girly voice, "Mommy, mommy, I want to shoot up into the sky and pop!"

Just an innocent childhood outburst? Yes, of course. But also something more. Notice what the little girl was saying.

There was not just excitement in her words, but fascination, wonder, awe. She was not just watching the fireworks; she identified with them. Not some white-coated experimenter standing at a distance, objectively observing the phenomenon, she wanted to stretch out and actually become the fireworks. Something spontaneous within propelled her not only to take in the experience but also to embrace it and become one with it. Not enough to see the fireworks, she wanted to enter into them, grasp them, comprehend them, know them from the inside. She wanted to be the fireworks.

I saw in her exclamation the unfiltered workings of the human spirit. The spirit within us is outgoing, open to all that is. The spirit goes out to anything that it encounters. It expresses itself in wonder, marvel, awe. In that awe we go beyond ourselves. We break open and stretch to embrace the novel and fascinating. Not simply embracing reality, in some way our spirit allows us to actually be what we embrace. In some way we become what we experience and know; whatever we experience and know becomes a part of us. Just as we are what we eat, literally, we also are what we experience. Uncensored, unthinking, spontaneous, that little girl exquisitely expressed this dimension of our humanity.

Through understanding, through affirmation, through appreciation—through an identification that is spiritual—we take into ourselves and somehow become whatever we experience. Our experiences make us who we are. The built-in capacity for self-transcendence that makes us human gears us toward the whole universe of being. *Whatever is* is, in principle, available to us. The range of our spirit—its curiosity, its wonder, its fascination, its questioning, its grasp—is open-ended. Our spirit is infinite in scope. To make this point, the medievals described the human spirit as *capax infiniti*: capable of infinity, open to the unbounded. The functioning of the human spirit reveals that we, ourselves, are somehow already that unboundedness, which leads us on and toward which we incline.

## POSING QUESTIONS AND BEING IN LOVE

Consider this other example of the human spirit in action. Consider what it means to ask a question.

To question is to already reach beyond what we currently know. We may be here, but our question stretches out to there, to a place we do not yet know. We anticipate reality. We somehow already have a sense of what there is. Our questions only serve to fill in the details. Our questions want to make concrete what we already somehow anticipate.

We recognize when our questions are answered and when they are not—even though in asking a question, we obviously do not know the answer. Yet not any answer will do. We know that some answers just do not make sense. They do not fit our valid expectations. Our questioning already anticipates what the answer must be like. We recognize when we are being given a snow job. We realize that political "spin" is actually misrepresentation. We understand the difference between reality and fantasy. In asking and answering questions—if we are honest—we move more and more deeply into reality. Our very being is geared toward reality. The very mechanism of our questioning imposes this orientation.

Moreover, a correct answer to one question tends to provoke other questions. And answers to them elicit still more wondering. Why are snowflakes all six-sided? Because of the shape of ice crystals. But why are ice crystals six-sided? Because of the structure of water molecules, $H_2O$. But why is $H_2O$ the shape that it is? And we could pursue the questions down to quantum physics and the quarks and leptons that structure our physical universe, and we would still be left wondering why these ultimate particles or energies are as they are. Our questioning is expansive. If we pursue this unfolding of questions—unless, as in the case of the poor fireworks girl, people suppress our natural curiosity and spontaneous delight or unless, unfortunately, we learn through mechanized schooling that knowing means memorizing given responses and reproducing them, parrot-like, on demand—we would never stop questioning until we understood *everything about everything*.

Such comprehensive understanding is the ideal goal of our human minds, given free rein. Yet, if we were ever to reach that goal, knowing everything, we would be like God—at least insofar as Western theology has understood God. Of course, in this world such an achievement is beyond us, yet Christian talk of union with God in another world envisages exactly such a human fulfillment: the beatific vision. Whether our spiritual capacity ever reaches that heavenly fulfillment or not, we must at least admit that, in this specific sense, the human spirit does literally reach out godwards.

This link with God should confirm that our human capacity for self-transcendence is, indeed, spiritual. Evidently, then, we can legitimately speak about the spiritual without bringing in God, yet examination of the spiritual easily points us back to God. Just examining our penchant for questions reveals the spiritual quality of our wondrous nature. The spiritual is a dimension of our everyday, ordinary activities—such as asking an honest question and expecting an honest reply.

Consideration of our loves leads to the same conclusion. Generally, our loves are few, and they are often small. We are so caught up in ourselves! We long to break free of our own narrow outlooks and to experience delight in others and their novel perspectives. No wonder we prize falling in love— or art, music, nature! They draw us out of ourselves, and we get caught up in them. We and our personal world expand when we love. Though too little actualized, our beings are geared to all that is good and beautiful. Like the fireworks girl, we want to go out of ourselves and take in the wonder, we want to be one with it all. Unless we have deadened our souls, we would want to love all that is loveable and to delight in its beauty and marvel. We berate ourselves for our pettiness, for our inability to give more, for our self-centered offenses against even those we love the most. We ache to love more deeply, more purely, more truly.

Were we ever to achieve that ever distant goal and love all that is loveable— to dream the impossible dream—we would love universally, love without restriction. And, again, through such loving we would be like God. Love is potentially that big. No wonder John the Evangelist wrote that God is love.

So, as I elaborated in *Sex and the Sacred*, human love is not just a physical urge, and love is not just an emotional bonding. Human love is also a spiritual reality. Love opens us to everyone and everything. Totally fulfilled love would have us embrace the universe. Examining the spiritual dimensions of the human mind, again we arrive at the same conclusion. Talk of love—if we don't mean mere sexual craving or emotional longing—is talk of spirituality. Love is an expression of our spiritual core.

## MOVING BEYOND SPACE AND TIME

Does this consideration of mere questions and love seem too ordinary to be spiritual? Oh, how we underestimate the marvel of our own makeup! Routinely we touch the transcendent and do not even advert to the fact.

Appreciate, for example, what Pythagoras did in explaining the right triangle. Realize what wonder we were engaging in our high school geometry class.

Pythagoras had the insight that the combined area of the squares built on the sides of a right triangle would always be equal to the area of a square built on the hypotenuse. Hence, the famous formula, $a^2 + b^2 = c^2$. We can memorize this formula and use it to solve problems.

I used this formula, for example, to figure out how high a floor-to-ceiling bookcase could be if I wanted to build it on the floor and then raise it up into place. I knew the bookcase could not actually be as high as the ceiling, but what was the tallest the finished bookcase could be without getting wedged against the ceiling while being raised upright into place? Computing a hypotenuse, the diagonal of the side of the bookcase, gave me that length.

Apart from allowing such routine application—whose value should not be underestimated—what had Pythagoras actually done? He gave us a formula that applies to any triangle *everywhere and always*. He tapped into something ubiquitous and eternal. In his formulation of the triangle, he actually transcended all space and time. Pythagoras formulated a purely spiritual reality. No wonder, then, that Plato was stunned by mathematical insight and theorized that ultimate—that is, perfect—reality exists in a realm of Ideas or ideal Forms.

The purely spiritual reality, which Pythagoras and Plato experienced, does not exist as such in the world of space and time. Pythagoras's theorem captured the ideal. It expressed a perfect right triangle. But where is there a perfect right triangle in the physical world? A perfectly flat wall? A perfectly level floor? A perfectly square corner? (I ask these questions remembering the unexpected complications of my task in building that bookcase!) Nothing in the physical world actually matches Pythagoras's theorem exactly.

We cannot draw a perfect right triangle. The drawing requires lines, and lines have thickness. The thickness of the lines would confuse the calculation. We cannot even imagine a perfect right triangle. The mental image would also need to have lines of some thickness. But geometry's lines are pure abstractions: length without thickness, a "locus of points," which have location but no dimension. We cannot imagine Pythagoras's right triangle—but we can understand it. Through understanding, we grasp exactly what Pythagoras meant and exactly what a right triangle is, and anybody who understands it grasps exactly the same reality. We can grasp perfect right-triangleness, which applies to any and every right triangle in the physical universe but exists as such in none of them. Pythagoras's theorem expresses an insight that transcends all space and time—as do innumerable other human achievements of understanding. Insight is a spiritual act that takes us beyond and enriches the physical givens.

Still, Pythagoras's ideal formula does apply to the physical world. The formula helped me build my bookcase. As Aristotle pointed out—differing with Plato and disputing the reality of his World of Ideas—Pythagoras discerned the ideal *within* the concrete. He grasped the universal within the particular. He touched the spiritual within the mundane. The product of his "mere" human mind in the physical world was a spiritual achievement that transcends the merely physical world.

## RELATIVIST REACTIONS TO PYTHAGORAS

Purists will object that the Pythagorean theorem is not actually correct. It is not about reality, everywhere and always, because it applies only in two-dimensional Euclidean space. Later geometers noted that a right triangle drawn on a sphere, for example, does not respect the Pythagorean theorem. Think of two lines drawn from the pole to the equator. The lines intersect with the equator at right angles, but the resultant triangle differs from a right triangle drawn on a flat surface. Even more seriously, Albert Einstein has shown that real space is not Euclidean. We would need the equations of general relativity theory to actually compute accurate lengths since time must be taken into account as a fourth dimension of physical reality.

Of course, technically the purists are right, but their objection merely strengthens my case. Instead of considering Pythagoras, we could ponder the equations of Einstein. What he did was to advance Pythagoras's contribution—which is perfectly adequate for most situations—and offer equations that do, in fact, apply to the whole of the physical universe.

In the present discussion the difference between Euclidean and Einsteinian space is beside the point. Compared to Pythagoras, Einstein offers an even more astounding example of the transcendent capacity of the human spirit. Even more than Pythagoras, Einstein abstracted from all space and time and expressed what holds everywhere and always and under every frame of reference. Einstein's was also a spiritual achievement.

But the purists might persist. They might argue that, if Pythagoras was wrong, Einstein may also be wrong. In postmodern inconsistency, they might even go on to insist for certain that we really know nothing for certain and our intellectual musings—and theirs?—might have nothing at all to do with reality. If so, exploration of the spiritual within the human mind is just a wild goose chase.

Well, I would read the history differently. That Einstein surpasses Pythagoras does not show that we are incapable of accurate knowledge. On the contrary, Einstein's precision shows that we are capable of ever more accurate knowledge. That we make mistakes does not prove that we cannot know. On the contrary, the finding of a mistake confirms all the more that with patience, effort, and dedication, we can come to know accurately. It is not that we cannot trust our own judgment or that we cannot know reality. Rather, it is that we continue to know reality better and better. The universe is just more complicated than we first imagined—as we have come to know!

Of course, we do not have the final truth! We do not achieve Truth with a capital "t"—whatever that means! We do not come to understand everything about everything or love all that is loveable! But these facts do not mean that we know nothing at all or that the goal of our plodding quest is not infinite. We walk on an unfolding path of ever more accurate understanding and ever increasing breadth of love. In the ideal that path leads to complete and accurate explanation. That is where our minds lead. Our minds are geared to the universe. We are not locked into the here and now. We naturally transcend space and time. While being here and now, we have insights that apply everywhere and always, and our loves touch the eternal.

There is a transcendent dimension to our minds; there is a spiritual component within us. It is the source of basic human goodness, the concern for honesty and truth, the moral sensitivity common to all religions. It is, I suggest, the ground of all spirituality. In its essence, spiritual growth is the ever deeper incorporation of our inborn spiritual capacity into our developed selves and our habitual functioning.

## QUANTUM LEAPS OF FAITH

I apologize for this detour into contemporary physics. Unfortunately, in these challenging and desperate times, it is necessary to address esoteric science when discussing spirituality. To propose my down-to-earth understanding of spirituality, I must blow the whistle on confusing complications. I would alert you, dear reader, to current popular trends that weave together disparate strands of over-simplified postmodern science—take, for example, the movie *What the #$*! Do We Know?*—and turn spirituality into a fairytale as in times of yore.

Many current "gurus" appeal to relativity theory and quantum physics to explain the spiritual. In the process they often portray a spiritual world out of synch with everyday life, and they demean the importance of our "merely" human and rational minds—forgetting that it was the human mind that came up with relativity theory and quantum physics in the first place. They speak of spirituality as if it were some alien experience that only a select few, if anyone, could ever understand or achieve. Ordinary folk are expected to "take on faith" the "wisdom" that those few offer. Once again, as in the religion of old, we are to find spirituality in mystification and blind faith.

In the postmodern world, "spiritual gurus" ask us to mistrust our human insight, reasonable judgment, and basic good sense and to regress to a premodern worldview. Rationality, logical argument, and appeal to evidence are supposedly limiting. The hunches of faith and the opinions of self-appointed preachers are to provide knowledge as secure as hard-won, evidence-based conclusions. In the attempt to preserve faltering unthinking religion, all science—except, incoherently, the most esoteric—becomes the enemy.

To be sure, science does have its drawbacks, especially in its thoughtless application—usually politically and financially motivated—that squanders our natural resources, trashes the environment, and overly mechanizes our living. Moreover, by their very nature, the conclusions of science are tentative: all we can have is "the best available opinion of the day," and it will need to be constantly refined and, in some cases, even reversed. Thus, a critical stance toward the scientific enterprise is wholly appropriate. Indeed, science-bashers should remember that a critical stance is of the essence of the scientific enterprise itself. As in medicine, so in all science, we always need to get a second opinion; we always need to confirm a given experimental outcome.

But in the postmodern world, the outright denunciation of science or the sophomoric application of its most subtle findings often lead to unwarranted claims—that we really understand nothing for certain, that science is just an opinion as whimsical as any other, that cultural bias inevitably distorts our every claim to facts, that the best we can do is to trust our hunches and go with what we feel deeply. Supposedly, science is just a modern myth as fanciful as alchemy and leprechauns. (I must confess, I feel foolish writing these things: they are so outlandish. But let me assure you, university professors actually hold and defend these views.) Supposedly, we are to abandon the conclusions of modern science and its method of appeal to evidence and return to intuitions, suppositions, pious beliefs, folklore, and mythology.

If we did, the result would be regression to primitive religion and superstition. Tradition, revelation, custom, ancient authorities, and local beliefs would tell us what life means. In more educated, but still ignorant, circles, popular distortions of quantum physics serve to shore up contemporary notions of a "spiritual" realm. We end up in magic, fantasy, and imagination—and we are to take this result as "spiritual" because it is mystifying.

Thus, the religion of the "New Age" becomes just another version of that old-time religion. On the very same basis—supposed revelation, claimed metaphysical insight, popularized "science," appeal to knowledge from celestial messengers—this new faith in crystals, vibrations, and quantum leaps competes for the allegiance of souls with the traditional faith in God, angels, and heaven. In this situation, there is no reconciliation of old and new. There is no advance to deeper and surer understanding. There is no moving on, as from Pythagoras to Copernicus to Newton to Einstein to Heisenberg, in natural next steps. Rather than growing up with the ages, spiritually we remain fantasizing children. Whereas before it was revelation, visions, and inner voices; today, relativity theory, quantum physics, and string theory provide the smoke screen to keep the fantasy going. Therefore, to flag the confusion, I delved into these technical matters.

I am suggesting that spirituality is nothing otherworldly or esoteric. At least for the present, I want to keep God and otherworldly realms out of the picture—as well as other vaguely understood contemporary notions. So I took a detour into some technical material. My purpose was to check bedazzling speculation and to bring us back down to earth. My insistence is that we ourselves are, in part, spiritual. We can experience the spiritual by attending to our own minds. We can understand the spiritual by pondering our own functioning. Our very minds open onto the transcendent and the eternal. Pythagoras's theorem—or, if you want to push the issue, Einstein's relativity or any of a series of cumulative scientific breakthroughs—provides a clear example. The basis of spirituality is our own human spirits, and it is accessible to anyone who cares to attend to the functioning of his or her own mind. In ourselves, on the basis of experiential evidence, we can come to know what spirit is.

## AN INITIAL SUMMARY

Talk of the human spirit is difficult because spirit is elusive. The story of the fireworks girl, attention to questioning and loving, and consideration of the advance of science suggest what the human spirit is. Already certain characteristics of spirit come to the fore.

The spirit is dynamic; as a higher expression of the thrust of biological life, the spirit moves and lunges ever forward. The spirit is open-ended; it is geared to all that is; in its wonder, marvel, and awe, it would embrace the universe. The spirit is transcendent; it is not limited by space and time. The spirit is goal-directed; it leans into reality, toward what really is. The spirit is cumulative; ever adjusting, ever correcting, it builds toward its ideal fulfillment. The spirit requires accuracy; its hope of fulfillment must rest on sure ground, and it registers dissatisfaction when this requirement is not met.

The spirit is unitive; it somehow becomes whatever it embraces and, thus, leads us to become one with the cosmos, moving toward an ever more comprehensive integration.

To say that the human spirit has these characteristics is to say that we do, as well, for, in part, we are spiritual. Our human spirit makes us what we are. The spiritual is what makes humans human. To describe the human spirit is to elaborate the distinctive characteristics of human nature.

These characteristics are also typical of what people say about spirituality: it is awe-filled, dynamic, transcendent, outgoing, truth-oriented, good-willed, open-ended, cosmic, unitive. In attending to the human spirit, we are already actually speaking about spirituality. We are treating spirituality apart from God or religion. Nonetheless, I suggest, this spirituality is itself a core aspect of religion and its very source as well as the basis of the discovery and reverence of God.

Without attending to religion, we are speaking of something common to all religion. We are building a bridge that might link the various religions. We are proposing a basis for spirituality that fits the whole human family. We are making inclusive space within spirituality for people who are not religious and might not believe in God. We are pinpointing the source of the basic goodness in those "Protestants up the hill," and the Jews in New York City, the Muslims in the Near East, the Hindus in India, the Zen Buddhists in Japan, and all of us, fellow humans on a shrinking planet, struggling to make sense of postmodern life and to live it in peace.

# 4

## The Structure of the Human Spirit

Our world is getting smaller. Through mass media, the Internet, and air travel, people on the other side of the globe are effectively our neighbors. As the planet shrinks, like sibling rivals, we seem to be fighting more. When we get too close, our differences show. And religion is often the source of the differences and a cause of the squabbles—and even worse, of terrorism, atrocities, and full-scale warfare. Somehow we need to come together as a loving family. Despite its rhetoric, religion has not provided us a common basis.

As an alternative, our common humanity might offer such a basis. Yet talk of it also seems all too vague. We hear of "the human spirit," our "common humanity," and "the demands of justice" all the time. The establishment of the United Nations and a World Court are encouraging. Nonetheless, compared to what is needed, such talk and first-step actions have done little to better our world. Indeed, our own American government refuses to acknowledge a World Court or to sign treaties to eliminate nuclear weapons, to preserve the environment, or to outlaw cluster bombs and civilian-mutilating land mines.

Perhaps a more precise understanding of the human spirit would help move things forward. Perhaps a more solid grounding for talk about the human spirit would bring people together.

In fact, more solid grounding in more precise understanding is available. It is possible to point out not only the general characteristics of the human spirit but also the specific "structure" of its makeup. It is possible to move from mere inspirational talk via symbols, metaphors, and stories to a detailed and ordered account of the human spirit. Such an exposition is the focus of this chapter.

The work of the Canadian philosopher-theologian Bernard J. F. Lonergan (1905–1984) inspires what I am writing here. Lonergan was interested in human knowing, something we all do but seldom think about. He was well aware that, unless we know how we know and what "to know" means, we could never deal with the pressing issues of the postmodern world—because many of our biggest problems depend on claims about the truth and claims about how, if at all, one knows the truth. Being a theologian as well as a philosopher—his treatise on the Trinity is said to be the best since Saint Thomas Aquinas—Lonergan realized how religious notions such as revelation, infallible teaching, and inspired and inerrant texts sometimes clash with the conclusions of science and how the shift from ancient to classical to quantum physics has complicated the meaning of science itself.

Lonergan spent his life analyzing human consciousness—or what he also freely called "the human spirit." His most important work is *Insight: A Study of Human Understanding* (1957), and his second most important, dealing with religious knowledge, is *Method in Theology* (1972). The University of Toronto Press is publishing his collected works, a projected twenty-five volumes.

Lonergan's position, basically simple but surprisingly far-reaching, is more profound, by far, than anything else I've come upon through decades of comparison. Lonergan discerned four shifting levels—or facets or aspects or foci or emphases—within the functioning of the human spirit. In technical terms, he called these four "experience, understanding, judgment, and decision." Interrelated in a precise configuration, they constitute the dynamic structure of the human spirit. In considering the fireworks girl in the previous chapter, our questioning and loving, and scientific advance, we have already seen something of the "pieces" of this structure. This chapter puts the pieces together in a coherent whole.


## THE SPIRIT AS BEING AWARE

The human spirit is awareness. Our prime experience of our spirits is in wonder, marvel, awe. Aristotle said that wonder is the beginning of all science and philosophy. Because of our spiritual nature, we are presented with things that impinge on our consciousness—sometimes so strikingly that they amaze us. We take note. We focus our attention. We become aware of things. We become enthralled. The human spirit is our built-in openness to experience—awareness. Like radar, it is sensitive to any incoming data. Whenever we are aware, our spirit is functioning.

Said otherwise, the human spirit is empirical. *Empirical* is a word used to describe the modern sciences; to be empirical simply means to rely on evidence. The sciences are empirical because they are not mere speculation, but they rest their conclusions on data, they rely on evidence.

However, the empiricism of modern science tends to be narrow; it limits the range of acceptable evidence. Usually only what is physically verifiable counts as evidence. Usually only sense data count—what can be seen and heard, observed and measured, experienced by others as well as by oneself. These qualifications characterize empirical science. But the data to which the spirit is sensitive are of many different kinds. We are aware not only of the data of our senses. We are also aware of inner experience, the data of our consciousness—such as emotions, images, memories, questions, insights, hunches, thoughts, and choices. We are even aware of our own awareness: we know that we are aware; we know the difference between sleep and waking, between dreaming and thinking. These inner phenomena cannot be detected by sight, sound, odor, touch, or taste, nor can anyone have access to them except the person experiencing them, but they are real, nonetheless. The empiricism of the human spirit is universal. The spirit is open to anything there is to be experienced, including itself.

In fact, the whole discussion in this and the last chapter appeals to evidence. The evidence in question is the experience we have of our own spirit's functioning. To this extent, the presentation here is scientific: it rests on relevant evidence. This is to say, I am developing a science of the human spirit—or, more accurately, I am reporting Lonergan's development of this evidence-based, this scientific, account of the human spirit. And I am applying Lonergan's analysis of human consciousness, or spirit, to ground a scientific spirituality. For this reason, like science in any other realm, this account of spirituality should be valid universally; it should apply to all religions and cut across all cultures. Indeed, the very talk about "structures" of the human spirit suggests a scientific enterprise. The aim is to name the essential dimensions that make the human spirit what it is. This aim is scientific.

The scientific nature of this enterprise rests on the very characteristic of the human spirit to be open, aware, receptive to input. The spirit is open to all things, including itself. The spirit can experience itself. When we are struck by wonder, marvel, awe, we are experiencing the human spirit itself in the very act of our experiencing whatever else is there to be experienced. The spirit is not only aware; it is also self-aware; it is awareness of awareness. Open to our own openness, we note that a first facet of the spirit is openness, receptivity to incoming data.

## THE SPIRIT AS HAVING IDEAS

Openness or awareness is the first dimension of the human spirit. Lonergan suggests that from this first dimension there arises spontaneously a second. Be attentive to your own mind and its working and see if the following is not so: no sooner are you aware of something impinging on your consciousness than you begin to ask, "What is it?" "How can it be?" or "Why does it work?"

Confronted with input, our dynamic human spirit shifts to another mode of operation. Originally open to data, our spirit now seeks to understand the data. We want to make sense of whatever we are experiencing. So we begin to question. The same human spirit is functioning, but its focus has changed. It is working at a new level.

On this second level of spiritual functioning, insights occur. We wonder, we ponder, we struggle with a question. Then, suddenly, we get a flash of understanding. We have an insight. From the insight we usually generate a concept, we come up with an idea, an inner expression of what we understood. Then we usually go on to produce some external expression of our understanding: a formulation, a verbalization, a symbolization. We put our understanding into words. Having understood, we propose a hypothesis or a theory about the understood.

Usually, what I am outlining step by step goes on nearly instantaneously in our minds. We take this process for granted and hardly ever advert to it. Still, on some occasions, when we grapple with a particularly difficult question, we might become aware of the struggle to understand, the actual insight itself, the effort to generate a concept, and the need to find the right words or symbols to express it. My intention here is to relate what actually goes on in our minds. I have observed this process in my own mind. I hope you can also recognize it in yours. Perhaps, grappling with what I have written, you can recognize in yourself what I mean to say.

Insights are spiritual acts. They are pure expressions of the human spirit. Pythagoras's theorem resulted from insights, as did Einstein's equations. Our solutions to everyday problems, and to major ones, are also the result of insights. Our spiritual nature, functioning in its second dimension, allows us to go beyond what is there in front of us and, through a flash of intelligence, to somehow reconfigure the whole set. After days of puzzling, while I was relaxing at the gym, it finally dawned on me how I could fix a favorite necklace of mine: I'd find a glue that acts like solder and holds even metal together. Similarly, a baffling puzzle is blatantly obvious once we figure it out. Our insight—the solution to the puzzle—allows us to see it in a new way, to grasp a pattern in the chaos, to make sense of it, to understand. This is a process of self-transcendence. It leads us to a perspective that is beyond the data right here and now, and it makes us, now understanding something new, different from what we were. Through understanding, we go beyond the given, and we go beyond ourselves. We add intelligence to the data, and our understanding moves us into, makes us a part of, a bigger reality. We and our world expand. This is a spiritual movement.

Hopefully, as I continue to unfold the structure of the human spirit, you are having insights. Making sense of the words on this page, you will at the same time be generating evidence within your own mind about the very spiritual functioning that is the topic here. Hopefully, your present attention to the workings of your mind, even as you strive to understand my writing, will fill out the meaning of my words and make my abstract statements concrete. You will find personal examples for what I say.

I am sorry that I cannot provide more help. Only you can experience the workings of your mind, and what I am talking about is available to you only in your own mind. Apart from putting out the descriptions that I offer, I can do nothing to expose your mind to you. I cannot display your mind on this page. Only you can attend to your mind to try and grasp what I am writing.

## THE SPIRIT AS ACTUALLY KNOWING

Have an insight, come up with an idea, state a hypothesis, and the human spirit spontaneously shifts to a third mode of operation. New questions come to the fore: "Is it so?", "Is that idea right?" The concern now is to be correct, to make an accurate judgment.

It's one thing to have an idea; it's quite another to have a correct one. Our very being senses the difference. Our spirit is structured to be satisfied only with what actually fits. After all, on a first level of operation we were aware of data. That awareness is not lost when we shift to a second level of spiritual operation and attempt to understand the data. Nor is that awareness of the data or the idea generated from it lost when our spirit shifts focus again. When we generate an idea, a possible explanation, the criterion of correctness is already within us, and it emerges spontaneously: Does the idea actually fit the data? Does the explanation hold? Within the realm of my own awareness, do all the pieces fall neatly together?

The same spiritual capacity is operating throughout, and it is operating as a unit. Though its emphasis has shifted, it is still the same capacity dealing with the same project: to attain reality. The question about accuracy arises in the context of both the data and the proposed explanation. The concern at this point is to determine whether the proposed explanation does, indeed, fit the data. Are all the essential bases covered? Are all the relevant questions answered? Has the thing been explained? Does the answer actually fit?

This new kind of questioning calls for a new kind of insight. The concern is no longer to understand, but to confirm a proposed understanding. The concern is not to come up with a creative suggestion or a possible whole string of them, but to judge whether this or that specific suggestion is on target. This other kind of insight is the realization or the determination that "yes, the idea is correct," or "no, the idea is not correct." This other kind of insight is a judgment of fact.

Achievement of a positive judgment of fact—"yes, this is so"—moves the whole spiritual enterprise another step forward. From marveling and wondering and from suspecting and supposing, our spirit leads us to a grasp of what really is. We make another advance in self-transcendence. We move from personal experience and creative understanding to actual reality. We know. We have a sliver of truth, and we are different because of it.

This third function of the human spirit is obviously spiritual. If for no other reason, it is spiritual because it regards truth, and truth is a religious concern and a religious claim. The concern for truth lies at the heart of religion.

But the concern for truth is not strictly religious. It is the very focus of the third dimension of the human spirit. The fundamental meaning of "truth" is the recognition that an idea squares with the relevant data. Not something specifically religious, truth is essentially a concern of the human spirit. By the same token, then, the fundamental criterion of truth lies within the human spirit—not in the heavens, not in belief in God, not in appeal to revelation. We can claim to know reality, to know something of the truth, when our idea squares with the available evidence. If an idea does not square, if it is obviously without grounding, we would have to do violence to our very being to affirm that the idea is true. Our very makeup constrains us to reject ungrounded claims. We know when something fits and when it does not. We recognize a "snow job" or political "spin" when we encounter them.

Try to deny what I have just written. You would only be demeaning yourself. Try and argue that I am claiming too much, that our minds are just not so, that we really don't know truth. Try—and in the very production of your denial, in the act of denial itself, you will only confirm in practice what you are trying to deny in words. Here is what I mean. You deny because you want accuracy. You hesitate to agree because you are unsure. Your very being requires that an argument clinch the point, and you recognize when it does not. But the need of the human mind for accuracy is precisely what I am affirming. Your reaction of thoughtful denial expresses this very need. This need shows itself in you even as you question its reality.

I see no way around the constraints of Lonergan's analyses—except in postmodern excess to foolishly reject all concern for reasonableness as foolish. Take the process of human wonder, thinking, and knowing at all seriously, and you end up where Lonergan did. He certainly was onto something groundbreaking.

The spirit's own aching for truth explains why religions make so much of the truth—but, once recognized for what it is, this same spiritual aching limits what religions can legitimately claim as true. To recognize that the criteria of truth are built into our very being turns the tables on religion. Religion can no longer propose any old idea and require belief—not in the name of venerable tradition, not in the name of revelation, not even in the name of God. Once we understand the criteria of truth, all assertions—even those of religion, even those supposedly "revealed," even those about God—must respect these criteria, or the assertions cannot be true. Beliefs without grounding, unreasonable beliefs, need to be exposed and rejected. Once clarified, the spiritual nature of humanity itself makes demands on religion. Spirituality takes precedence over religion.

## THE TENSION BETWEEN RELIGION AND SPIRITUALITY

That last point is hardly novel. In recent decades many have professed that they are spiritual, but not religious. Increasingly, our age claims that spirituality is more important than religion.

I would agree, but I would nuance this claim in two ways. First, I would note this: since spirituality is an aspect of religion, it does not make good sense to pit spirituality against religion. To do so is to illogically pit religion against itself. True, spirituality is only one facet of religion, but it is, indeed, a facet of religion, and the most crucial one. True, too, attention to spirituality can purify religion. But said more accurately, with increased attention to its own spiritual core, religion can purify itself. It is a mistake to suggest that spirituality and religion are opposed or that one could choose between them.

On the one hand, spirituality comes from religion. We get our sense of spirituality from our religious upbringing or from the religious "coloring" of our social environment or from our delving into the religious traditions.

On the other hand, spirituality becomes religion. New spiritualities eventually turn into new religions, and then they usually devolve into new versions of that old-time religion. Followers of new spiritual movements can become as closed-minded, self-righteous, and bigoted as any religion ever was. And some spiritual movements are as outlandish as any institutionalized religion is. So, spirituality has no bragging rights over religion.

Second, I would also make this point: it is possible to sort out such nuances about spirituality and religion only after you understand what *spiritual* really means. For example, analysis of the human spirit shows that the criteria of truth are built into our human makeup. Then, it follows, it's not personal preference or family tradition or religious belief or supposed revelation from God, but the squaring of an idea with the relevant evidence that is the meaning of *true*. By appeal to the spiritual, the specification of *true* allows us to challenge religious teaching. In this sense, thus specified, spirituality does take precedence over religion—as many have suggested. However, Lonergan's analysis explains why this precedence holds. To be sure, many people challenge religion for being spiritually inept; but few can explain precisely how the challenge is valid. Few can say exactly what spirit and spirituality are and why some religion is spiritually destructive. Lonergan's account allows for such exactitude.

Thus, discussion here has moved beyond mere assertion and opinion about the spiritual and away from vague appeals to spirituality in criticism of religion. Discussion here is sketching the very structure of the human spirit and, in light of this structure, raising pointed questions about religion.

Again, it must be obvious that this discussion about something as everyday and ordinary as human knowing is truly about the spiritual. Concern for truth is a third dimension, or level, facet, or aspect, in the structure of the human spirit.

## THE SPIRIT AS CHOOSING AND DOING

Hit upon a correct understanding, arrive at some fact, actually know something of reality, and the functioning of the human spirit shifts into yet a fourth mode. The shift is from thinking to doing. In light of what we know to be the facts of the matter, the human spirit expresses itself in a new line of questioning: "What are you going to do about it?" "How are you going to respond?" "What will be your follow-up?"

Our living is not just mental; it takes place in a physical world. Living in a world of time and space requires making decisions and opting among choices. Confronted with new knowledge, we ponder its implications. Confirmed, for example, in the realization that religion must be subordinate to spirituality, we begin to wonder about our current religious commitments. Our pondering eventually brings us to the point where we make some decision. This decision is a spiritual function—although, more than in the case of the other dimensions of the human spirit, this spiritual function shows in the physical world: we do something.

Our decisions change our world. In the process, they also change us. We form ourselves by the decisions we make: we not only shape our world, we also shape ourselves. Just as the fireworks girl wanted to shoot up into the sky and pop, our spiritual nature leads each of us to become the reality that we affirm. As we make specific choices, we more and more become the kind of person who makes that kind of choice. Our very capacity for spiritual acts reacts back on itself. One peculiarity of the human spirit is its capacity for self-formation. Our choices make us who we are. We can make or break ourselves.

We can act in such a way as to enhance our human capacities or in such a way as to diminish ourselves. Although we could probably never destroy our spiritual potential completely—as they say, "Where there's life, there's hope"—we can move toward the point where, Darth Vader–like, we dampen and shut down the whole of our spiritual dynamism. The case of drug addicts is an extreme example: they end up unaware of their surroundings, uninsightful about their living, unconcerned about the truth, and enslaved to their addiction. The habitual liar presents another example, eventually unable to see the difference between his or her own lies and the truth. Blinded to their own doings, the professional criminal and the power-drunk politician offer other examples. And the fanatical religious believer, trapped in a make-believe world, presents still another. Ironically, the decision-making power of our human spirit—"free will"—can even undo itself. We humans are powerful creatures—and dangerous.

This notion of self-formation explains what spiritual growth means. Spiritual growth is nothing other than the ongoing enhancement of our own spiritual capacity. We enhance that capacity by using it constructively. So openness begets more and more openness; insight elicits more and more insightfulness; honesty fosters more and more ingenuousness; and goodwill nurtures ever-increasing capacity for love. These self-induced changes affect not only our external behavior but also our very capacity to behave. Sage use of our spirit increases the very capacity of our spirit. We grow spiritually.

The self-formative quality of the human spirit explains why religions are concerned about good living. They all include ethical requirements, and they all predict dire consequences for unethical behavior. These predictions are not made to scare us—though they should. These predictions simply express the reality of our situation.

Sometimes those consequences are projected into another world: purgatory, hell, a next life of negative karma. There is a spiritual lesson consistent in all these varied teachings: we cannot reach our personal fulfillment—we could not endure seeing God face to face, for example, or we could not achieve enlightenment—unless we are perfected in our very being. The lesson is that spiritual fulfillment involves self-induced changes in our makeup, the purification and perfection of our hearts and minds, not passive reliance on external powers such as "grace" and supernatural interventions. Spiritual fulfillment is a matter of human growth and potential.

More to the down-to-earth point, the effects of positive and negative living are this-worldly. Even as the days, months, and years of our lives go by, our choices, ethical or unethical, affect the quality of our experience. Our spiritual capacity expands to the extent that we use it well, and our lives are richer to the extent that our spiritual capacity expands. This very possibility for richer living is the meaning of *ethical*. The good is that which conduces to a more fulfilling life, overall; evil is that which is harmful and destructive to the process of living, overall. The effects of good and evil are not simply in the external world; they also show in ourselves, in us who do good or evil. If "virtue is its own reward"—fulfillment, richly satisfying life, happiness—vice also carries its own punishment: the debilitation of our very beings, the narrowing of our perspectives, the diminution of our capacity for experience, the shutting down of our sensitivities, the deadening of our "souls." There is no absolute need to look to another life; we already enjoy our rewards and bear our punishments in this life.

An understanding of the structure of the human spirit explains how these matters are so and why the religions teach what they do. This understanding also makes clear what the religions actually ought to be teaching, with what nuance, and why.

## WHAT'S LOVE GOT TO DO WITH IT?

My mention of love in connection with the fourth facet of the human spirit deserves specific comment. As they say, "Love is a many splendored thing." For this reason, love tends to be illusive. It includes more than a physical dimension: presence, touch, and sometimes sexual sharing. And it includes more than an emotional dimension: affection and sometimes infatuation and romance. It also includes a spiritual dimension. This dimension expresses the fourth level of the human spirit—decision, choice. Choices have to do with values, and loving means valuing. Loving means concern. Loving means dedication to the good of another person. To love someone is to prize and cherish her or him, to wish him or her all the best. To love is to choose and affirm another person.

From this point of view, the essence of love is its spiritual dimension. Being physically close to a person or even having sex does not necessarily imply love. Likewise, becoming emotionally entangled with someone does not necessarily guarantee love. People fall in love all the time and "cannot live" without each other, but their behavior toward each other often reveals little caring; they are just "hooked" on each other, and they use each other to fulfill their own needs. To love is to recognize the value or goodness in someone and to affirm it. To love is to affirm that person in his or her very being. The physical attraction and the emotional entanglement might or might not even support the spiritual affirmation. Obviously, then, they are not essential for love. The spiritual component is. Without it, what might be called "love"—English has only one word for the whole confusing lot—is hardly love, at all.

Thus, as is commonly said, love is a spiritual reality. But at this point we can also pinpoint the nature of the spiritual component of love: it is an expression of the human spirit functioning on its fourth level. To love is to discern goodness and to value it, to choose it, to affirm it, to commit oneself to it.

Related to love, related to ethics, related to religion, related to the self-formation of our own persons, choice or decision is a spiritual matter. It is the fourth aspect or facet or level of the human spirit. The human capacity to choose and the exercise of this capacity are spiritual.

## SUMMARY ABOUT THE STRUCTURE OF THE HUMAN SPIRIT

The human spirit is a dynamic, open-ended, self-constituting, self-regulating, self-transcending, cosmic dimension of the human mind. It is geared to the universe of being, all that is. It allows us not only to experience and know reality but also to affirm, embrace, and become one with it. The ongoing actuation of the human spirit moves us more and more deeply into reality. These qualities of the human spirit are not random. They cohere in one and the same human spirit, variously they express it, and in a particular way they interrelate. The human spirit has a structure.

The structure of the human spirit is fourfold. The human spirit is experience, understanding, judgment, and decision. These four emphases express the shifting and interrelated functioning of the human spirit.

In a logical sense, these four function in a particular order. As I presented them, experience and awareness of data lead to questioning and understanding; these, in turn, lead to judgment and knowledge, which finally lead to decision and behavior.

But, in actuality, the order varies. For example, our choices limit what experience is available to us, so in this sense decision comes first. But again, our knowledge limits what our choices might be; moreover, our prior knowledge—especially in the form of prejudice: prejudgment or premature judgment—also controls what further understanding we might allow ourselves to have, so in this sense knowledge comes first. But yet again, our understanding limits what knowledge we can have, and our understanding might also limit what we become aware of: we frequently overlook important details because some premature idea already controls our minds. So in this sense understanding comes first.

In the end, then, none of the facets of the human spirit comes before any other absolutely. They function in a shifting pattern, serving whatever need happens to be most pressing. And they all affect one another, as I just illustrated. The four levels make up one sole reality: the human spirit. It is multifaceted and structured in its makeup, but it is still just one reality, a marvelous reality that involves us ever more deeply in an awe-inspiring universe.

# TWO-PART VERSIONS OF A FOUR-PART STRUCTURE

In chapters 1 and 2, I spoke of the spiritual in terms of "meanings and val-ues." I also used alternative paired terms to suggest the same thing: credos and commitments, or beliefs and ethics, or understandings and evalua-tions, or ideas and ideals, or visions and virtues. In this chapter I am pre-senting the human spirit as a fourfold affair. Why the difference? Because in this chapter I am going into more detail.

Notice that the first three facets of the human spirit have to do with knowl-edge. Knowledge is correct understanding. Or said another way, knowl-edge (the third facet of the spirit) is understanding (the second facet) that squares with the data (the first facet). The first three facets of the human spirit share a similar concern. Sometimes more loosely, sometimes more precisely, this same concern could be named credos, beliefs, understand-ings, ideas, or visions. Also note that the first three facets of the human spirit parallel the textbook account of the scientific method: science arrives at sure explanation, knowledge, via observation (the first facet of the spirit), hypothesis (the second facet), and verification (the third facet).

On the other hand, the fourth facet of the human spirit relates to values—or, again, sometimes more loosely, sometimes more strictly—to commit-ments, ethics, evaluations, ideals, virtues.

So the two-part formula, meanings and values, is just a shorthand way of referring to the fourfold structure of the human spirit. Meanings and values—and those other pairs—are just simplified, more suggestive, some-times more poetic ways of invoking the fourfold essence of the human spirit.

To that list of shorthand pairs, we could add another: knowledge and love. As just noted, knowledge suggests the first three facets of the human spirit, and, as explained above, love relates to the fourth.

Furthermore, knowledge and love recall yet another parallel pair. Ancient and medieval philosophers spoke of the higher functions of the human mind as intellect and will. Again, the reference is not exact, but the thrust of the reference is on target: intellect relates to knowledge, and will relates to love.

I make this point to show that what I write about the human spirit is nothing distinctive, novel, or esoteric. With precision brilliantly added by Lonergan, I am just summarizing a perennial teaching of the Western Tradition.

For millennia, philosophers and theologians spoke in these same terms about the human spirit. Unfortunately, in our era this understanding has been lost. We have taken the spiritual as a characteristic of religion, pro-jected it up into heaven, and forgotten its relevance to everyday life. When recently we have tried to free the spiritual from its religious sarcophagus, we continue to treat it like something otherworldly, metaphysical, or divine, and we continue to overlook its connection with our own self-transcending minds.

In this third millennium, as our planet shrinks and we face increasing religious diversity, we can no longer afford to mistake the true nature of the spiritual. The human spirit is our hope for a truly global community—but only if we extricate spirituality from competing religions and esoteric metaphysical claims. Thus, I am attempting to clarify what spirit is, and to do so I am pulling in any associations that might help. I would also suggest that, if we understand what spirit actually is, we can understand its connection with religion and belief in God, and we can understand how it might get tangled up with esoteric, metaphysical musings.

In chapters 5 and 6, I will explicitly talk of God and otherworldly beliefs. Here I only want to elucidate the human spirit. My two-part formulas are just shorthand versions of the full fourfold structure of the human spirit.

## GIVEN STRUCTURE AND EFFECTIVE FUNCTIONING

All along I have been presuming that there is a correct and a mistaken way to use one's spiritual capacity, and I have freely used the term *ethical*. Again, these notions are nothing novel. In one way or another, every human being on this planet recognizes the difference between a lie and the truth, kindness and cruelty, prejudice and fairness, and openness and narrow-mindedness. But once again, this analysis of the human spirit actually grounds these commonplace notions—good and bad, right and wrong, better and worse. This analysis explains where these notions come from and why they are as they are: they are built-in requirements of the human spirit.

The human spirit has a particular structure. Then, it only makes sense that the spirit must function in a particular way. As they are designed, so things work. The computer is a great example. Struggling with it, people often declare that a computer has a mind of its own. That is to say, it will only work for you if you follow the particular procedures that are programmed into it. To get the best out of any piece of equipment, you use it as it was made to be used. The same holds for the human spirit. Its structure dictates its proper use.

On a first level, the spirit is receptive to incoming data. This openness to input is the fundamental requisite of any further spiritual functioning. If nothing new comes in, nothing new can happen. The whole system shuts down. Therefore, a first requirement of the human spirit is to be open-minded.

It's easy enough to say, "Be open-minded," but harder to actually follow through. Is there anyone who does not think that he or she is open? But we fool ourselves so easily! The Freudians even have a name for our unconscious self-deception: defense mechanisms; and the first of the defense mechanisms is denial. We simply blind ourselves to our own reality. We deny that things are as they are. We think we are being open when, in fact, we are not. We recognize denial easily in the people around us. What makes us think that it is not also operating in us?

This matter of denial is psychological. It opens up a whole other set of considerations that I have not yet addressed in this discussion of spiritual growth. We are not pure spirits functioning in an ideal setting, and I am hardly suggesting that we are. For better and for worse, our psychological makeup—and our biological makeup, as well—have major influences on our spiritual functioning. This matter of openness offers a prime example, and chapter 7 will address these further considerations in detail. I am well aware that the picture I have projected thus far is extremely idealistic. But, after all, I am proposing an ideal form—like Pythagoras's formula, Plato's Ideas or Forms, and Einstein's equations. I am presently suggesting a scientific account of the human spirit apart from other considerations that do, in practice, impinge on its functioning. Rest assured, in due time I will give the darker side of the human situation its due.

Here, simply note a first requirement of the human spirit: be open. Our very being imposes this requirement on us. No external authority—not parents, peers, society, religion, or God—but our very selves make this demand. The very outgoing nature of our human spirit calls us to be receptive, attentive, awake, open. Well aware that we sometimes deceive ourselves, we need to strive to be open-minded to the extent that we are able. Otherwise, we shut down our own self-transcendent possibilities.

Second, in the face of incoming data, the human spirit spontaneously seeks to understand. So, to the extent that we are able, we should be questioning, inquisitive, wondering. We should foster curiosity and exercise our intelligence. We should constantly make good use of whatever IQ we have. We should make every effort to try and understand. To the extent that we simply "take things on faith," go along with the crowd, buy the party line, or stop trying to make sense of things, we shut down the open-ended functioning of our human spirit.

Third, in the face of ideas, the human spirit wants to be correct. So we should be honest about things. We should evaluate the evidence, bravely criticize our own bright ideas, honestly judge whether an insight is valid or not. Otherwise, we begin building castles in the air—and they are sure to eventually fall down. Without honesty, we have no real future. As Jesus imagined the matter, we are a house built on sand.

Of course, we are hard-pressed to be honest on our own. We all have our blind spots, and we all have different areas of giftedness and expertise. We need one another to keep ourselves honest. Others fill in the gaps of our own shortcomings. So the process of spiritual growth is never an isolated enterprise. We need one another. We need community. We need a group of fellow truth-seekers to help us keep on track. The very thrust of the human spirit is outgoing, so true spirituality is never solitary. For this reason, spirituality and religions—organized communities of seekers—always go hand in hand.

Finally, in the face of new knowledge, we need to act. We need to decide and do something. The requirement of the spirit in this case is to do what is called for. Popularly said, we are to "do the right thing." But deciding what is the right thing is the challenge. Oftentimes an array of options stands before us. In chapter 5 of *The Transcended Christian*, I present a extended discussion of how the spiritual traditions help us know what option to make.

Attention to the human spirit suggests two guidelines for decision making. Act in accordance with the known truth of the matter, and act in such a way as to enhance the open-ended functioning of the human spirit.

It must be obvious that a secure future requires that we act in accordance with what we know to be the facts. You cannot build a future on misconceptions. But in themselves the facts do not yet specify our choice. The challenge of successful living is that in the face of the same facts a number of legitimate options are often available. Either the surface roads or the expressway will get us to our destination. Which we take is up to us, and often the choice makes no big difference. But when the difference does matter, the second guideline comes into play: make the choice that best serves human growth overall. As best as you are able, in light of what you know to be the truth, keep the system flowing. Do the loving thing. Build a solid future. Foster growth. Choose life. As Lonergan says, choose value, not just mere satisfaction.

## THE TRANSCENDENTAL PRECEPTS

The fourfold structure of the human spirit implies four general requirements: be open, be questioning, be honest, and be loving. Lonergan phrased these four more succinctly and more technically: be attentive, be intelligent, be reasonable, and be responsible. He called these four the "transcendental precepts."

They are transcendental because they apply across the board to anything and everything that people do. Their application knows no limits.

Besides, they are transcendental also because they specify no particular, concrete behaviors. They do not tell us exactly *what* we are to do; rather, they say *how* we are to go about whatever we do: attentively, intelligently, reasonably, and responsibly. What the final, legitimate conclusion should be is up to us to determine.

Specific requirements might not always hold. For example, we have the Commandments, "Honor your parents. Do not steal. Do not lie." But if a parent is mistaken, we should not obey. If a person is starving, he or she has a right to take food. If the bald truth will cause more harm than good, we sometimes need to obscure the truth—as in the famous case of the mother superior who, confronted by Nazi SS troops, denied outright that there were Jews hidden in the convent when, in fact, there were: those soldiers had no right to that truth or to the lives of the Jews. Sometimes the good is more complicated than the simple rules of morality. To make a crying child take a bitter medicine may not seem loving at the time, but we all know that it is. Sometimes the truly loving action seems harsh; hence, the talk of "tough love."

The transcendental precepts avoid the complications of particular, concrete requirements and specify only *how* one should act, not *what* one should eventually do. In this sense, these requirements of the human spirit are broad and open-ended. They are transcendental. They apply across cultures and relate to various religions. They offer a basis for wholesome and growth-producing living around the globe. Growth-producing living is precisely their intent. What they prescribe is action that, on all fronts and levels, fosters life.

Yet they are precepts. Without being absolutist, they are nonnegotiable absolutes. They truly are requirements. Nonetheless, these requirements are not laws imposed on people from outside. These requirements emerge from the makeup of our own being. For this reason they are absolutes.

Only "the devil" would object that these open-ended requirements skew and bias our functioning. Only "the devil"—that is, pure evil—would suggest that being open to the issues can be misleading, that wanting to understand is wrong, that basing our judgments on the evidence is narrow-minded, or that acting to produce the most growth is counterproductive.

Sometimes echoing the diabolical, our contemporary world goes astray to insist on personal freedom in the extreme: "It's my life; I'll do whatever I damn well please." We have warped the very notion of ethics. We take ethics to be external: the arbitrary rules of varying cultures or the morality of differing religions or the required procedures of professional agencies or the personal, deeply felt preferences of you or me—as if genuine ethics could vary from person to person, place to place, and time to time, as if the very same response in the very same circumstances could be wrong for one person but right for another, as if differing religions make things right or wrong by their mere decrees, as if dancing were really wrong for Baptists but not for Episcopalians or Methodists, or as if eating pork were truly evil in itself for Jews and Muslims but not for Catholics except on the Fridays of Lent. No wonder we react against moralists! No wonder some moralists are so far out in left field! We labor under widespread ignorance about the true meaning of morality.

Genuine ethics or morality—I use these terms interchangeably—grows out of our own humanity. The fundamental requirements of ethics come from our selves. The transcendental precepts are built-in. They are part and parcel of our spiritual makeup. They spell out what is needed for effective living. They express what is for our own best interest, overall. They define genuine or *authentic* humanity. We are authentic to the extent we embody the transcendental precepts. Any deviation from them results in dehumanization.

## KNOW THYSELF, TRUST THYSELF

Do not "take on faith" what I am presenting here. Look into your own mind and heart. Check out your own life experience. See for yourself whether or not what I present here fits. The stakes in this enterprise are too high for us to be accepting random opinions. We cannot build our lives or create global community on the basis of mere personal preference. We need to build on what grounds us all. We need a common foundation in our own selves. It is this foundation that the transcendental precepts claim to articulate.

Test within yourself the validity of this claim. Do you ever find yourself confronted with new phenomena? Do you ever wonder what they are? Do you ever question your understanding to make sure that you are right? Do you ever agonize over what would be the right thing to do?

Attend to your own experience. Don't take my word for it, or anyone else's. Raise questions. Entertain doubts. Research the matter. Consult with others. The more honest exploration you do on your own, the more we will all be working toward consensus.

I welcome questions about my presentation. I encourage doubts. In your own mind they provide the data you need to understand what I am writing—and to confirm or reject it. Questions that rise in your mind about this supposed "structure of the human spirit" exhibit the very open-ended functioning of the spirit about which I write. Doubts that arise are themselves evidence to support this presentation: they show that your own mind requires you to be sure before making a commitment. Your willingness to question and your honesty in raising doubts reveal you to be a person of human genuineness and personal authenticity: you spontaneously trust the requirements of your own mind. Such authenticity is precisely what this presentation intends to spell out. Don't take my word for it. Find it in yourself.

## A SPIRITUAL CHALLENGE TO RELIGION

Once while I was lecturing on nonreligious spirituality, a Biblical Fundamentalist confronted me with this objection: "How can you talk of spirituality without ever mentioning Jesus?" I responded with another question: "To what would Jesus object in anything that I've said?" The Fundamentalist had no answer. The obvious answer is "nothing."

The religions would not want to go on record as opposing the transcendental precepts. In general, they would support them—but especially the last two: be reasonable and be responsible or, in my popular rendition, be honest and be loving. The religions tend to emphasize truth and love.

However, if the truth actually be told, one peculiarity of the religions is that they tend *not* to support the first two precepts: be attentive and be intelligent or, in my popular rendition, be open-minded and be questioning. Especially the "religions of the book"—Judaism, Christianity, Islam, Mormonism, which claim to have the final truth from God and wherein fundamentalism is rampant—tend to downplay open-mindedness and questioning. Their "revealed" doctrines are supposed to be the last word, and people are to accept them on blind faith. In contrast, Bahá'í, for example, teaches a more balanced understanding of revelation as periodically updated.

This analysis of the human spirit raises serious questions about religion. Religious fanaticism comes precisely from the unwillingness to be open to other evidence and from the reluctance to question and seek deeper understanding of existing beliefs. Fanaticism comes from close-mindedness and mistrust of human intelligence. Where close-mindedness reigns, even the religious advocacy of truth and love becomes suspect. Without a foundation in openness and questioning, how could such advocacy be trustworthy? "Truth" could be just a codeword for official policy, and "love," just the biased requirements of the institution. Religions that oppose open-mindedness, questioning, research, and study oppose the very God-given engine of spiritual sensitivity and growth. Sad to say, the tragic flaw of much religion is that it stomps out the very spirituality that is its charge—even as the misguided parents of the doomed fireworks girl suppressed the essence of buoyant life in her and her little brother.

Evidently, this analysis of the human spirit cuts deep. Sometimes when we give precise meaning to the language religious and spiritual movements use, their teachings become suspect. Of course, we foresaw this outcome from the beginning. Spirituality is always a sensitive and dangerous enterprise. Once we have a clear understanding of what spirit and spirituality mean, this understanding works back on any claims about these matters. Hallowed religion and sacred personal belief are no longer immune to criticism.

## PURIFIED RELIGION AND GLOBAL COMMUNITY

The present analysis, grounded in the evidence of our own minds, is in this sense scientific: it is an explanation grounded in the relevant data. Hence, here, again, we see an example of how science can clear up confusion and purify traditional beliefs. Proposing a scientific approach to spirituality, I am constructing a spiritual basis for a worldwide community.

I highlight a common spiritual core on which humankind as a whole can rely. This core legitimates criticism of religion; it allows us to winnow out the religious wheat from the chaff. Then, without either losing spiritual commitment, on the one hand, or buying into any particular religion whole hog, on the other, we have an approach that could bring our world together in peace.

Universal positive effects of religion are not commonplace, but the promising effect of scientific explanation is well known. In the field of medicine, an understanding of infection might discredit cherished folk practices, yet it still fosters the health intended by those practices. The same is true for psychiatry: neurological misfiring often explains and exposes as superstition what used to be called demon possession, yet treatment restores the sacred sanity that the religious diagnosis envisioned.

In the present case, at issue is a science of the human spirit. It inevitably raises questions about the adequacy of religion. There is no need to apologize for this questioning. We cannot avoid questioning religion if we are ever to unite the diverse peoples on our shrinking planet. In light of the known structure and functioning of the human spirit, the next two chapters will consider some key religious notions and examine their validity. The goal is to invigorate the healthy growth by pruning away dead or rotting branches.

# 5

## The Problem of God

In South Side Pittsburgh where I grew up, we had a strong sense of community. The same was undoubtedly true in every village, tribe, and nation in the premodern world. Everyone pretty much believed the same as everybody else, so everybody got along. When petty disagreements arose, at least we agreed on the principles to settle them. At the core of that shared worldview in South Side Pittsburgh was our belief in God. Luckily, there was no doubt about God. Our Catholic faith of that era left little room for uncertainty.

But the times have changed. Not only is there fragmenting debate within the Catholic Church itself; but the same word *God* also obviously means different things to different people committed to different religions. When "God" can excuse the destruction of the World Trade Center, the Israeli occupation of Palestinian land, the Arab terrorist attacks on Israel, the territorial disputes between India and Pakistan, the relentless "troubles" in Ireland, the murder of personnel at abortion clinics, the bashing and killing of gay men and lesbians, the requirement of proven ineffective "abstinence-only" sex education in the United States, the Vatican prohibition of condom use in the age of AIDS, the suppression of women in most countries of the world, the mass suicides of the Peoples Temple in Jonestown, Heaven's Gate in San Diego, and the Branch Davidians in Waco, and the subway gassing by the apocalyptic cult Aum Shinrikyo in Japan—belief in "God" has become a problem.

This chapter explores the notion of God and proposes an understanding that would allow God to be God and us to be us without confusing the two.

## THE ABUSE OF GOD

As it turns out, *God* really means whatever I and mine hold ultimately dear. Putting the name "God" on it makes it no more valid than otherwise. We are all well aware that people's image of God may be one thing and God in Godself something quite different again, so we now wonder whether belief in God can have any validity at all. Is belief in God just a way of passing the buck? Do we let "God" take responsibility for what we and our culture have concocted?

In most cases, unfortunately, the answer is yes. All societies develop their particular understanding of the world and its proper functioning. Having done so in good faith, societies tend to presume that their understanding is from God, and this presumption is perfectly reasonable—as far as it goes.

A well-known example is the Ten Commandments and the other laws included in the Hebrew Scriptures. Supposedly, God revealed to Moses these detailed requirements for daily life. Another case in point is conservative Islam's insistence that Allah requires society to be structured as it was in the sixth century. Again, the Vatican insists that God personally forbids the ordination of women. In American society, the phrase "for God and country" makes a similar connection between public policy and divine approbation. Every society believes that its ways are divinely inspired. Today's problem is that we are aware that all those ways can differ and God starts looking schizophrenic.

The same kind of thinking applies on the personal level. Often, as individuals, we appeal to "God" to ground our most cherished beliefs when, really, we may just be using belief in God to excuse our own irresponsibility. Unwilling to grapple deeply with the hard questions of life, we fall back on religious beliefs and accept them without thinking, "in the name of God."

This strategy is unapologetically blatant among Biblical Fundamentalists. When condemning homosexuality, for example, they confidently insist that it is not they, but God's word in the Bible, that makes the condemnation. They forget that massive scholarship comes to a different conclusion about the Bible's teaching so that their claim about God must depend on their personal choice to read the Bible in a particular way. In the process, they are excused from exploring the real reasons for their fervent opposition to homosexuality. In the very least, an honest response would have to admit that the Bible's teaching on homosexuality is highly debated and, therefore, uncertain. The same kind of rationalization applies to Fundamentalist beliefs about the treatment of women or the disciplining of children.

This same religious rationalization was at work in the Vatican's 2003 statement opposing gay marriage and its 2005 statement forbidding gay seminarians. Disregarding historical, theological, and social-science evi-

dence, the Vatican has solemnly enshrined all the standard negative stereotypes about lesbians and gays, "in the name of God."

## MISGUIDED NOTIONS OF GOD

In these confusing times, when we are better at criticizing beliefs than at
proposing secure ones, what validity does the notion of God hold? Does my
criticism of "God," here and in chapter 2, make me a godless atheist, as
some have said? Are all of us doomed in the postmodern world to give up
belief in God?

The answer depends on what we mean by "God." And in most cases, like
those in the list above, our belief in "God" may be misguided.

I understand that in alcohol-and-drug-rehab circles there are three principles about God: "First, there is a God. Second, you are not God. And
third, God is not Santa Claus." If we are honest about it, however, for most
of us "God" is, indeed, an adult version of Santa Claus. We think that, if we
are good little boys and girls and if we ask nicely, "God" will step in and
give us what we want. In my experience, both personal and professional,
when people say they believe in God, they mean that there is a spiritual
force that answers prayers, rewards good living, and personally, deliberately, and explicitly intervenes to change, adjust, and manipulate our lives
in particular directions. If someone does not accept that, like a puppeteer,
God is pulling the strings of life and history, that person is accused of not
believing in God.

Often, when we turn to God, we expect a miracle. We carry over into
adulthood the childish notion that makes Freud correct: God is just
Mommy and Daddy projected large into the sky. Just as, seemingly magically, they stepped in to catch us when we were about to fall or backed us
up when we had a challenging school assignment, so, it is said, "God is
there to care for us in all our needs."

Isn't that phrase exactly what religion teaches? To be sure, there is a legitimate understanding of that phrase. In some sense, God *is* there, and in
some sense God *does* care for all our needs. But this sense is subtle, and it
does not always cover what *we*—even with good reason—think our needs
are. So, depending on how you take it, that phrase could well be misleading. It is surely misleading to the extent that we continue to think of God as
a wonderworker in the sky.

I do not mean to offend as I express these thoughts. The criticism I make
applies also to me. We all need to mature in faith. Despite my considerable
education and lifelong experience, I must admit that often I catch myself
childishly praying to God for a miracle: "God, please let my car start"; "God,

please let me find some money to cover the bills on my desk"; "God, please let me feel better so I don't have to make a doctor's appointment." Like others, I also fall back on my childhood emotions, and I find myself expecting God to take care of things that, as an adult, I ought to take care of myself—even as traditional religion teaches: "God helps those who help themselves." But we learn about God at so early an age that God becomes part of our childhood sense of magic, and what is learned early and with profound emotional charge sinks deeply into us and is hard to uproot.

## PRAYER—CHILDISH AND MATURE

In chapter 2, I said that God cannot be comprehended, so every notion of God is a hypothesis, a theory, a supposition. But, I added, some hypotheses are better than others.

The hypothesis of God as a heavenly Santa Claus, who responds to our prayers and good behavior, is wanting. For one thing, our prayers often go unanswered. Oh, the true believer will insist that God always does answer prayers but God's answer may not be what we ourselves would want. How very clever! And, of course, there is no way to prove or disprove this assertion. This fact is the very problem with such metaphysical claims: whether they are true or false is beyond any possible adjudication; there is absolutely no way to show whether they are true or false, so in the name of supernatural faith people can advance the most outlandish of claims. They are indeterminables. Even so, in light of how events often turn out, one would be hard-pressed to insist that they were a good God's response to our prayers—not only in the case of the deceits, thefts, murders, and heartbreaks that we perpetrate against one another but also in the case of the deformities, storms, accidents, illness, and death that befall us because of natural causes.

In fact, there is a valuable lesson in the claim that God answers prayers. It is the lesson that we should not give up hope. To continue to pray means to continue believing in good things to come. And, indeed, we should continue trusting, continue hoping, continue striving. We should keep on keeping on despite what happens. Doing so is the only way to live well.

So that lesson is certainly sound—but it does not support the notion of God as a wonderworker, and it also applies to people who do not believe in God. This is to say, the lesson in the advice to pray to God—not to give up hope—could be had apart from prayer and apart from belief in God. This valid human lesson is not necessarily tied to religion although religion is a regular spokesperson of this lesson.

In addition, asking things of God forces us to put our wants into words. As self-help gurus tell us, the first step toward getting what you want is to be clear about exactly what it is. Formulating our wants—for example, in prayer—helps us get them clear. So prayer may, indeed, help us attain what we want in some cases—not so much by getting God to act on our requests but by focusing our own capacities on specific goals.

There could be yet another valid meaning of prayer. In prayer we often mention this and that specific need. Well, offering our list of needs to God could be a way of acknowledging that we trust God in every last detail of our lives. The popular phrase, "Let go, and let God," captures this attitude: there is only so much we are able to do; much of life is out of our hands. So if in prayer we mention our needs but do not literally expect God to work miracles, our prayer could express a fully legitimate religious attitude: sane surrender to the natural process of life in things both big and small; courageous, unswerving, and virtue-filled trust—this is true faith—that overall the universe is unfolding as it should.

But how many of us pray without really expecting our requested answer? If we did not expect those answers, would we continue to pray? If we did continue to pray not expecting answers, what would our prayer look like? It would certainly not be the commonest form, the prayer of petition. It would more likely be wordless prayer of quiet surrender, mere resting in awareness of the presence of God. I treat these different ways of praying in *Meditation without Myth*.

Prayer to God as to a heavenly Santa Claus is wanting. Such prayer suggests that God did not do the work of creation very well. If God needs to step in periodically to adjust the system, the universe and the laws that God built into it appear to be faulty. Such a notion presumes an inadequate God.

Besides, if we truly believed that God oversees all happenings, we would not feel a need to ask God to change anything. As Jesus pointed out, God knows what we need even before we ask, so asking is not the essence of prayer. If we do pray to have God step in and make changes, we evidently do not really believe that God is caring for us. Our very prayer for divine favors suggests that we lack faith. On all fronts, the notion of a God who answers prayers is problematic.

## GENUINE TRUST IN GOD

If we do not expect God to miraculously grant our requests, what are we to do? Just accept things as they are, working with them as we are able and, otherwise, being grateful for the experience?

Yes.

The comedian W. C. Fields grew up in Philadelphia, but he utterly hated the place. When asked what he would like to have carved on his tombstone, without hesitation he replied, "I'd rather be in Philadelphia."

The very experience of being alive can outweigh all its negatives. When I sometimes lament that I am growing old, some wise friends remind me that this is better than the alternative. Unflagging appreciation for life can be a sustaining attitude.

Consider what such an attitude would imply—that we own our status as mere creatures, that we humbly accept the life we have been given, that we make the best of any situation, that we feel true gratitude in the face of every small beauty and joy, and that we delight in the very adventure and challenge of being alive. Is this not the attitude we admire in people who, despite whatever setbacks, go on to make their contribution and live a fulfilling life?

Would not such a positive attitude toward life also include—whether spoken in words or merely implied—a quiet reverence for Whatever-It-Is that is behind the whole enterprise of life?

Such a positive attitude, even in the face of life's challenges, would certainly express profound faith. Religious believers would call this attitude "faith or trust in God." Nonreligious folk might simply call this attitude "belief in life"—as in the Jewish toast, *l'chaim*. In practice, this attitude would be the same whether religious or not. The explicit words put on it—belief in God or belief in life—would hardly matter. What matters is trust in what is.

That same, affirming attitude toward life is central to Eastern philosophy. I see that attitude in the well-known Eastern teaching that all is illusion. People often misunderstand this teaching and think it means that nothing is real. But, as best as I can determine, the meaning is psychological; it is about how we think about things. The meaning is not ontological; it is not about the actual reality or nonreality of the things we think about. No doubt, things are real. But we often distort their reality by thinking of them wrongly. The following story about an Eastern guru brings home the point.

This guru's son had died, and the guru was distraught. This reaction confused his disciple, who asked, "Master, why are you upset? Do you not teach that all things are illusion?" The guru responded, "Yes. You are right about the teaching. But my son was a very big illusion."

The point is not that the son was not real. The point is that, like any proud parent, the guru had projected grand dreams upon his son, and these dreams were shattered. Our dreams and expectations, our self-serving schemes, distort the realities before us. We see them through our individualistic and self-centered eyes. Our perception is entangled in strands of personal preoccupation. In Western terms, we are "ego-involved." Thus, we manipulate and warp reality to fit our own designs. We live in a web of illusions, not within reality. Thus, for the unenlightened, all is illusion.

The spiritual solution is to release our grasp, to give up our manipulative and distorting designs, to surrender our illusions. The solution is to trust reality as it is, to let things be.

This "letting things be" does not suggest that we just sit back and do nothing. It is a mistake to categorize Eastern philosophy as passive. Look at the Dalai Lama. Look at Thich Nhat Hanh. Look at any of the great Eastern spiritual leaders teaching among us in the West. They are hardly do-nothings. They launch and sustain powerful spiritual movements. Though fully enlightened, they are fully engaged in the affairs of this world. But they are not attached to them! They are not ego-invested! Detachment is the issue.

Detachment is also a central concept in much Western spiritual teaching. For example, detachment is a key virtue among St. Ignatius of Loyola's Jesuits: they are to throw themselves whole heartedly into every worthy project but, after having done their best, let the chips fall where they may and let go of final results. They are to trust that God is working God's inscrutable will in whatever outcome.

A similar attitude characterizes Taoism—with its awareness of the complementary energies of yin and yang, dark and light, passivity and activity, ebb and flow. Taoism's ideal is to move with the natural course of things and in this way to live effectively. The ideal is to engage the very forces at hand, not resist them, to achieve one's goal. The martial arts embody this ideal. Not by pushing and forcing, not by manipulation and aggression, but by graciously moving with the natural flow of energy, one overcomes. In a similar vein, there is the story of the enlightened, expert butcher who never had to sharpen his knives: he cut so skillfully along the natural grain of the meat and bones that his knives never met resistance.

The basic attitude underlying all those perspectives is a kind of trust. You recognize reality for what it is; you accept the natural configuration of things; you enter into their flow. Because you are at one with the universe, you can advance your cause. You do not pretend to be able to make things fit your own schemes. You do not imagine you could magically transform life to meet your own imaginations. You give up illusions. You let go of attachments. You move with the current. You take things as they are, and in this way you tap into the available powers! You trust the given universe, and in this way you work with the forces of the universe on your side!

Now, there's a clue to an understanding of "God" that makes good sense! God is not a celestial Santa Claus who can change reality to square with our wishes. God is the creative power that has set up and sustains reality as it is. Working with reality as it is, we work hand in hand with God. Acknowledging reality for what it is, we reverence the God of the universe, who made things as they are. The trusting soul has no need for a God who grants favorites special favors.

I have a friend whose Brazilian grandmother taught him early and well, "God is for thanking, not for asking." Many of us never got this lesson, and some will fight it tooth and nail—although across religions the essence of spirituality is often said to be gratitude. From the Christian tradition, the very word for the service of Holy Communion, *Eucharist*, means thanksgiving.

Pointing to a valid understanding regarding "favors" from God, Jesus noted that God lets the rain fall on the good and the evil alike, and lets the sun shine on them all, as well. A nonbelieving friend of mine playfully made the same point once when, against all odds, we easily found a parking space. His comment: "See how the Lord takes care of those who don't believe in Him."

My friend was making fun of popular religion but was also showing his profound religious wisdom. If there is a God at all, God is not the heavenly magician who periodically suspends the laws of the universe in response to our requests. Rather, God is the source and sustainer of the universe and its laws, so whatever happens must *in some way* be attributed to God—even the random success in finding a parking space. In this indirect way, on a good day, one could optimistically and accurately say, God is, indeed, caring for our every need. And every day, feeling supported or not, one would at least have to say, God is behind everything that happens.

## THE QUESTION ABOUT EXISTENCE

Although it leaves us wondering about the bad things that happen to us, the notion of God as the source and sustainer of the universe holds up. It is the answer to a question that puzzles anyone who pauses to think: where did we and this vast universe come from? Physicists, chemists, and astronomers might push the explanation of the universe creation back to a few milliseconds after the Big Bang. But what explains the Big Bang itself? Where did *it* come from? Explain as much as we might about the universe's functioning, the question about the very existence of the universe still remains. Philosophers have asked this same question in a more provocative form: why is there something rather than nothing?

Nothing we know needs to exist absolutely. That I am here, and my world, is a matter of chance—my good fortune. I could as easily have never existed. Why do I exist? Why does anything exist?

Our human mind, with its spiritual capacity for understanding, expects that reasonable questions have answers. The question about the existence of things is reasonable. It must have an answer.

But what answer could we give? In our scientific enterprise we have been somewhat successful in explaining what things are and how they function—

presuming all the time, of course, that they exist, that they are already there to be explained. To some extent we know the "laws of the universe." But to say where the universe comes from? To account for its very existence? This question is surely beyond us.

Nonetheless, we know there must be an answer. If there is not, we must begin to consider that, ultimately, nothing makes sense, all is meaningless—because the very notion of "making sense" includes the whole. To make sense means that all of the pieces fit together, all of them. If we are aware of parts of our world that do not cohere with the rest, we cannot pretend that our world makes sense—unless we keep ourselves from thinking about the big picture. If only part of our life makes sense and the rest is chaos, we have to consider that even the sense we have might well be a fluke. Integrated with the whole, the sense we have might well prove to be illusion, totally off base in light of the bigger picture. "Partial explanation" is an existential oxymoron: if we cannot account for the whole, we really do not have an accounting.

A few precious strands of meaning in a sea of meaninglessness lose their viable meaning. They have no solid basis; they lack a sustaining context. They float randomly; they are disconnected from the whole. But by nature and definition, the random and disconnected is not meaningful. Meaning means that things cohere, they fit together, they make sense.

Understanding always presumes wholeness; it implies comprehensive coherence. If the questions around the fringe of our lives do not have answers—not just that we do not know the answers but that there are none, period—well then, overall, our world does not make sense. Oh, we may have an island of sense, our everyday world in which life hangs together well enough. But if this island of meaning ends in dark cliffs on the brink of chaos, the surrounding meaninglessness challenges, relativizes, or even disqualifies whatever meaning we make on our island. The surrounding darkness ever threatens to overwhelm our single point of light.

To get on with daily living, we can and do ignore the big picture; we put off the looming questions. But deep down inside, we know that we may well be fooling ourselves. Unless the whole makes sense, we are really hard-pressed to maintain the meaningfulness of our personal island. We are unwilling—and, indeed, constitutionally unable—to live in a meaningless world. If we allow that we do know anything at all, we know that our question about the existence of things must also have an answer. Otherwise, all our knowledge falls under suspicion. Our question-asking, reasonable minds might simply be part of a grand hoax. There must be an answer to the question about the existence of things.

Our own sense of worth is entwined with this expectation of an answer. Our self-respect depends on there being an answer. That we would have legitimate questions that have no legitimate answers brings our own selves into doubt. If our reasonable questions do not have answers—especially the most profound of questions—our very reasonableness forces us, paradoxically, self-contradictorily, to disqualify our reason itself. Our minds must be askew. Our human makeup spontaneously asks questions and confidently expects answers. If there are no answers, in honesty we must admit that our minds are essentially flawed. We must be deviantly oriented: we expect meaning when there is none. To expect an answer to questions is to trust our own minds. If there is no answer to this one reasonable question, how can we expect and trust answers to any reasonable questions?

To believe that there is an answer to the question about the existence of things is to believe in ourselves. If "God" is to be the answer to the question about existence, belief in God and belief in ourselves are two sides of the same coin. This is not to say that God is just an idea that we concoct, but to say that, trusting our minds, we might naturally be led to affirm the existence of God.

If legitimate questions have no answers, our minds must have nothing to do with reality. Our minds must be merely deceptive devices of creative self-distraction. What we call reality must only be our individual, self-deluded constructions, the sheer, extravagant productions of our imaginations. This line of reasoning—if reasoning has any meaning at this point—typifies radical postmodern nihilism. Because postmodern living is so complex, we are inclined *to choose to distrust*—catch the irony—our own minds. Seemingly, our era so alienates us from ourselves that we discredit our innermost, spontaneous beings. At the heart of the postmodern dilemma lies the inability to trust our experience to account for human knowing, and the conclusion—catch the irony again—is that we cannot really know anything. But if human knowledge is invalid, nothing we know is real. The word *real* has no meaning. Indeed, for us "self-demeaners," there could be no real reality, for what reality there might really be is supposedly out of bounds to us.

That supposed set of affairs is absurd. Absurdity indicates error. In fact, we do conceive of reality. It is part of our computation. Evidently, then, reality is not beyond us. It pertains to our experience and to the universe which we construct for ourselves.

In light of these considerations, we are left with two options. Either we accept our minds as geared toward reality, or we discredit ourselves as knowers. But if we are not knowers, can we know the supposed fact that we are not? If human knowledge has nothing to do with reality, what validity could this supposed knowledge about knowledge have? It discredits itself along with all other knowledge claims. The postmodern denial of realistic human knowing is a spiraling rat hole that leads one deeper and deeper into self-deprecating absurdity. This descent is not an option worth pursuing.

## G-O-D AS THE ANSWER TO THE QUESTION

The very makeup of our being expects an answer to reasonable questions. We are structured this way. Such is our nature. The best that is in us insists that there is an answer, that our world is meaningful. So, trusting ourselves, we draw the natural conclusion. We state what in all reasonableness must be affirmed: there is an answer to the question about the very existence of things; something does explain existence itself.

But in all honesty, we must also admit that we do not know what the answer is. While we continue to ponder the question, we put a name on the answer that we do not yet have. We suggest that we call whatever it is that explains the existence of things G-O-D. In algebraic equations we use an $X$ to name an unknown whose value is necessarily implied in the equation but whose value we cannot yet state. In a similar way, we use the term *God* to name the expected answer to our question about the existence of things, although we cannot say what God is.

*God* is our name for an unknown. *God* is shorthand for "whatever explains the existence and ongoing functioning of the universe." Saint Thomas Aquinas stated repeatedly that we do not know *what* God is but it is completely reasonable to affirm *that* God is—because there must be something behind the whole shebang (ah, not Aquinas's word). Whatever that something is, we call it "God."

God is an Unknown. God is the Great Mystery behind the existence of things. To say it otherwise, God is Creator.

Do we think we know what "Creator" means simply because we put this word on it? Can we explain how it is that things came to exist, how they continue to be, how they function to produce newness in the universe, each according to its proper nature?

The medieval world spelled out the implications of the notion of creation; they are the three issues that I just questioned. To say that God is Creator means that out of nothing God fashioned a universe and set it in existence. By sheer dint of logic, creation must be "out of nothing," *ex nihilo*, because apart from creation there is nothing with which God could construct a universe. This first aspect is called simply *creation*. But nothing created exists in itself; no creature exists per se. No creature is a necessary being; no creature is self-explanatory as regards its existence. Rather, every creature is contingent: each just happens to exist. Now, if no creature exists by its own self, it must be—by simple logic again—that every creature remains fully dependent on the Creator not only in its coming into being but also for its continuing to be. This second aspect, God's keeping things in existence, is called *conservation*. Finally, creatures function and act according to the natures the Creator gave them, but in so acting, they introduce novelty into creation. But nothing new can come to be without the creative activity of the Creator. This third aspect of creation, God's supporting creatures in their every productive activity, is called *concurrence*.

This elaboration makes clear that the Creator is active in creation and remains intimately involved in the activity of every creature: divine providence is part and parcel of the full notion of creation. The Creator-God is not the eighteenth Century Deist God who, it was supposed, set creation in motion, as a clockmaker builds a timepiece, and then sat back, uninvolved, to watch it run. Insistence on divine conservation and concurrence keeps the notion of Creator rich and full. The development of physical matter from subatomic particles to elements and complex molecules, the astounding emergence of life on the basis of routine chemical processes, the evolution of myriad species over millennia upon millennia, the eventual appearance of full consciousness in human beings, the gradual human understanding of matter, biology, and even the mind itself—the unfolding of creation clearly exhibits a directedness even as understood by secular science. What more could be needed for faith to see God at work in creation? To keep God actively involved, there is no need to suppose extraordinary interventions that would adjust and suspend the laws of nature periodically. There is no need to imagine God as the great Santa Claus in the sky. God can love and care for us—is creating us not gift enough?—without in addition having to work miracles for us.

Those are some of the details about creation that theologians have worked out over the centuries. Those details spell out the logical implications of affirming a Creator: a necessary being that would account for the appearance and ongoing existence of all contingent reality. There are the details, and there are even some technical terms to go with them. We can say much about this topic.

However, when all is said and done, how much do we really understand the Power, the Force, that set the universe in being and order and keeps it functioning? Do we know what creation is in itself, how it occurs, or what it means? Does naming creation, conservation, concurrence, Deism, divine providence, and necessary and contingent being mean that we actually understand the Creator, creation, or existence? No way! Not at all!

We rightly insist that there must be some answer to the question about existence. We carefully deduce the logical implications of the expected answer and list them. We can quote technical terms to name these implications. In the case of an $X$ in an algebraic equation, after listing all the known details about $X$, we are able to go on and solve for it; we determine the exact value of $X$. Can we do the same after listing the details about *creation*? Can we "solve" the puzzle and now say what *creation* means? Do we understand anything more about the Creator than the affirmation with which we started? Not at all. We only appreciate more profoundly the Mystery with which we are dealing. With Aquinas we are left to say that we know there is a God but we do not know what God is. Calling God *Creator* merely puts a more sophisticated term on *X*, the Great Unknown.

Unfortunately, many religious folk never get that lesson. They take the names *God* and *Creator* and start using them as if we knew what they mean. They tell us what "God" thinks and wants, what "God" requires and expects, what other people had better do to keep "God" from getting angry, what plan for the entire world and universe rests in the mind of "God." They—we—talk about God as if we knew what we are talking about. We do not. Correctly, we know this "something" must exist, and shrewdly we name that unknown. But putting a label on the unknown does not mean we know what the unknown is.

The best we can do before this kind of God is to bow in reverent silence. The best we can do is to go with the flow, to work within the system, to humbly accept life for what it is. As soon as we open our mouths and begin to speak words about God, we only express our ignorance; we project our own petty thoughts onto God. This result is the same whether we speak in petitioning prayer or in instructive preaching. Imagining a God who grants favors is projecting our own schemes onto heaven. Telling others what God is and what God wants of them is pushing our own agenda. Whatever we say about God is more our own thoughts than God's reality. The true God of the universe remains ever an unknown.

I do not mean to suggest that we have no way of knowing right and wrong, better and worse ways to behave. What I want to suggest, throughout this book, is that we can know these matters without knowing God or involving God in the discussion. Our knowledge of right and wrong is our own. We figure out, as best we can, how we ought to live. We attribute our solution to "God" only because we know that, whatever God is, God would certainly approve of behavior that enhances creation and disapprove of behavior that is harmful and destructive. God is on the side of being, life, growth, expansion; this is what God stands for. To add talk of God to this concern is to be redundant. To maintain this concern and omit talk of God in this case is to lose nothing substantive. Figuring out what fosters life and growth in the concrete, we propose our rules of ethics. The specific conclusions, the moral requirements we profess, these are our own. Rules of ethics and morality are human productions. In different situations, given new information, our conclusions would have to change. They do not enjoy eternal, infallible validity as if they were literally God's own. To involve claims of "God" in our ethical discussions actually distracts from the telling issues: it puts a divine seal of approval on a particular human opinion; it obscures the responsibility that we ourselves bear to make informed, wise, and fair decisions; it blurs the this-worldly consequences of human behavior that morality is supposed to address; overall, it does a disservice to the Divinity and humanity alike. To invoke "God" to resolve our this-worldly concerns is to draw conclusions from an unknown. Being intelligent, we should keep otherworldly indeterminables out of the discussion of this-worldly indispensables.

"God" is that which set the universe in existence and sustains it in being. As such, this reality, God, whatever it is, is fully beyond our comprehension. This God invites us to wonder and awe, reverence and trust, humility and gratitude. Claims to know God and pleas to change God are childish fantasy.

## THE GOD OF THE MYSTICS

Do we lose something in speaking of God as the Great Unknown that created and sustains the universe? God as the Power behind all things? "The Force" from *Star Wars*? Of course, we do. We no longer have a God whom we can picture, talk to, and entreat. God is no longer the image of the Divine Father or the Eternal Loving Mother. Even Jesus spoke of God as *Abba* (Daddy): "Our Father, who art in heaven." As the Great Unknown, God becomes impersonal, a power, a force, an energy—or, at least, God no longer seems to be a person as we understand persons to be.

Growing up is hard to do. So many of us have aches in our hearts that date back to unremembered childhood! We long to be held and caressed, to be protected and cuddled. We hardly find such response among fellow human beings. Most of them are struggling to satisfy these same needs for themselves, so we are not able to attend well to one another. We have only God to turn to, so we want God to be someone or something to which we can relate.

The understanding of God that I am presenting hardly fits that bill. How sad! How truly unfortunate! How heavy is the human burden! Yet, as I argued, the God I present is the best notion of God available. Other notions do not work. They cause many of our problems. Indeed, they often cause that very emptiness in our hearts that leads us to make God into a surrogate parent: looking to "God" for comfort rather than learning to love one another, we mistreat one another and just increase our need to avoid reality, whose hurtfulness is, for the most part, of our own making. We are caught in a vicious circle, and we draw God into it. We look to God for an escape from the challenges of life while, in reality, our infantile notion of God prevents us from engaging life seriously, so we live shallow lives, miss opportunities for growth, and continue to feel boxed-in. Naive notions of God just spin us round the circle ever more quickly.

At some point we need to break the vicious circle, to step out of it. We need to acknowledge that God is not like us, that God is not what we would want God to be, and that—alas, without a comforting God—we need to embrace the reality in which we exist. We need to learn to let go of our childish notion of God and, growing up bit by bit, let God truly be God and let us take up our proper responsibility for our lives and our world.

In fact, the great religious traditions support such an understanding of God, challenging though it might be. For example, the oldest religious texts in existence, the Vedas of ancient Hinduism, include hymns describing the origin of creation. One hymn ends with a humble acknowledgment that all such explanations are mere speculation, that we do not know how things came to be—that even "the One who is above the heavens" may not know! Likewise, a standard maxim in the East teaches, "Those who say do not know; those who know do not say." This maxim refers to the ultimate mystery of life, to the most profound of religious experiences. The lesson is that the ultimate is unknown, fully beyond our poor human means of comprehension or expression. Likewise, the Bible has God say, "My ways are not your ways. As far as the East is from the West, so far are my ways from your ways." Similarly, when Moses asked God's name, the response was enigmatic: "I Am Who Am." Nobody even knows for certain how to translate the Hebrew. Other possible translations are "I Am What I Am," "I Do What I Do" and "I Will Be What I Will Be." In every translation, the point is the same: God is not to be pinned down. No one should ever get the idea that he or she has a handle on God. No one knows God's name. For this very reason the Jewish tradition forbids pronunciation of that revealed name and, along with Islam, outlaws images of God. Likewise, images of the gods in Hinduism have peculiar, sometimes grotesque features. They remind us that God is nothing that we know or would expect. Universally, the religions suggest that we should not expect to find in God someone like ourselves.

The mystics and enlightened ones speak in a similar vein. Striking, for example, is St. John of the Cross's account of mystical encounter with God: "*Nada, nada, nada*—nothing, nothing, nothing." Those who claim to have experienced God firsthand—a claim that must itself be taken with a grain of salt—often speak of the Void, not of ecstasy, bliss, or rapturous fulfillment. Those who would seem to know most about God portray God as Mystery, Unknown, Darkness, Vastness, Emptiness, Untouchable. The God of the mystics is not the cozy warm fuzzy that we often make God out to be.

The philosophers and theologians make the same point. If God is a person—and they say that God is—God is not a person in any way that we understand persons to be. Nor is God anything else in the way we understand it to be—good, loving, intelligent, existing. To supply a reasonable answer to our question about the existence of things, God and all that God is must be beyond anything we know. If God is just more of the same of what we know in the universe, how could God ever be the source of the universe? The universe does not account for its own existence. How could a "god" of the same stuff as the universe ever account for it?

If God exists, God exists in a way fully incomprehensible to us. Everything we know is temporary and passing, just existing by chance. In contrast, to explain the existence of such ephemeral reality, God must be eternal and perfect, existing by necessity. We have no idea what that means.

If God is good, God's goodness fully surpasses any human notion of goodness. We calculate the good from within limited perspectives and short-term views. In contrast, to be the ultimate, positive explanation of all things, God must be goodness as an infinite, already fulfilled reality. Again, we have no idea what that means.

If God is intelligent, God's intelligence must be different from ours. We understand step-by-step, switching and turning as we collect and check insights and gradually piece an explanation together. In contrast, to be the explanation of all things, God must understand everything about everything in a single, all-encompassing insight. Who knows what it is like to understand everything about everything in a single idea?

Likewise, the existence and structure of the universe suggest that behind it lies an intelligent and freely creative being. As we have seen, the spiritual qualities of intelligence and freedom, intellect and will, knowledge and love, are the very hallmarks of a person. So God, intelligent and free, must be personal. But if God is a person, as a personal being, God is not a person in any way that we could grasp. God's intelligence and creative freedom transcend anything we know in this world or anything we could imagine. So the very characteristics that would make God a person exceed anything we understand of such characteristics.

Well, then, is God a person or not? Intelligent and free, God must be a person, but perfectly so, God is no person in any sense we know.

Therefore, to conceive God merely as Ultimate Power, Originating Force, Creator, is not to deny that God is personal. It is only to admit that we do not really know what God's personhood means.

Yes, the understanding I present seems to make God out to be a thing—a power, a force, merely an energy behind all reality. However, this feeble human description does not imply that God is not a person, someone to whom we can relate. We may be perfectly correct in relating to God as a person. It's just that, in relating to God, we need to be careful. All too easily we turn God into a projection of our own needs and imagination. Above all, to us God is Unknown. God is Mystery. Therefore, to relate to God accurately and usefully, we need to let go of childish notions of God. We need to move toward the experience and understanding of the mystics, saints, theologians, philosophers—*Nada, nada, nada.*

The push toward a global community, which is driving the third millennium, is forcing us all to embrace a highly refined notion of God. The movement of history is calling us to stretch toward a new mode of religious faith. Today we are all pushed to hold what formerly only the mystics and sages held about God.

Of course, this stretching entails a loss. Every growth entails loss. Becoming an adult means leaving behind the enchantment of childhood. Yet growth also entails unsuspected gains, as every adult can attest. At this point in history, the very God of history is calling us, forcing us, to move on. God requires that collectively we take another step forward in maturity. God requires that we relate to God as Someone veiled in unknowing. The unfolding of our world and the advance of the universe require that we stop using the Unknown to answer our questions and begin to take full human responsibility for the world that the Creator put into our hands.

## DETERMINING THE WILL OF GOD

A viable notion of God leaves us almost as much in the dark as we had ever been. So those who say they do not believe in God, who live rather in unknowing, may come closer to a realistic statement than those who claim, oh, so loudly to know God. Whatever we say we know about God is *our own* statement; it comes from us, not from God.

An understanding of God as the Great Unknown works—because it does not claim to say what God is. It only makes the reasonable assertion that there is some such reality.

The problem is that, once we have the word *God*, we think we know what God is. Then we begin making all kinds of claims about this God. We project onto God our most cherished beliefs. We begin to fill the empty category *God* with our fondest hopes and desires and with our deepest fears and prejudices, as well. Then we construct competing religions telling us what God is and what God wants. Then we have people hating and killing one another in the name of God.

Oh, to be sure, it would be more reasonable to say some things about God than others. Not all statements about God are inane. For example, if God is the source and sustainer of the universe, surely God favors whatever supports and advances the cosmic process, and surely God opposes whatever hinders or short–circuits it. No problem with this statement! Phrased in open-ended terms, it says nothing specific. It speaks only about "whatevers." It leaves intact the unknowing that surrounds God.

But to specify those "whatevers," to determine exactly what supports or hinders ongoing cosmic process—ah, there's the challenge. To meet this challenge, we have to do our homework. As best we can, we ourselves need to figure out what truly is to the good. We cannot naively look to God for answers. When we turn to God for answers, the buck turns around and stops with us. We need to come up with our own answers. We need to fall right back on our own God-given spiritual capacity, our collaborative openness, questioning, honesty, and goodwill. We need to rely on the principles spelled out in the previous chapter. The human spirit, with its given structure and built-in transcendental precepts, is our surest—and God-given!—guide. So our search for truth and goodness must retreat from heaven and come back down to earth. There is no other possibility when believing in a God of Mystery, the Unknown God, the Power behind the universe. Alternative notions of God lead to arrogance and megalomania.

After we have done our homework and settled our difficult questions, yes, then we could say that our honest conclusions are, as best we can determine, "God's will." If our conclusions really are honest and goodwilled, sincerely open to all the evidence, truly striving for the good of one and all, then our conclusions would be of God—because, if anything, "God" stands for the good; "God" implies what is positive and up-building; "God" points to existence, being, ongoing process, life, health, advancement, fulfillment. Whatever expresses this positive thrust can legitimately be said to be of God. However—and here's the rub—what this positive thrust means concretely, in our own everyday here and now, needs always to be researched, assessed, and reconsidered.

Committed to God, the true God of Mystery, we could affirm no pregiven answers as if they had miraculously come directly from God in the sky. To insist absolutely on pregiven answers, to unbudgingly affirm claims of "divine revelation," is to turn religious teaching into idols. Such idolatry is exactly what all the fundamentalisms entail. Christianity has even coined a word for blind worship of the Bible: *bibliolatry*. Judaism, Islam, and Mormonism, would do well to coin parallel words. When we set up past teaching as our Absolute, we no longer reverence the infinite and unknown Power behind the unfolding universe; rather, we take as our god the finite icons of particular past places and times.

The answers we were given, those we learned from our religion—where did they come from? Our ancestors came up with those answers before us just as we need to come up with our own answers today. In their own time and place, our ancestors grappled with the hard questions of life, and in response they proposed their best wisdom. Having done their inquiry in good faith, they were honestly able to say that the answers they derived were "from God." That is to say, as best they could know, their conclusions are what God would affirm—because their conclusions, as best they could know, advanced life and growth in all openness, honesty, and goodwill.

When we inherit those answers and learn that they are "from God," we need to be careful not to overlook the process through which the God of the universe works. God is that which set up the universe, keeps it in existence, and sustains its functioning. Human beings are part of this universe. So if humans are functioning properly, functioning as they were made to function, functioning as God made them to function, they can legitimately say that the result of their functioning is also "from God."

However, the process at stake—set up and sustained, yes, by God—is human through and through. Its link with God is always indirect. That link always passes through the human heart and soul. The only guarantee that the result is truly "from God" is that these hearts and souls are pure. The only guarantee is that the functioning that led to our conclusions was what it ought to be: proper, humanly genuine, authentic.

Luckily, about these qualities there is no mystery. As noted in the last chapter, the criteria of genuine humanity are the transcendental precepts. They were in place when our ancestors grappled with the questions of life, and these precepts remain in place as we do the same. The transcendental precepts are our constant compass and guide. The process they specify is the spiritual constant throughout the ages. It is the link between our dealings on Earth and the God of Mystery.

In the last analysis, it is not belief in God, but adherence to the transcendental precepts, that legitimates any belief or assertion. In the last analysis, belief in God is secondary and even irrelevant. Indeed, skewed belief in God is actually dangerous; it subverts authentic process. If we leave God to be God, Awesome Mystery, then belief in God takes on a minor role in addressing the concrete questions of life. Indeed, insistence on belief in God in a pluralistic society becomes a dangerous distraction. Insofar as people insist on God, their God is most likely the projection of their own preoccupations. Insofar as people believe in the Unknown God of Mystery, they have no need to impose God on others.

## HOLDING ONTO GOD ONLY LIGHTLY

An adequate notion of God both preserves belief in God and frees society from screeching preaching about God. A refined understanding of "God" takes urgency about God out of the picture. Yet even without belief in God, society is not left without a spiritual compass. Human authenticity performs the function that belief in God used to fulfill, and now God is left simply to be God—the Mystery, the Force, the Power, the Creator, who/which calls us to reverence, gratitude, humility, and awe. To the extent that belief in God fosters such attitudes, it is useful. To the extent that belief in God fosters other attitudes, it is problematic.

God is part of the metaphysical superstructure of religion, the indeterminables, which I noted in chapter 2. The differing metaphysical superstructures of the different religions, as I said, are what we need to let go of or, at least, to hold onto only lightly. When insisted on, those metaphysical beliefs, impossible to prove or disprove, fully indeterminable, only serve to provoke unending dispute. My discussion of God in this chapter gives an example of how a metaphysical belief can be both reasonably affirmed and lightly held.

Reasonableness inevitably leads to holding metaphysical beliefs lightly, for honest analysis shows that they cannot be proved one way or the other. Nonetheless, some of them—such as belief in God, as just shown—may be more reasonable than others.

Which is which? How does one tell? The test will always be fidelity to the transcendental precepts. On a shrinking planet, spirituality takes precedence over religion. Only those aspects of religion that support spiritual advance—as discussed in the previous chapter—could possibly be legitimate. Baha'u'llah, founder of Bahá'í, taught this lesson boldly: it is itself a religious act to turn away from religion that is divisive. In the third millennium, religion that is destructive can no longer be tolerated.

But destruction must be measured in terms of actual, this-worldly outcomes. Notions of reward in heaven and punishment in hell are irrelevant to the discussion. These otherworldly indeterminables are as useless in answering concrete questions as is appeal to personal belief in God. Believe in God as much as you want, you still must determine for yourself how you are going to live—and passing the responsibility off to God ("The Bible tells me so") does not take you off the hook ("The Bible as *you choose* to interpret it?!"). Matters on this planet are different from those in heaven or hell. These we can observe, examine, follow, study, discuss, and resolve. In coming to our most reasonable conclusion, we have lost nothing: if we wished, we could also refer our conclusion back to God. Who could sanely claim that God would want human destruction? Or, contrariwise, that God would forbid something that has no discernible ill effects? Even the barbaric account of Genesis 22, wherein God supposedly asked Abraham to sacrifice his only son, Isaac, ends with God's forbidding this murder as a lesson to future generations. Wherever this lesson has not yet been learned, religion deserves no respect whatsoever. A god in the heavens whose precepts make no sense in the face of the transcendental precepts on this earth could be no legitimate god at all.

In light of the analysis of spirituality that I am presenting here, conflicting beliefs about "God" and "God's will" should become moot. They need to be relegated to the world of speculation and imagination from which they derive, and our world needs to get on with the pressing task of building a wholesome human community. This task is essentially a spiritual one, as I suggested in previous chapters, so my condemnation of strident religions is hardly a diabolical act. Rather, I am advancing a godly deed: to restore God to God's place of reverence and awe and to call humankind to its unavoidable responsibility. With such a deed the true God of the universe would surely be well pleased.

Other metaphysical questions besides God also bedevil religion and our postmodern world. The following chapter addresses some of them: providence, religious experiences, mysticism, and afterlife.

# 6

## Otherworldly Beliefs and Spiritual Community

Intoxicated as a child by drinking in the experience of a harmonious community, I continue to dream of a world at peace. The movie *Equilibrium* presented a not too distant future in which all the world was at peace. But the cost of the peace was extreme. It had been concluded that the cause of discord was the wide range of human feelings, so every person was required to take daily injections to dampen sensitivity and prevent emotions (just like Prozac and Paxil, Zoloft and Cymbalta, in our own society!). Then the world proceeded undeterred along a rationalistic course. Of course, as the story unfolded, humanity reasserted itself, that rationalistic plan for world peace eventually failed, and people again delighted in the beauties of life—and, presumably, also indulged again in its atrocities.

This book might seem to be proposing a similar solution to the challenge of our pluralistic age: level all religions and, in the process, also dampen the sensitivities of our souls. Of course, this caricature is not what I am suggesting, but the concern is worth addressing.

In fact, our world cannot tolerate religious pluralism if each of the religions continues to proclaim that it alone is true. Religious pluralism is viable only if we can discern a common spiritual core to which all the religions could adhere. Beyond that core but without violation of it, the various religions could propose their unique perspectives. Just as a common humanity allows multiple cultural expressions, which can be mutually enriching, a common spirituality could fire a variety of religious expressions, equally enriching. To uncover such a spirituality is the purpose of this book.

However, this approach might seem to be watering down religion and homogenizing faiths, and such a shift may be too much for us to take. Surely, some true believers will object to the very whisper of what I propose.

And to be honest, there may be aspects of religion that are dear to each of us, and some of them seem absolutely legitimate—like belief in God, for example. We would not want to clumsily sweep the table clean and be left with anemic and sterile religions. We would not want to be forced to dry up our souls so that we could live with a unified pluralism.

For that reason, the previous chapter looked into the question of God and proposed a belief in God that is fully welcome. The suggestion was that we can continue to believe in God, but also leave room for people of good-will who do not. In practice, authentic belief in the God and honest lack of belief in God should not make a big difference.

But not any notion of God is acceptable, and the understanding proposed in the last chapter is not what most believers currently hold. Nonetheless, that understanding is, in fact, what the greatest theologians, mystics, and sages have held across religions and throughout the ages. Now globalization is forcing us all to get with the program. Our age is calling us to stretch to a more nuanced understanding of God—just as our postmodern world is demanding a balanced sophistication about every other aspect of the sciences and the humanities. We are in fast-changing times on all fronts.

Besides belief in God, other religious questions also need attention. In this chapter I address some of them: trust in divine providence; visions and voices, angels and entities, and extraordinary religious experiences; the experience of God and mystical union with God; and life after death and life before life. What validity could these varied and even conflicting religious notions retain in a global community of the postmodern era?

## TRUST IN DIVINE PROVIDENCE

My criticism of petitionary prayer in chapter 5 was rather severe. I think it naive to believe that prayer makes God change God's mind. Yet I allowed that asking God for favors could express a valid spiritual attitude, namely, trust that God cares for every little detail of our lives. Technically, such care is called *divine providence.*

How can we understand providence apart from a God who periodically steps in to alter the laws of nature? For example, there are particular biological processes at work when a person is sick or dying. Should we expect God to suspend them?

It is enlightening to realize that we did not know of these processes when our traditional religious beliefs were formed. Only in the seventeenth and eighteenth centuries did we begin to understand that nature functions through routine mechanisms, which can be explained and even controlled: the fall of bodies toward the earth; the orbits of moons around their planets and of planets around the sun; the role of nutrients in plant growth; the functions of the lungs, the heart, the brain; the possibility of immunization against disease; the cause of illness in germs and poor hygiene. Indeed, not until the mid-1800s did we even know that it takes the union of both an egg and a sperm to produce a new conception and that the man's contribution, not the woman's—*pace* King Henry VIII—determines the sex of a child. People used to attribute these processes and their failures to the miraculous work of God, the intervention of spirits, or the evil work of sorcery and witchcraft. Religion actually opposed scientific interventions as interference with God's providential will: the use of fertilizers to increase crop production and lightning rods to prevent storm damage. Current debate over the use of contraceptives to regulate births and prevent disease is a remnant of that older mentality.

When the forces of nature were not understood, it was reasonable to petition God for prosperity, protection, and progeny. But we live in a new era, not only an era of scientific understanding regarding even some of the workings of the mind but also an era of multicultural awareness, global communication, and space travel. Today, to pray for healing is to want God to change the processes of nature in specific, privileged cases. Against this backdrop of history and in light of ongoing scientific advance, such prayer is no longer reasonable; it is superstition.

If God does not miraculously step in to change the course of events for our advantage, how does God guide the unfolding of the universe, and how does that guidance express care? How could we still believe in a caring God without turning God into a celestial Santa Claus?

The summary answer is this: God cares for every individual part of the universe by caring for the whole. By structuring the universe as a whole to function in a particular way, God guides the functioning of all the parts that make up the whole. God has no need to step in and adjust the individual elements; the overall process channels all their functioning toward the good end that God built into the universe.

The universe is set up to function in a particular way. Overall, the laws that govern the universe guide its unfolding. From the Big Bang to the formation of atoms and complex molecules, to the emergence of vegetative life, to the formation of sensate animal life, to the appearance of self-conscious humanity, to the proliferation of cultures, societies, and civilizations—we can trace an order in the structure and unfolding of the cosmos. This order is obviously built-in; it is the order we discover when we study the universe. This order is also working in a particular direction. The cosmic order reveals increasing complexity of structure and an expansion of capacities.

From a theological perspective, that order is what it is because that is how God created it. God determined the order and, keeping the universe in existence and concurring with the activities of every creature, God sustains the order. That is, the functioning of the universe is under the sway of God—not because God steps in to direct and guide events, but because God set up and maintains the order that directs and guides them. God guides the universe by having structured it in a particular way. And God guides every particular aspect of the universe by making it a part of the overall functioning.

This understanding works well enough regarding nonhuman aspects of the universe, for they operate as they were made to. Unlike humans, they do not have the capacity to determine their own lives and even to make self-destructive decisions that counter their natures. God's plan unfolds naturally in the physical, vegetable, and animal realms. But the role of humans within the whole adds further complications.

First of all, we need to admit that the natural working of the universe causes difficulty for us humans. Because we too, in part, are physical, vegetable, and animal, we are also subject to the laws of nature. So we age, get sick, and die; we suffer from accidents and natural tragedies. We live within the limitations that bodies impose, and painful questions arise: Why do innocent people die in earthquakes, tornadoes, and tsunamis? Why are children born deformed, and why do they become victims of cancer? Why do our lives end always too soon?

The only answer faith in God can propose to such questions leaves us unsatisfied. Evidently, we, like the rest of creation, are caught up in a bigger process, and sometimes the process is not gracious to our individual preferences. We can only trust that, nonetheless, the process is for the good, overall; and, committed to the good, we surrender ourselves to the process, personal setbacks and all. To trust in life is to trust in God, so, in times of tragedy, we can only affirm that "God knows best." To make such an affirmation is simply to go on trusting in life despite its hardships. But to trust in life is to reverence the Power that set life in place and the Force that sustains it in its existence and operation. Belief in God carries no exemption from the sorrow that the processes of nature sometimes entail.

In Romans 8:28, Paul writes, "We know that all things work together for the good for those who love God." To clarify the point I am making, I would rephrase Paul's statement thus: "All things work out for the best for those who make the best of the way things work out." As I am explaining this matter, are not "those who make the best of the way things work out" the very ones whom religion would say are "those who love God"? Those who love God would surrender themselves in trust to the natural workings of God's universe. And trusting God, they would surely continue ever to make the best of whatever happens, for commitment to the good is what God stands for. To go on in this way is what trust in God means. To be undeterred by hardship is to believe in a good God. To go on living even in

the face of death is to embrace life as God has given it to us. This understanding, unsatisfying though it be, respects the notion of providence without turning God into a heavenly magician.

Once when I was lamenting the sometimes sad situation of the human
species, a wise woman encouraged me with an iron-hard version of faith. In
light of the thinking I just expressed, I complained that sometimes I feel like
just a cog in a machine. I do my part as best I can, yes, but in the end I am
just being used, worn out, and replaced. We humans just come and go by
the millions, so much potential untapped, so much talent never developed,
so many lives seemingly wasted, totally. And even in the best of cases, we
die. "Yes," she agreed, "perhaps just a cog in a machine, but consider whose
machine you're a part of!" Or, said secularly, consider what grand cosmic
unfolding we advance, living for a cause bigger than ourselves.

Can we continue to live in truth, justice, good will, and generosity although we know we will die? Can we believe in the good despite the seeming success of scoundrels, takers, tyrants, and egregious evildoers? Can our
trust in the overall unfolding of the universe match that of the Creator, who
set it up? Can we trust that our every small effort for love will not be lost in
the end, that we also will not be lost, and that a gracious and long-term
plan for fullness of life will inevitably reach its goal? Such trust, such believe, is what *faith* truly means. Faith is not that mere matter of pious
protest: "I believe in God," "Praise the Lord," "Allah is great," and other
such religious verbiage. Faith is that massive matter of commitment to the
good in a world of disappointment, heartache, betrayal, and death. The
faith that counts is not in a creed, but in the living. If we are cogs in a machine, then cogs we will be, but the best cogs we are able. If the universe unfolds on probabilities, emergences only possible through large numbers
over long intervals e and with considerable waste, then we will deliberately
be part of the flow, taking our chances on trust in the movement. We will
be part of God's universe, hurts and all.

But there is a further question. Dealing with the natural order of the created universe is one thing; dealing with the choices of human beings is
another—because these choices are not always in accord with the good.
People sometimes counter the flow of the universe and block the unfolding
process. People sometimes do evil. How, then, does God's plan for the good
continue to operate when people are free to throw monkey wrenches into
the works?

The same answer applies again, but it requires further elaboration. God
guides every particular aspect of creation by ordering the overall process. Although people are free to make their own choices, people still function
within the overall system. Accordingly, although human choices are, indeed, free, they are limited in their scope. There is only so much we can do.
There are lines we are unable to cross. In fact, we cannot fly just by flapping

our arms. We cannot become invisible by simply wishing it so. We cannot repress the surge of excitement or fear in us when we attempt a new adventure. We cannot deny to ourselves the reality of our own dishonesty. We cannot avoid the consequences of every decision we make. Even thieves, corrupt politicians, dishonest business executives, and dictators know these facts to be so, and shrewdly they do their best to "cover their tails."

Human freedom functions within an overall order, and the overall order eventually carries the day. We cannot go on bucking the system forever. The more we buck, the greater the resistance built up against us. We eventually wear down, and the system reasserts itself.

This set of affairs reminds me of the amusement park ride, bumper cars. Driven by playful patrons, awkward vehicles make their way slowly around a rink. The cars hardly progress in a smooth forward motion. Part of the fun of the ride is deliberate collision with other cars. So the movement around the rink is uneven, but it continues, and inevitably the cars make their rounds in the prescribed direction. Repeatedly some of the cars get out of line, but it is virtually impossible for any of them to circulate long against the flow of traffic. Despite all effort, the devious cars are bumped back again and again into the required traffic pattern. Like human beings in life, each bumper car has only a limited possibility for moving against the flow. In the end, the set order of the ride determines the overall movement. The deviates may slow and hinder the movement, but they cannot stop it.

The overall movement of life and growth that is built into the universe is also built into our very beings, and it always has the last word. Even the human spirit, our source of freedom and choice, is structured in a particular way. Choice must work in consort with awareness, understanding, and knowledge. That is, our choice is naturally geared to square with reality. When it does not, distortions result, and inner tensions build up. These inevitably find a resolution, and the structure of the human spirit springs back to its natural configuration. We exercise our free will within this overall structure, just as other facets of the universe unfold within a given order. That structure and that order ultimately guide the process, and within it there is only so much leeway. Our freedom is not so unbridled that it could subvert the universe. Said religiously: God is in charge.

We have proverbs to express this fact of life: "The truth will out," "What goes around comes around," "Hoist on your own petard," "Getting a taste of your own medicine," "Sleeping in the bed you made," "Honesty is the best policy." To be sure, hatred, hurt, fraud, and evildoing will have their day. But that day inevitably passes, and the reign of the good reasserts itself. "Justice will have its day." "The pendulum always swings back." Jesus used his own metaphor to make this point and spoke of a house build on sand.

It is the nature of falsehood and evil to eventually self-destruct. Such eventual self-destruction is the very meaning of evil and falsehood. Evil is negative precisely because it leads to a dead end. Falsehood is wrong precisely because it has no lasting future. You cannot build a life on deception and lies. Such a life eventually implodes. In contrast, whatever leads to further life and expansion is to be approved. Whatever has a long-term promise is, by definition, good. If virtue is its own reward, vice carries its own undoing.

Therefore, a spirituality for a global community need not jettison belief in divine providence. The two are fully compatible if providence is understood aright. Then, belief in providence would support authentic human living, and a religion that advocates trust in divine providence would, in its own way, be supporting the core spirituality that applies to all religions. Of course, those who are living this core spirituality, even apart from belief in God and divine providence, would still be engaged in the same positive living that is the goal of authentic believers. In either case, for believer and nonbeliever, the practical outcome would be the same. In the last analysis, there is no need to make an issue of belief in divine providence as such.

Truth be told, trust in providence offers little reprieve from the hardships of life. Nonetheless, this religious faith can be powerful and powerfully inspiring, and, when coupled with the shared belief of real community, it can be sustaining. Recall the response of the Eastern Pennsylvania Amish community to the October 6, 2006 mass murder of their girls at school. The community held together in mutual support. The people expressed acceptance of God's baffling will for them and offered forgiveness to the murderer and even compassion and support for that man's family, non-Amish but still members of their community, neighbors. And all the world watched in surprise and with profound respect. How different was this response from what is seen almost nightly on the evening news! For a few meditative moments, this striking show of trust in providence stopped the spinning of our self-centered society.

## VISIONS, VOICES, AND SPIRITUAL ENTITIES

People who are "into" spirituality often tend to seek out unusual experiences. Belief in angels, the use of crystals, consultation of mediums, alliances with spiritual entities, tapping into libraries in the sky, the reception of messages, apparitions of spiritual beings—in some circles these are taken to be the sum and substance of spirituality. If they actually are, what place have they in a "mere" spirituality of human authenticity?

That place will be small, and it must be significantly restricted. Those interests are part of the metaphysical superstructures of religion. They belong to that otherworldly slice of religious concern that can be neither proved nor disproved but appears, rather, to be gratuitous. These are the kinds of spiritual interests that, at best, divert people from the challenge of living in this world and allow them to fill their time and conversation with esoteric metaphysical factoids. And, at worst, such interests lead people to fight inconclusive and interminable battles. At best and at worst, these interests can be not only fanciful or ludicrous but also dangerous.

It is significant that the great religions have always downplayed other-worldly phenomena. Jesus said it is not those who cry "Lord, Lord" who will be saved, but those who do the will of God—that is, those who do good and live rightly: "I was hungry and you fed me, I was thirsty and you gave me drink." In his famous chapter on love in First Corinthians, Paul the Apostle said that speaking with the tongues of angels is useless unless we have down-to-earth charity. In his first letter, John the Evangelist warned against believing every spirit because some of them are false.

Likewise, Buddhist teaching warns against getting lost in the entanglements of the psyche by pursuing delightful experiences during deep meditation: enlightenment is not about achieving altered states of consciousness, but about living wide-awake at every moment in the real world and doing what is called for in every situation. The ideal of Tibetan Buddhism is the Bodhisattva, who refuses to enter nirvana until every sentient being is enlightened. The "return to the marketplace" in service of one's fellow humans is the end point of the meditative quest. Thus, the genuine religious message always points to down-to-earth, wholesome living—the very ideal required by the transcendental precepts.

Also from a psychological and psychiatric point of view, many purported religious experiences are suspect. St. Hildegard of Bingen's descriptions of her religious experiences match the symptomatology of migraine headaches. The raptures, voices, and visions that St. Teresa of Avila reported were likely the result of minor epileptic seizures or other neurological misfirings. The same seems true for the ecstatic experiences of the Prophet Mohamed, who was reported to periodically "zone out" for a moment in what was thought to be communication with an angel.

To be sure, these psychological explanations do not ipso facto discredit saintly people or their religious experiences. Such experiences are not what make a person holy—the very point I am making! What matters is that these spiritual leaders were able to use their experiences, however caused, to gain important insight and to transform their worlds for the better. If the proof is in the pudding, these spiritual giants proved themselves great by their deeds, not by their spiritual experiences. Seen from a critical perspective, in themselves the experiences were hardly "spiritual."

But many think spiritual achievement is about extraordinary religious experiences. So through meditation, austerities, and other practices, people set out to induce altered states of consciousness. Current spiritual movements advance this sort of thing. The assumption is that there exists a parallel universe of spiritual beings, and if we use the right techniques and are lucky, we can tap into that spiritual universe. There is a promise of profound new knowledge and fabulous powers that could preserve us from the ups and downs of life. Spirituality becomes an enterprise of escape from this world. I treat this matter extensively in *Meditation without Myth*.

Many people have found works such as *Letters from God*, *The Seat of the Soul*, *The Celestine Prophecies*, and *A Course on Miracles* motivating and reassuring. To this extent, such inspirational presentations of spirituality make a positive contribution. Metaphysical claims are fine as long as they do no harm, as long as they are innocent and innocuous; and they are positively welcome when they bolster commitment to the transcendental precepts. People are free to indulge their hopes and fantasies, and to do so is even helpful at times. Like a good movie, a novel, or the medieval legends of the saints and the lore of the Eastern gurus, tales of spiritual pursuit can be inspiring. The powerful song by ABBA, "I Have a Dream," touchingly makes the point that having something to believe in helps us face life—and death—with strength and purpose. However, when spiritual claims become unreasonable and are taken as solid fact, they inevitably become harmful, and they need to be challenged and contained. They no longer support good living but lead to irresponsibility.

On one occasion, for example, a colleague shared the story of a woman who knew she would win the lottery if she truly believed she would. Her belief was part of that often heard, adult foolishness—a leftover from innocent childhood fairy tales such as *Peter Pan*—that just believing in something hard enough will actually make it happen. As a sign of her firm belief, this woman ran herself into tens of thousands of dollars of debt, and she would not restrain herself—because to stop spending borrowed money would mean a loss of faith! She was trapped in a self-destructive, spiritual catch-22.

On another occasion I attended a free spiritual lecture presented by a husband-and-wife team. They promised to explain—in their paid workshops—exactly how, without ever needing to fill the gas tank, one could drive a car across the continent by simply imagining the fuel-gauge needle pointing constantly to "full"! Beliefs such as these are outlandish. Anyone up for buying a bridge?

What of angels and other spiritual beings with whom we might have contact? Do they really exist? Are the reported contacts real?

It is hard to answer these questions with certainty. Personally, I find these questions inevitably irrelevant. I have never seen a ghost. I wish that I would. I've tried. Life would be so much more fascinating if there were spirits floating about or even the latest version of angels, extraterrestrials who speak to us during sleep and invisibly accompany us through daily life. But that there are such things—I am unconvinced. Spiritual beings could certainly exist.

The possibility is real. And if they did exist, surely we could have contact with them. But how would one know for sure? To build one's life around mere supposition is surely misguided.

In the Bible *angel*—from the Greek for messenger—is a symbol for the presence of God, nothing more. Awesome beyond all creation, God's immediate contact would destroy mere mortals. So God graciously communicates through intermediaries. God sends His angels. Similarly, the Tibetan Buddhist tradition is explicit on this matter: its gods and demons are symbols for the contending forces within the human mind.

From a more scientific point of view, much, if not all, of what is attributed to celestial beings could be explained otherwise. After all, if the human spirit is infinite in scope, somehow transcendent of space and time and geared to all that exists, might these "spiritual entities" not simply be creations of people's own imaginations, and might not the "received messages" be the products of their own spiritual capacities? Most likely, yes. Automatic writing, free association, and the amazing creativity of our dreams suggest parallel cases of rather astonishing phenomena. Insights are often experienced as coming from beyond oneself, and we are often surprised by our own flashes of understanding. Add in the possibility of mental telepathy and clairvoyance—with which some people are definitely gifted and which can in large part be explained by unusual sensitivity to infrared waves, magnetism, and odors—and appeal to spiritual entities seems superfluous. We underestimate our own spiritual capacity, so it is hardly surprising that people would attribute the products of their own minds to some external being.

Besides, even if the spiritual entities really were more than symbols for the workings of people's own consciousness, how could one ever tell the difference? The result of such experiences—new wisdom, new focus, new motivation—would certainly be undeniable. But did these come from some external source or were they generated by the human makeup itself? How could one tell the difference, and what difference would it make, in any case?

Sometimes the "revelations" are just detailed accounts of some supposed other world. While it might be fascinating to learn about the intrigues of life in the spirit realm, such information—just as detail about the private lives of celebrities or the "royals" in Great Britain—is basically irrelevant to life in the real world.

Nonetheless, sometimes the "revelations" express real wisdom about human living—such as the need for forgiveness or the value of compassion or the importance of not losing hope or the assurance of the love of a dead loved one. In such cases, what does it matter where the understanding came from? What difference would it make if the claimed spiritual entity were a real being or only a psychic symbol?

If the acquired information is valid, its source is spiritually irrelevant. Not the existence of spirits, but the validity of the insight, is what matters. This point must be stressed: the criteria of wholesome living in this world govern this validity. Now and every time, we are thrust right back onto the human spirit and its built-in transcendental precepts. These are the only valid criteria of truth and goodness in our world. Intuitions, hunches, revelations—from whatever supposed or claimed source—must be checked out and confirmed before we act on them. Running one's life on hunches and suggestive suppositions is absolutely irresponsible. It is humanly offensive.

Thus, discussion of spirit realms is moot. On the one hand, claims about the experience of spiritual beings are not persuasive. On the other hand, in practice such claims are irrelevant. Insistence on metaphysical entities and debate about spiritual realms dangerously distract from the task of building human community on this earth.

Therefore, like notions of God and providence, reports of spiritual entities and extraordinary religious experiences can be allowed—as long as they do not result in bizarre, confusing, and destructive thinking and, even better, as long as they foster positive human growth. The measure of such growth must be the transcendental precepts and wholesome human living in this world. Other spiritual claims must remain ever peripheral.

## MYSTICAL UNION WITH GOD

One class of spiritual experiences deserves special attention. Through the ages, many have claimed direct experience of God. Such experience is the general meaning of the word *mysticism*. Moses, for example, was supposed to have been allowed to see God face to face and live. The Apostle Paul spoke of being taken up into the seventh heaven and having seen things that cannot be expressed in words. Mohamed, likewise, is said to have received communication directly from God, as is Joseph Smith, the founder of Mormonism.

Mysticism is a Western concept. It depends on an understanding of God as a being distinct—but not separate—from all creatures. As I will explain below, the Eastern understanding is different. Nonetheless, students of mysticism find it—in the guise of its close parallel: enlightenment—also in Eastern religions. The best known mystics are of the Western Tradition—Clement of Alexandria, Augustine of Hippo, Dionysius the Areopagite, Bernard of Clairvaux, Francis of Assisi, Meister Eckhart, Catherine of Sienna, Teresa of Avila, John of the Cross, Rainer Maria Rilke, Evelyn Underhill, Thomas Merton, Teilhard de Chardin.

Less suspect than talk of other spiritual entities, the notion of God does hold up, as noted in chapter 5, so the idea of direct experience of God is credible. Nonetheless, my conclusion here will be the same as that regarding the experience of spiritual entities: whether or not one had really experienced God would be hard to demonstrate, and in the end the significance of the experience would still need to be assessed. The mere claim to have experienced God must be met with reservation.

By this point, I may seem to be a fuddy-duddy, pooh-poohing all spiritual claims. I might seem to be writing off anything having to do with the supernatural world. But let my intention and my goodwill be noted.

My concern, on the one hand, is to clear the air of unnecessary spiritual claims because I want to propose a spiritual base that all humanity could hold in common. And it is precisely in the realm of the supernatural that different religious beliefs come into conflict.

On the other hand, I am being as open as I honestly can to claims about spiritual matters that go beyond any possible adjudication. After all, I am presenting a book on spirituality. I certainly do not deny the reality of the spiritual. I know that belief in spiritual realities is important to us human beings. We certainly do not live by rationality alone—nor is sterile rationality what I am proposing: Lonergan's understanding of the dynamic human spirit with its emphasis on nonmechanizable, creative leaps of insight is hardly narrow, modern, logico-deductive rationalism. The inspiration and imagination of art, music, story, and dance are crucial for our souls.

Thus, my response frequently comes down to a "yes, but." My sense is that this is the only honest response we can give. Insistence on anything more at this point in human history can be not only unhelpful but also downright destructive. We must hold to our metaphysical claims only lightly, if at all. So many of them are fanciful leftovers from another era!

If people say they experienced God, how could they ever know it was really God that they experienced? God is an unknown, so what would a pure experience of God be like? Who could ever say?

Besides, there is another perfectly viable explanation for the mystical experiences that people report. Perhaps they only experience their own human spirit in all its open-ended capacity. We have seen that the human spirit is a built-in dynamism that transcends space and time and is infinite in scope, geared toward all there is to know and love. If one were to experience this spiritual facet of the mind in pure form, one would seem to have moved outside the world of everyday life and into a realm that is potentially unbounded and beyond time. The very characteristics attributed to mystical experience—ineffable, infinite, and timeless—would be realized in an experience of one's own human spirit. Why, then, call this an experience of God?

Indeed, current psychological and neurophysiological research has even begun to explain the biological underpinnings of religious or transcendent experiences. We now have some fair understanding of the brain circuitry and neural functioning related to mysticism. In addition to meditative practice and other standard spiritual techniques—my *Meditation without Myth* reviews them in detail—we can actually induce transcendent experiences with mere magnetic fields or, of course, psychedelic drugs. Religious purists argue that these induced experiences are not truly religious or mystical, but the purists are not able to specify what that supposed truly sacred difference is in the experiences themselves. In fact, drug-induced altered states of consciousness—from the *soma* of the Vedas to the *ayahuasca* (dimethyltryptamine) of Central and South American peoples to the peyote (mescaline) and mushrooms (psilocybin) of the indigenous American southwest to the wine (ethanol) on an empty stomach in Christian Eucharist—has been a constant facet of the religious traditions. Unfortunately, pandering to popular religiosity and the book market, even some solid scientists have been using phrases such as the "God spot in the brain," "the God gene," the "'God' part of the brain," *neurotheology*, and *theobiology* to characterize the focus of their research. The uncritical identification of the spiritual and the divine is ubiquitous. Further institutionalizing this misidentification, researchers of psychedelic drugs and religious experience have coined the word *entheogens*—sources of God within—to rename the drugs to highlight their spiritual relevance. You don't have to be a theologian to realize that, if we can induce these experiences at will, they are hardly experiences of God—unless we believe in a god who is at our beck and call. But the realm of religion and spirituality is befogged with misunderstandings and contorted by political agendas, and the emotional nature of the topic easily obscures critical thinking. As a result, almost any unusual mental experience can get attributed to God.

Yet, how would one know the difference between any transcendent experience and the actual experience of God? On what grounds would one determine the difference? For want of other words, we might understandably call an extraordinary experience an experience of God and mean by this that the experience was of another order—stunning, mysterious, inexplicable, supernatural. But if God is the Great Unknown, how could we know that the divine characterization is correct? We have no idea what the experience of God would be like. More importantly, if we can explain mystical experiences perfectly well as experiences of one's own spiritual capacity, it is gratuitous to claim that these experiences result from direct contact with God.

We ought not to confuse the created human spirit with the uncreated divine spirit, God. Yet we make this mistake all the time. The history of Western mysticism actually explains how this confusion arose. It came from the blending of Greek thought about the mind with Jewish and Christian thought about God.

Plato, it seems, was astounded by the capacity of the human mind. He recognized, for example, that Pythagoras's theorem, $a^2 + b^2 = c^2$, conceives of a perfect and unchanging right triangle that exists nowhere in the physical world. So Plato concluded that this physical world is only a poor imitation of the really real world where all things exist in perfection. Thus, every right triangle in this world is only an imperfect copy of the real right triangle in the Ideal World or the World of Ideas or Forms. And the same goes for every other thing in the physical world. So, according to Plato, this world is not the real world, but only an illusion, an imitation, an imperfect copy. The real world is the spiritual world where perfect Ideas dwell.

Plato took this notion of another world seriously—even as many today believe in a spiritual world in addition to our spatial-temporal world. But, of course, the ideas that astounded Plato were "merely" the products of human intelligence. That there really was a World of Ideas different from our spatial-temporal world was pure supposition. After all, it was in this spatial-temporal world, in the body, that Pythagoras and Plato conceived of the perfect right triangle.

To complicate matters even more, the ancient Greek word *divine* did not refer to God as we understand God. The Greek gods, with their competitive intrigues and amorous affairs, were a far cry from the transcendent God of Israel, and early Greek thought had no idea of a creator. *Divine* meant simply perfect, and unchanging or eternal—like the idea of a perfect right triangle. So, in standard Greek usage, Plato could correctly refer to his Ideas and their World as divine.

When the early Christians were trying to make philosophical sense of the personal God of Judaism, the Christian thinkers found Platonic thought very helpful. From the Jews, the Christians had the notion of God as Creator. It made sense to think that God created the realities of this world according to some plan in the divine mind. Plato's notion of perfect and eternal Ideas fit well with the notion of ideas in the mind of God, so the two notions were fused. Supposedly, the World of Ideas was really the mind of God. In God's mind were the blueprints, the ideal models, for everything in the created world.

Thus, the human mind and the divine mind were identified. The perfect ideas that were the products of the human spirit were thought to be the ideas in God's mind. Saint Augustine and Saint Thomas Aquinas, for example, taught outright that human intelligence is *in some way* a participation in the divine intelligence. Meister Eckhart was condemned for pushing this notion too far and suggesting, very much as in Eastern thought, that the human mind actually is divine.

Identification of the spiritual with the divine is a perennial theme in philosophy and religion. In contrast to what I am arguing in this book, for example, this same theme currently controls the treatment of spirituality in psychological circles at the highest levels although, instead of speaking outright of God, psychologists finesse the matter by using the vaguer term *the*

*Sacred.* Thus, quite easily a pure experience of the human spirit might be associated with a supposed experience of the divine, God. My brief historical analysis even shows how this association arose in the West. A similar history applies in Eastern thought wherein "atman is Brahman" and "Thou art That," and deep down inside, we are supposedly God.

Having untangled the history, I am suggesting that this identification is a mistake. Too easily we think we are experiencing God when we may really be experiencing only our own human spirit. Although the misidentification has often been made, to experience the infinitely open-ended awesomeness of the human spirit is not necessarily to experience God.

Well, I can make my point and explain it, and it is hardly original. Nonetheless, both Christianity and Hinduism do speak of union with God. Then, should my assessment be revised? I still think not—because Christianity and Hinduism understand union with God in two different ways, which are incompatible. As I have been arguing, to invoke these religious beliefs proves nothing except that people hold such-and-such beliefs.

To explain union with God, Christianity relies on a set of complex doctrines. To account for union with God was, indeed, the source and purpose of these doctrines. Christianity believes that, because of the saving work of Jesus Christ, in addition to our own human spirit, God has also poured into our hearts the divine Holy Spirit. Then, by experiencing the depths of our own beings, we also experience the Holy Spirit, God, who dwells there. Thus, Christianity does explain the direct experience of God—begun in this life and perfected in heaven, the beatific vision—but not without affirmation of its central metaphysical beliefs: that God is Father, Son, and Holy Spirit (the doctrine of the Trinity); that through his life, death, and resurrection, Jesus Christ changed the ultimate meaning of human living to union with God (the doctrines of incarnation and redemption); and that to effect that union, the Holy Spirit comes to dwell in human hearts (the doctrine of sanctifying grace). Apart from these metaphysical claims, which are beyond proof or disproof, one could not coherently argue that we can experience God in Godself. The Christian assertion that an experience of the depths of our being is actually an experience of God depends on the belief that, through the saving work of Jesus Christ, God the Father has poured out the Holy Spirit into human hearts in order to lead us along the path Jesus first trod to the glory of God in heaven.

That Christian argument comes as a package. Take belief in the Trinity out of the picture, and there is no reason to claim experience of God, even though the experience itself remains what it ever was. Put belief in the Trinity into the picture, and the experience does not change—except that, without being able to prove or disprove the claim, one can now claim that the mystical experience is actually an experience of God. So Christian belief allows one to claim a direct experience of God, but the experience in question could also be interpreted and explained otherwise. My basic point recurs again: the metaphysical superstructure of religions becomes moot.

Hinduism also speaks of union with God, but in this case this claim is not the significant one. Unlike Judaism, Christianity, and Islam, Hinduism does not recognize an absolute difference between the Creator and the created but holds that, from the start, the deepest core of the human soul is divine. That is to say, for Hinduism the human being is already in some sense God—even as two of its central maxims state: "Thou art That," and "atman is Brahman," that is, roughly rendered, "The soul is God."

According to the Hindu understanding, to experience oneself is ipso facto to experience God; to be one with oneself is to be one with God, for every person is God. But the divine in us is clouded over and hidden, so we need to do meditation and perform other purifying practices. These move us closer to our own core and ipso facto closer to God. As a result—to express the matter now in Buddhist terms—the fully enlightened person lives in union with the Ultimate Power of the Universe.

Unlike in the West, Eastern thought never was guilty of mixing together the spiritual and the divine because in the East the two were never clearly sorted out in the first place. However, once we recognize the inviolable difference between the created human spirit and the Uncreated God, Eastern thought must also be seen as confusing two very different realities. By sheer dint of logic, the created cannot be the Uncreated.

Admittedly, I couched that Eastern teaching in the terms of Western theology. In fact, it is debated whether Brahman is equivalent to God and whether atman means soul or human spirit as we understand these notions. Nonetheless, scholars do find parallels between Eastern and Western thinking about these matters. Recent historical research about the development of Hindu thought also finds a conceptual fusing of the human spirit and the Ultimate such as what I traced in Western thought. In the end, however, the very fact that there is debate over these matters shows, once again, that there is no consensus across religions on metaphysical beliefs, not even on the most fundamental issues, like the nature of God.

In contrast to Christianity, Hinduism offers a different understanding of how a mystical experience is actually an experience of God—because deep, down inside we actually are God. It is the same understanding that occurs in Platonic thought, and this understanding is common to most Eastern thought as well as to Western Gnosticism, New Age religion, and much contemporary spirituality. But this understanding differs significantly from the logic of orthodox Christianity. For this very reason, among others, the so-called Gnostic Gospels were not included in the Christian canon. It is overly simplistic to suppose that the decision was purely political.

"Well, so what?" you might say. "Despite their differences, those religions agree that God is present within us. The basic point is that we are in union with God. The point is the same in both understandings, and it is what matters. Why quibble over details?"

As a scientist or theoretician, I would have to insist that the difference between those religions is major. This difference marks the philosophical fault line between Eastern and Western thought; and because of the different emphases in Plato and Aristotle, this difference also draws a dividing line down the whole of Western philosophy itself. There is a big difference between valuing this world as "really real" or, in contrast, rather, some other and spiritual realm. There is a big difference between accepting as the criterion of knowledge reasonable argument grounded in evidence and accepting as that criterion claimed revelation, some personal experience of a spiritual realm. This difference is *the* greatest challenge to the overall argument of this book. If we are unable to let go our tight hold on our cherished metaphysical beliefs, this difference will have to be resolved before our world finds any intellectual consensus. The prognosis is not promising—although Lonergan's work does offer hope. Thus, I would have to insist that there is a big difference between really being God and merely having God's Spirit within oneself. Frankly, given my understanding of *God*, that we would actually be God seems ludicrous to me: if we are God, what are we doing here struggling through our lives?!

Besides, there are logical inconsistencies in the assertion that we are God. If our souls are literally that poetic "spark of divinity," God would have to come in parts. Bits of God would be in each one of us. Or if we are truly God but not yet fully so, God would have to come in varying degrees of intensity. We would supposedly be God, but only a little bit so. We would enjoy the omnipotence, omniscience, and omnipresence of God, but they would be restricted by the bars of our earthly flesh. What sense do these limitations on God make? The understanding of God that I developed in chapter 5—"the best available opinion of the day," as scientists characterize their conclusions—does not allow for a God that can be divided or diluted. God either is or is not; so we either are God or are not. As in being pregnant, it makes no sense to speak of being "a little bit" divine. The notion of "partial divinity" is an oxymoron. The suggestion that humans really are God "deep, down inside" makes neither logical nor conceptual sense.

Granted, Genesis 1:26 says that we were created "in the image and likeness" of God, and in chapter 4, I spoke of our moving "godward" and becoming "godlike." But having characteristics that are similar to God—transcendence of space and time, infinite capacity for knowledge and love—is not the same as actually being God. There is no fudging the difference between creature and Creator. *A* cannot be *non-A*; the *created* cannot be the *Uncreated*.

Therefore, for purely logical reasons, not doctrinal ones, I find the Christian explanation more coherent. Granted, talk of a Trinitarian God and of a divine incarnation is hard to swallow, but at least these doctrines preserve the distinction between the Creator and the creature, which can be reasonably argued and is not dependent on religious faith. If we are going to insist on direct union with God, this dizzying Christian explanation or some variation on it must be the best we have to offer.

In contrast, the Hindu understanding raises serious logical and conceptual problems. At stake are the difficult questions of whether and how our human minds could actually know anything for certain. (Recall that these were the questions that Lonergan's analysis of the first three levels of consciousness, or spirit, claim to answer.) To get beyond these problems, any logical argument in the Eastern mode seems to ends up disqualifying logic. In a maneuver that is at least as complicated as belief in the Christian Trinity, the standard way out of the logical contradiction—Ken Wilber is lucid in advancing this maneuver—is to appeal to some kind of "transrationality."

Consider the case. Eastern philosophy suggests that this world is not real but is just an illusion, so our knowledge in this world does not hold ultimate validity. This world is not the really real. In technical terms, Eastern thought distinguishes between *relative* or *conventional* knowledge (in this world) and *ultimate* knowledge (in the meditative or mystical experience of the All). In meditative experience, all is one; there are no distinctions between this and that, between now and then. But ultimate knowledge trumps relative knowledge. Therefore, supposedly, our this-worldly knowledge of a multiplicity of different and related realities is mistaken. Yet this philosophy makes its statement with a multiplicity of words in this relative, conventional, illusory world. Arising from and formulated within this non-real world, how valid could this statement itself be? The this-worldly claim that this-worldly knowledge is only relative is itself relative; it enjoys no ultimate validity; it discredits itself. To get around this obvious logical contradiction, this philosophy insists its statement is beyond logical thought; it is transrational. But what does *transrational* mean? Of course, no one can explain what it means because the notion is beyond reason; by definition transrationality is beyond explanation. Instead, we are told, "If you experience it, then you'll know." In the meantime, are we to "take it on faith"? Is this solution any different from belief in the Trinity? To me the end result sounds like that "old time religion" all over again.

I discuss these intricate philosophical matters in detail in *Religion and the Human Sciences*. The key to resolving the East-West difference is the realization—in Lonergan's terms—that experience is not knowledge. Experience (Be attentive) merely provides the data that understanding (Be intelligent) and verification (Be reasonable) account for. By design, meditative experience lets go of all feelings, images, questions, ideas, distinctions, thoughts, concepts, and propositions. As a result, the experience undeniably includes moments that transcend space and time and, thus, present an undifferentiated unity. But regardless how deeply felt, this experience is not knowledge. Knowledge entails statements, propositions. But to state—as Eastern philosophy does—that the experience was such-and-such is to have already moved outside the mere experience and to have added insight to the data of the experience, to have added an interpretation. But other interpretations are possible. I submit that, with an adequate theory of knowledge, it is possible to give a profoundly insightful and logically coherent account of the unitive meditative experience. And it differs from the standard Eastern account.

In sum, there is a serious and important technical difference between the Christian and the Hindu understanding of union with God. It would be dishonest to fudge the difference.

But then, on the other hand, well, for practical purposes I could agree that we could stop quibbling over technicalities and just ignore the details. Christianity believes that God is a Trinity of divine persons who have miraculously intervened in human history. Hinduism believes that the Ultimate Power of the universe, Brahman, is the depth of the human soul, atman. Apart from logical analysis and in the realm of inspirational religion, both beliefs could appear equally appealing or equally fanciful. So why insist on one or the other? Take them both with a grain of salt, and focus on their implication: in one way or another, God is present and acting in us, and we are destined for full and perfect union with God.

In fact, that down-to-earth suggestion has been my point all along. In the end, there is no resolving the differences among metaphysical beliefs. One set may be more coherent than another, but there is no available data on which to prove or disprove even the coherent set. We are left with pious speculation. In the case of metaphysical beliefs, we must hold them only lightly. Unbudging insistence on them is unwarranted. Even worse, it is often the cause of our religious wars.

So take "God" to stand for all that is right and good, perfect and noble. Believe that in some way God is in us, moving us to be more godlike—that is, more honest, loving, goodwilled, and geared toward unbounded positive growth. In this case, insistence on the direct experience of God and on union with God could not help but foster wholesome human living. To the extent that it does, insistence on mystical union with God would actually be something welcome—because in practice it would nurture good living in this world.

There! I have legitimated belief in "mystical union with God."

But by the same token, I have made this legitimation optional. Good living is again the bottom line. The transcendental precepts ultimately determine what *good* means. And the transcendental precepts hold sway whether one believes in God or not. All these spiritual questions come back to the same human core of spirituality.

Therefore, like the other issues we have considered, mystical union with God becomes a moot point. Accept or reject a theological account of mystical experience—but only lightly so, in either case—and the consequences for wholesome life on this planet remain the same. Beliefs about the experience of God and union with God are not worth fighting over.

## LIFE AFTER DEATH AND LIFE BEFORE LIFE

One of the most distressful aspects of being a human being is the awareness of death. We just cannot believe that we will come to an end, poof! and cease to exist. Our minds are too far-reaching; our creativity is astounding; the dignity of the self-aware person seems inviolable. Yet we are more than spiritual; we are also animal. We exist in our bodies, and our bodies wear out, as does everything physical. Even our most sublime ideas are housed in our biological organisms. So we are caught in a dilemma. On the one hand, our spiritual nature transcends space and time; we can grasp what is eternal and timeless. On the other hand, we die; our bodies cease to function, and we go to our graves. Both these facts are undeniable, and they tear us apart.

Religion proposes solutions to this dilemma by including beliefs about life in an otherworldly realm. Variations on this belief are fascinating. Most project some kind of spirit world and suggest that, after life in this world, we will live on in that other world.

It is striking that the Jewish faith traditionally has not included belief in an afterlife. You were to live your life as best you could, be grateful for the life you had, graciously surrender it at the end, and you would be remembered with gratitude by your family and friends. There was no sense of incompatibility between belief in a loving God and the extinction of the human being at death. Jews celebrated God's goodness in their living. They were grateful to have lived at all. They had no expectation that God should extend someone's life beyond the grave.

The reasoning behind that ancient Jewish attitude toward death is important to note. The human dilemma is to be torn between the spiritual and the biological. Most religions resolve the dilemma by emphasizing the spiritual; they propose a spiritual realm in which our lives continue. Very down-to-earth in its stance, Judaism insisted that to be human is to be both spiritual and physical; one dimension without the other is not a human being. We are not just spirits encased in bodies—as Plato, and most Eastern thought, and, unwittingly, much popular Christian thought would have it. We are our bodies. So when they die, so do we die. To go on living in some spiritual realm would not be to continue as a human being at all, for humans are bodily beings. Judaism's insistence on the goodness of the material world leads to the conclusion that there is no human life apart from this world. Rather than being a pessimistic fatalism, this Jewish attitude is really an affirmation of life—but life as we know it, human life in this world and in the body.

Christianity grappled with that same dilemma but came to a different so-lution. Christianity does believe in life after death—but in its strictest form, that belief includes bodily life. Resurrection of the body is a central tenet of Christianity: "resurrection of the dead and life everlasting" is the phrase in the Nicene Creed. Like Judaism, Christianity cannot conceive of human life apart from life in a body, for the human being is bodily as well as spiritual. So life in heaven is life in a "glorified" body. Of course, no one can say what a glorified body is. Life with God cannot be physical life as we now know it, but, to be human, that life must somehow be bodily, nonetheless, so, it follows, the body must be transformed—hence, the glorified body.

Although Christian belief included resurrection of the body as a central tenet, most contemporary Christians do not understand life after death in these terms. The popular notion is that we are body and soul and at death the body goes into the grave and the soul goes to heaven. The unspoken as-sumption is that we are really just souls, and we use our bodies for a time and then discard them. Strictly speaking, this belief is not Christian, but it is what most Christians hold.

In fact, that popular Christian belief is Platonism all over again: this world is not the real world; rather, there is a spiritual realm, and it is the re-ally real; and to it, heaven, we go when we finally die. Of course, part and parcel of this understanding is that this physical world is not very worthy; it is something to flee. It is imperfect and passing. In these very statements are echoes of an older Western spirituality, inherited from the Desert Fa-thers and the medieval world, a body-denying, otherworldly spirituality that still thrives in many religious circles. In *Sex and the Sacred* I discuss at length the connection between the body and spirituality.

Finally, the Eastern solution to the dilemma of body and spirit is very similar to the Platonic. Our real identity is the spirit within us. We use our bodies only in passing. This world is not the real world but only a kind of distracting entanglement. When we die, our spirits are freed from our bod-ies. Our spirits unite with the All, and we are dissolved into it. In Christian belief, we retain our individual identities—like the three persons in one God—even after death. In Eastern belief, we lose that individuality.

Eastern thought also includes another belief that differs from the Christian—the possibility of living a human life again and again: reincarnation. In one way or another, all religions insist on the need to be perfected before reach-ing ultimate fulfillment. Catholicism, for example, proposes purgatory as an intermediate state between this life and a life with God. In purgatory one is purified of any sin not sufficiently repaid in this world. In contrast, Protestantism believes that as Christians we are "covered over" in Christ, so when God looks on us, God sees the perfection of Christ and not our inner depravity. Thus, the perfection of Christ allows us to slip into heaven. East-ern thought uses reincarnation as the means of reaching perfection: one must live a human life over and over until one gets it right. Only then does one break the cycle of rebirths and enter eternal bliss. Thus, in Eastern thought we not only have belief in life after death, but we also have belief in multiple lives before this life.

Obviously, there is an array of religious opinions about the great beyond, and they all have their advantages and disadvantages. Reincarnation solves the problem of the need for final purification and for making up for one's wrongdoings, but reincarnation devalues our bodily life in this world.

If my true identity is some spiritual being who periodically descends into a body to take on successive historical identities, what validity does my presence in this world hold? When you speak to me, to whom are you really speaking? Remember, I am not only Daniel but also a long number of other identities as well; I could even say that I am not really Daniel, at all: Daniel just happens to be my current expression. Then who is this person behind the expression that you encounter? And how personal is the encounter when what you encounter is not really me? Of course, Eastern thought goes even further and insists that you are not really you, either, and I never was or am a distinct identity, in any case, but we are all just passing historical expressions of the All, the one and only reality. So why worry about personal identity? It is just an illusion.

The Eastern approach, like the Platonic, subtly devalues this world—as a trial, as a test, as a school, as an expression of something else. So nothing in this world can be granted ultimate validity. Take this implication to its logical conclusion, and we must live in doubt about the value of this world's achievements and our own conscious experiences. Following this approach, in some sense we and our world do not ultimately matter.

The popular Western belief in separation of the soul from the body logically implies the same problem—even though in this case we only go around once. While belief in an immortal soul does guarantee life after death, this belief demotes our earthly life to second-class status. Then, living for another world, not fully committed to this one, we easily ignore our responsibility to make this life worth living. We drift off into bizarre forms of self-denial and rely on magical rituals. We become blind to the this-worldly consequences of our religiously inspired behavior. The extreme example is the suicide bomber who gladly dies to this life in order to inherit a promised spiritual one. After all, this world is not really real, anyway!

At the other pole is the Jewish belief that death is final. This belief does affirm the validity of the physical world, but this belief disappoints the perennial human hope for ongoing life.

Finally, the official Christian belief in bodily resurrection from the dead affirms life after death, maintains the identity of the human person as both body and spirit, and insists on the eternal validity of our one life in the physical realm. These emphases are all to the good. But this Christian belief also raises difficult questions. What does resurrection mean? What is a glorified body? Where is the person while his or her body obviously lies in the grave before the final resurrection at the end of time? To be sure, Christian thinkers have proposed coherent and impressive answers to these questions—recently involving the Einsteinian equation of matter and energy as well as quantum-physics perspectives. Such answers, however, though not unreasonable, depend on elaborate speculation. But of course! Do not all the other opinions do so, as well?

Thus, I come again to my recurrent point: we have an array of religious beliefs, they conflict with one another, and none of them can be proved or disproved. These beliefs about life in a spiritual realm are part of religion's metaphysical superstructure. These superstructures are but webs of informed speculation. What reality they carry is hard to know. There can be no certainty in these matters. They are indeterminables. Therefore, to insist on them absolutely—or to deny them absolutely—is not helpful. These religious differences are beyond resolution, and in a pluralistic world they easily become occasions for conflict. Realizing that each of them is but a hope, a longed-for dream, we do better to graciously let go of them or else to hold to them only lightly.

That phrase, "to hold to beliefs only lightly," expresses our true situation in this world. Despite the infinite capacity of the human spirit, in practice there is much we do not know and much, it seems, we could never know. We live in unknowing. We live amidst mystery. To live with openness, honesty, and goodwill is to own this uncertainty.

Our aspiration for life after death is real, but our religious answers express only hopes. A hope is not the same as a firm belief or sure knowledge. We hope in trust and unknowing, in poignant longing and inspired expectation. Hopes provide vision and joyful motivation, so hopes are precious and good. What a wonderful thought that, after we die, we and all our loved ones will be reunited in an eternal celebration! But that such is the case, we really do not know. Living in hope is still only living buoyantly with uncertainty.

Perhaps when we die, we simply cease to exist, period. Or perhaps we go on to a new life such as some religions promise. Or perhaps we pass to another plane and live through another of an ongoing series of levels or universes, as portrayed in the sappy but exceedingly popular 1970 fable *Jonathan Livingston Seagull*. Or perhaps we get caught up in a further existence that is totally beyond anything that we can now imagine. Who can say?

In whatever case, in some way all the religions agree that most important is to live well here and now. Without virtuous living on this planet, we should not even hope for any blessed fulfillment in some hereafter.

Since wholesome living in this world is what matters, I suggest that metaphysical speculation about afterlives is a moot point. Whether there is an afterlife or not, our best bet is to live well here and now. Apart from good living we have no chance for a rich life either in this world or a next. Our concern, then, must be to build wholesome community on this shrinking planet. Then, whatever life there may be to come will take care of itself.

## CONCLUSION

I am proposing a spirituality for a pluralistic, global society. Such a spirituality must at least express what is common to all humanity. As such, this spirituality cannot buy into the wide range of metaphysical beliefs found in the world's religions, yet this spirituality must be open to such beliefs and respectful of them to the extent they merit respect.

In this chapter I have examined the main metaphysical religious beliefs. I have expressed why, in honesty and goodwill, one could let go of such beliefs altogether and, alternatively, how much of these beliefs one could retain without violating the human core of spirituality.

Our hardest challenge is to live a wholesome life in this world—to follow always the transcendental precepts, to live in openness, questioning, honesty, and love, attentively, intelligently, reasonably, and responsibly—and, at the same time, to live without the certainty that the religions provide. The challenge is to accept the human predicament with eyes wide open and, while reaching in self-transcendence toward the infinity of the universe, to live with one's feet planted solidly on the ground. Stretched between heaven and earth, we exist in a limbo state. Being honest about our situation, we need to live with radical uncertainty yet without giving up hope. Maintaining this balance is the challenge. In fact, all the world's religions at their best propose that delicate balance as the goal of spiritual perfection. Faith does not mean having the answers, but living in trust in the face of the questions.

However, more than a spiritual ideal, living with uncertainty is also a psychological challenge. Not just the human spirit, with its clear perception and penetrating gaze, but also the human psyche, with its murky channels and grotesque gargoyles, plays into the human mix. Our inability to live with uncertainty is more a psychological weakness than a spiritual flaw. After all, it is our emotional state—anxiety, fear, terror—that makes uncertainty unbearable. The next chapter delves into psychology and examines how the human psyche affects the working of the human spirit. There we will look squarely at the dark side of human nature and the prospect of bringing more light to our inner selves.

# 7

# The Psychological Housing
# of the Human Spirit

The community in which I grew up was stable and coherent, but it was not as idyllic as my descriptions thus far might have suggested. Of course, there were problems in the neighborhood, and, of course, these centered on "problem people." In my own generation, there were some kids who, as they said, were "bad." They got into fights, broke into people's yards, and sometimes were caught stealing. Drug abuse was not a problem at that time, but drinking and smoking were also "bad" things that some of my peers did.

Among the older generation, the most prominent vice was overdrinking, alcoholism—but nobody called it alcoholism at the time. As in all "moral" failure, the problem was supposedly a matter of "willpower." Most people were able to drink moderately, and others periodically just did not want to. But many of the heavy drinkers were simply unable to stop drinking, despite the pleas of their families, the warnings of the priest, and their own best efforts. They displayed their drunken excesses before the whole community, bore the shame, and continued to drink.

My own struggle with teenage "sexual temptations" seemed a parallel case. This thing came upon me all unexpected and uninvited, and I knew it was wrong—as well as I could have known anything to be wrong at that time: the church had declared all sexual thoughts, desires, and acts mortal sins. So wearily and weekly I confessed my "sins," did my penance, made a firm resolution not to sin again, received Holy Communion, prayed for strength, involved myself with wholesome activities—and inevitably ended up "sinning" again.

Juvenile delinquency, overdrinking, sexual acts—all were lumped into the same category: sin. All supposedly resulted from moral weakness, and all had the same remedy: personal determination and the grace of God. It had never occurred to me—I don't know if it had occurred to anyone, certainly not to any of my peers—that these were very different kinds of behaviors. I now see the sexual exploration as a normal and wholesome part of growing up, not to be faulted at all. The alcoholism was due more to addictive biological processes and deep psychological needs than to ill will. And the youthful misconduct was in part normal adolescent rebellion and in part the result of dysfunctional family life, often related to the alcoholism.

Of course, to some extent personal choice also played into those negative behaviors. I am no crass determinist; I do believe in free will. As spiritually endowed human beings, we *are* responsible for our behaviors to the extent that we are free. With exercise, the range of our personal freedom can expand as we gradually extricate ourselves from a tangle of biological urges and early psychological programming.

However, that range of personal freedom and responsibility is smaller than we like to believe. If my own experience with teenage sexuality was any indication, sometimes biology and psychology take their course outside of any possible, personal control—or, at least, in many cases to rely on iron-willed control is unreasonable and counterproductive: there must be better ways to expend one's energy than by fighting futilely against one's own constitution.

An enlightened understanding deals with the "passions" by exploring, channeling, and diffusing them, not by attempting to bottle them up, to repress and restrain them. Like an unvented boiler, a bottled-up person eventually explodes. Preaching, prayer, and willpower are simply not effective in correcting personal failings. Most personal failing is only in the slightest way dependent on free choice. Culpable wrongdoing, real malice or deliberate cruelty, evil perpetrated in the heart—what religion would call "sin"— does occur, but not in simple one-to-one correspondence with the external, destructive behaviors. We are not always completely responsible for what we do.

Nonetheless, an older understanding saw such failings simply as spiritual matters—in much the same sense that I have been using the term *spiritual* in this book: matters of meanings and values or of beliefs and ethics. Supposedly, the failings arose from a misunderstanding of what life was all about, what "God" wanted, and from an unwillingness to toe the line. Appeal was solely to the self-transcending and self-determining dimension of the human mind. With additional appeal to the power of God and amazing grace, this same, myopic approach lives on in that old-time religion. There, simple conversion to Jesus or pious reading of the Good Book is supposed to miraculously eradicate the problems in one's life. Thus far in this book, but without appeal to God and grace, I have also emphasized that spiritual dimension, and I risked giving the impression of a naively opti-

mistic picture of the human situation. This chapter redresses the balance by
delving into the messiness of the human condition.

## PSYCHE, ANOTHER DIMENSION OF THE HUMAN MIND

Nowadays we are all aware that the human mind is complex. Spirit is, indeed, one dimension of the mind, but another dimension must also be
recognized—what Lonergan called *psyche*. The psyche includes aspects of
mental experience other than the spiritual, such as emotions, memories,
imagery, and personality. In contrast to the open-ended, transparent, lucid,
and self-transcending dimension of our minds, these other aspects are
fixed, stable, dark, cavernous, mysterious, and sometimes threatening. In
fact, once spirit is recognized as a distinct dimension of the mind and its
structure delineated—an achievement that appears all too simple after Lonergan's genius work—the psyche also stands out in clear relief as a different
dimension of the mind. It is the psyche that often trips off negative and destructive behaviors.

We are familiar with the makings of the psyche. Today, everyone knows
what emotions are—the feelings of excitement, joy, peace, anger, disgust,
hurt, sadness, fear, anxiety, and the like. Even people who realize that they
are "out of touch" with their emotions have experienced emotions strong
enough to break through on occasion.

We also know what mental images are: pictures in the mind. We conjure
them up to figure out problems, and we recall them from dreams or indulge
them during daytime musings. We would also be open to the idea that not
all mental "images" are visual; call them "representations," and the idea
makes better sense. There can be auditory representations like a song or
somebody's voice that replays in our minds. And there can be kinesthetic or
bodily representations like feeling touched or hugged or beaten up—that
"weight" on your shoulder or that warm embrace that grandma used to
give. "Images" of smells and tastes can also occur.

And we all know what memories are: recollections of past events. Sometimes they haunt and torment us, and sometimes we gladly relive them.

It also takes little effort to realize that these psychic phenomena all hang
together. Our mental images are often related to our memories; in fact, they
often express memories. And our memories and images are laced with emotions. Recall that high school scene of your freshman year, and all the excitement or embarrassment of the moment comes rushing back.

Emotions, memories, mental imagery—they are of a kind. Working together, in large measure they make us behave as we do. They set up patterns,
they constitute habits, they support tendencies, they have us reacting in predictable ways. There are the jovial types of people, and the serious types, the

cautious types, the temperamental types, the aggressive types. These "types" are different personalities, different ways of being a person. Personality also hangs together with emotions, memories, and imagery. Our past, preserved in our memories, powered with emotions and projected in images, is the stuff of our typical behavior patterns, our personality. Our pasts have formed and shaped us, and we carry that history in our psyches, and we reenact it in our living.

## INTERACTION OF PSYCHE AND SPIRIT

The patterns of the psyche are programmed in; they are formed as our lives unfold, especially in the earliest years. Of course, some of our psychic makeup also results from our biology—sensitivity, alertness, openness to novelty, energy levels, mood fluctuations. But much of the psyche also results from our histories. Past experience shapes and prunes our psyches and, thus, our personalities. Not so, our spirits. The human spirit is forward-looking and open-ended. Rather than being fixed by the past, it opens onto a new future. The spirit restructures and re-forms; it is a principle of change and growth.

Though inseparable in the human mind, spirit and psyche really are distinct: the two always go together, but they are not the same thing. We might not have an insight without reliance on a helpful image—for example, that the human spirit operates on "four levels"—but just picturing the image is not the same as grasping its meaning. Or we might not come upon a new outlook without a surge of emotion—for example, that the basis of spirituality is in the human mind and not in belief in God—but just feeling the excitement or the anxiety is not the same as actually taking in and beginning to process the new data.

It seems obvious to me that two different dimensions reside in the human mind; they constitute the mind. But until Lonergan, their distinction had been obscured. I know of no psychological theory that clearly differentiates the two. Psychology conceives the mind as one reality and deals with it globally. This statement is true of Freud's id-ego-superego model, of current object-relations theory, of Jung's personal and collective unconscious and archetypes, of behaviorist stimulus and response, of the contemporary cognitive movement, and even of humanistic and transpersonal psychology. These psychologies *presume* a self-transcending dimension in the human mind, and they *presume* a programmed-in fixity, and they *presume* a heaving and shifting reality globally called the "mind," but they never sort out the psyche and the spirit as different aspects of the mind, and they never treat them in their own right.

As I already noted repeatedly, the pinpointing of the spiritual as a dimension of the human mind challenges traditional religion and refocuses all discussion about spirituality. Similarly, clearly distinguishing the psyche and spirit challenges modern psychology—and all the human sciences—and provokes the realization that spirituality is actually an unavoidable psychological concern, a matter of the human mind. Both religion and psychology are challenged. Religion is forced to realize that human problems have no simple spiritual solution, and psychology must acknowledge that the solution to human problems is in part spiritual. Psychology is left needing to deal with deep issues that it used to conveniently shunt off to religion, and religion needs to let go of some of the concerns that it is used to claiming as "spiritual."

## UNDERSTANDING AND ACHIEVING SPIRITUAL GROWTH

One key to understanding human behavior is the interaction of the psyche and the spirit within the human mind. Although inseparable, the psyche and the spirit really are two different dimensions of the human mind. They both demand attention, and they must both be given their due.

The psyche and the spirit cohere in a shifting tension. The fixity of the psyche accounts for mental stability, mental health, and the dynamism of the spirit results in growth and change. The spirit cannot soar freely toward its open-ended goal, embrace of the universe, because the psyche often holds the spirit in check. Likewise, the psyche cannot ever remain comfortable with patterns from the past because the spirit keeps pushing for movement and change. In a healthy person, this tug and pull goes on over the years, and gradually, healthily, the personality shifts.

With ongoing personal growth, the structures of the psyche more and more accommodate the dynamism of the spirit. The person becomes one whole, moving in a single direction, integrated, geared overall toward the open-ended goal of the human spirit. The psyche now supports the movement of the spirit. Needed memories appropriately arise; useful images easily emerge; emotions support, rather than confuse, the clear working of the mind. Psyche and spirit work harmoniously to facilitate positive change in the person. Personal integration and spiritual growth are underway—personal integration, because the change depends on harmonization of various inner facets of the person; spiritual growth, because the change depends on ever further sensitivity to the dynamic human spirit.

As should be obvious, personal integration and spiritual growth are one and the same. Increasing spirituality is "simply" a matter of integrating the human spirit ever more into the permanent structures of one's being.

Increasing "spiritualness" is "merely" a matter of having the psyche—and the body—more and more readily support the open-ended dynamism of one's human spirit.

This account of spiritual growth proposes the ideal. Like Pythagoras's $a^2 + b^2 = c^2$, this ideal, too, is never realized perfectly in the real world, in our world of space and time. The ideal explains in theory how the process of spiritual growth actually works although the actual working in any particular case never attains the ideal.

This state of affairs does not imply that the theory is useless or wrong. Should we give up striving to reach an ideal, should we declare that every ideal is but some personal or cultural fiction, simply because we are understandably hard-pressed—even as the theory explains—to ever reach the ideal? Of course not! The theory is neither wrong nor useless. Like any scientific theory, it merely expresses the nature of spiritual growth in the abstract, apart from this or that particular case. The theory expresses what is common in all cases apart from the specific differences that color the actual instances. As is true of any scientific explanation, we can also explain the process of spiritual growth without being able to perfectly actualize it.

In most actual cases, aspects of the process of spiritual growth are curtailed. Consider, for example, how our infant and childhood experiences shape our thinking and influence our behavior for the rest of our lives. To some extent or other, despite all goodwill, our parents or caregivers are simply unable to meet our every need. If for no other reason, the caregivers lose patience or run out of energy. Or, oftentimes, they do not know what we need: the baby is crying and the parents are frantic to help, but they do not know what the baby wants. Besides, every child is different. It would take a genius of a caregiver to know how to adjust and shift to meet every specific need of every child during those critical early years. And some caregivers are far from genius. Some are downright abusive. So growing up, we sometimes feel neglected, isolated, hurt. Naturally, we get angry. But the anger of a child is pretty useless in the face of powerful adults. Besides, what child could admit that his or her parents are ugly and mean? What child can afford to write off his or her caregivers? The child simply cannot face the world alone, and on some level the child is well aware how helpless and vulnerable she or he is. So these negative experiences get repressed; they go underground. Apart from long and expensive psychotherapy, much of this process is not remembered at all. We carry it in our gut, not in our explicit memories.

It is as if these early emotional events never occurred at all. But they did, and they live on in the shadowy caverns of the psyche—repressed hurt, forbidden anger, punished curiosity, violent hatred, painful isolation, confused affections, guilty self-blame, aching unworthiness. These corrosive forces get lodged in the depths of our hearts, and like the puppeteer's strings these forces control us as they secretly manipulate our reactions to later experiences. There is a war going on in the depths of our own mind, and we are hardly aware of the conflict.

Thus, the healthy tension between the psyche and the spirit gets distorted. The psyche is misshapen, its inclinations, misguided, and the natural spiritual urge for fuller life veers in the only direction the psyche allows: self-protectiveness, competitiveness, vindictiveness, self-assertion, self-disgust. For these psychological reasons, in large part, youthful vandalism, alcoholism, and other "sins" occur, not because people are wicked, evil, or unconverted.

A human is not a free-floating spirit like the mythical angels. In the human being, for better or worse, the spirit resides in the body alongside the psyche. Psyche and spirit live together and depend on each other for survival. As in the nuclear policy of "mutually assured destruction" of the Cold War era, if one goes down, so will the other. So psyche and spirit settle for the best working compromise under the circumstances. The end result is satisfaction of the most basic of all needs: self-preservation and survival. But the shape of such individual survival is often at odds with the needs of personal fulfillment and collective survival: personal bonding, a just society, a wholesome way of living.

## THE FORMATION AND RE-FORMATION OF THE PSYCHE

Growing up, we are amazingly and spontaneously sensitive to the demands of the people around us. For survival's sake, we had better be. We want to engage them; we want to please them; in the end, we want to be like them. After all, theirs is the only reality we know, so to us their ways define what "normal" means. Besides, at some level of our juvenile minds, we are well aware that we could not survive on our own. We just have to fit in.

However, no family is—or could be—perfectly responsive to the varied needs of the little ones, so in every case, finding one's place requires creativity. Usually unconsciously but sometimes with astute planning, we do what it takes to fit in. Our natural gifts determine the direction our survival plan will take, and in the process those innate propensities get overdeveloped, and less conspicuous or less rewarded talents get ignored. One child becomes the family clown and sidesteps issues by joking. Another learns to avoid disagreements by disappearing into the woodwork. And still another wins approval by becoming the favored bright light of the family and the hope for a better future for all. In each case, the strategy works, and it forms a personality.

But come graduation time and exit into a bigger world, and the necessary compromises that got us through to adulthood often prove counterproductive.

After some painful encounters, we begin to realize that something is askew. In quiet moments, we feel only half-real, and we ache in the depths of our souls. People around us and we ourselves get tired of our always joking, or disappearing, or playing the hero. The old strategies no longer work. We have developed out of balance; we are one-sided.

We can ignore this realization and hunker down for a dull and ultimately bitter life. The circus and sideshows that our society amply provides—popular "entertainment," VCRs, DVDs, SUVs, CDs, RVs, beautiful bodies, fast cars, luxurious houses, expensive jewelry, stylish clothes, incessant travel, designer drugs, high finances, power and manipulation—might afford anesthetizing distractions for much of the time. Rigid, conservative, uptight religion or novel, fascinating, self-aggrandizing spiritual pursuits offer a disguised and more subtle version of the same strategy of escape: in this regard, Chögyam Trungpa Rinpoche wrote masterfully of "spiritual materialism."

Buying into these distractions, we become part of the self-serving, competitive, hard-hearted, and cruel forces that control our world. Thus, to a large extent, the "evils" of our world depend on initially innocent and oftentimes unconscious psychological quirks: consider psychologically Adolf Hitler, Richard Nixon, Margaret Thatcher, Bill Clinton, George W. Bush, Condoleezza Rice, or Saddam Hussein. Usually, our guilt is only that we tune out the subtle cues that tip us off to our truth and we reluctantly surrender to the seemingly inevitable. Or worse, done with awareness and deliberateness, this surrender is "going over to the Dark Side," as *Star Wars* phrased the matter: we culpably choose to be less than we know we could be.

Or else, realizing our one-sidedness, we can take on the lifelong challenge of re-forming ourselves. We can engage the project of making space in ourselves for the more subtle and far-reaching dimensions of our being. Said another way, we can begin to restructure our psyche so that it is more in tune with our spirit. We can let our inner principle of self-transcending life take the lead, and we can bring all the facets of our being into harmony.

Talk shows, self-help books, and counselors abound to help us with this project. To a lesser or greater extent, these resources are all useful, and we would do well to take advantage of them. In this chapter, I can only hint at the realm of personal growth that has opened to us in the last century. My modest attempt is but to situate that realm in an even bigger panorama and to focus the role of psychological healing in spiritual growth.

In contemporary jargon, the project of self-help and personal growth is called "psychological." I am suggesting that psychology, the science of the mind, properly regards the human spirit as well as the psyche. So the project of self-help and personal growth is also a spiritual project. Even apart from explicit concern about God or religion, to honestly and humbly take up this project *is* to be on the spiritual path. My highlighting the human spirit, its structure, its inherent transcendental precepts, and its interaction with the psyche clarifies what spiritual growth entails as understood at this point in history.

## A FREUDIAN PERSPECTIVE ON THE PSYCHE

The shape of the psyche is critical for the unfolding of the human spirit. In a fearful personality for whom all novelty provokes anxiety, the human spirit can hardly be open to incoming data, and the self-transcending movement of the human spirit is stymied. In a dogmatic personality for whom all truth is already revealed, insight into oversights is blocked, and awareness of inconsistencies in belief is not allowed, so in critical areas the self-transcending spirit cannot function. In an insecure personality for whom every new fact threatens the status quo, an honest judgment that "yes, it is so," is unlikely to occur. In a protective personality for whom every other person is a rival, a loving decision to be tolerant and forgiving can hardly be tolerated. Because growth means letting go and trusting in a hoped-for future, the pressing needs of a defensive psyche cannot permit the transforming movement of the human spirit.

I have seen those very mechanisms at work in Biblical Fundamentalists who objected to my interpretations of the scriptures or my prescriptions for sexual ethics. I have watched them follow my argument point by point and then, at the moment of conclusion, seen their eyes glaze over as they dismissed my presentation and reasserted the reassuring beliefs they had always held. At such times, I have been reminded that they are totally unaware of their blind spots. Meet them later, and they offer their hand like a bosom buddy. I have learned that it is utterly impossible to follow through on a logical argument with them. They simply do not see the obvious and cannot acknowledge what is blatant. They are convinced that they are right and that their irritating proselytizing is goodwilled and helpful. In the case of us all, I have marveled at how solicitously our own minds preserve us from actually experiencing experiences we could not digest—and I have wondered what blind spots may be controlling my own worldview.

Sigmund Freud and his daughter Anna had names for the unconscious maneuvers that protect us from threatening experience: defense mechanisms. Through *projection* we attribute to others the flaws that we are unwilling to acknowledge in ourselves. Through *reaction formation* we invest in a crusade against vice so that we do not have to admit that this vice is our own. Through *rationalization* we find reasons to believe that what is not the case actually is. Through *displacement* we vent our hostility on a safe target instead of on the person to whom the hostility really belongs. In so many clever ways, we are able to stay distant from our true selves and feel content in believing that we actually are what we admire. Among the defense mechanisms, *denial* is father of them all: we simply become honestly oblivious to the facts.

In their own devious way, the defense mechanisms are actually healthy. They help preserve sanity when we really could not stand to face the truth. Thus, they provide a perspective on the one-sidedness we might develop during childhood. In the face of otherwise insurmountable obstacles, they allow us to survive with some semblance of sanity. In conspiracy with the human spirit, the intent of their misguided thrust is always wholeness and health. Of course, still seeking greater health, increased experience exposes them as flawed solutions. Then, an even healthier approach is to learn to deal with threats up front and more creatively or, at least, to be aware when our needed defenses are operating so that we are controlling them and they do not control us.

Defense mechanisms are basically healthy. In the case of the death of a loved one, for example, denial makes us gratefully numb so that we cannot experience what has actually happened. Then, little by little, over months and years, we are able to gradually restructure our lives without the physical presence of the dead loved one. We could not bear to face the reality of death in one fell swoop. Even the fully enlightened guru suffered from the "illusion" of his dead son.

I have witnessed the functioning of healthy denial in my experience as an LSD subject at Maryland Psychiatric Research Center. My first experience of the drug was devastating to my self-image. In retrospect, it was as if I were stripped naked and saw my natural self for the first time, genitals and all. But like a deep-sea clam shell, my mind had snapped shut. I was impervious to what I must have experienced under the drug. My image was that layer by layer my psyche had been unpeeled. Then, bit by bit as the weeks advanced, the pain of that transformative experience seeped out. The shell opened and shut, opened and shut, as regular as a clock. I found myself morning and evening given over uncontrollably to mourning for about a half hour at a time: deep, rocking sobs, freely flowing tears, crying more intense than I'd known since childhood, and fears—soon proven unfounded—that if I surrendered to the pain, I would get lost in it and never come back.

I had no idea what specific losses I grieved. I only knew that I had to let the grief flow. In fact, I was given no choice. A wisdom deeper than my conscious mind was director of the show. That wisdom was the work of my wondrous human spirit beyond my explicit awareness or deliberate control. I surrendered to it, and the process took its healthy course. And I learned tremendous respect for an inner mental process that knows better than

"I"—it is I!—what is right for me. It protected me from the devastation, then gradually let me absorb it, and finally remade me.

Because the psyche functions in collaboration with the human spirit, because the spirit is geared toward an open-ended fulfillment, and because that fulfillment only comes with integrated wholeness, our inner being conspires to move us along a healthful path. I saw that process lucidly through the influence of LSD, but Enlightenment philosophers, romantics, and psychologists have been describing that process from varied perspectives for centuries. Freud offered one perspective; Carl Jung offered another.

## A JUNGIAN PERSPECTIVE ON THE PSYCHE

Jung spelled out what constitutes, I believe, the structural elements of the psyche—the archetypes. These are patterns that get built into our minds simply because they are aspects of experience consistent across all human life. For example, we all have fathers and mothers, encounter wise elders, confront female and male stereotypes, experience falling down and getting up, get sick to our stomachs, fear threatening animals, face the challenge of life, struggle to find ourselves, and so on. Our experiences cluster and solidify around such commonalities, and each of them characterizes one of Jung's archetypes. Hence, in the most general of terms, the archetypes or psychic patterns structure our outlook on the world. They make up the very templates of our experience. All incoming data and outgoing decisions get filtered through them. Our human spirit itself operates through them.

The feminine and masculine archetypes—anima and animus—provide an easy example. Our day has made gender a topic of frequent concern—as regards heterosexuality, homosexuality, bisexuality, feminism, transvestism, transsexualism, androgyny, "metrosexuality," and cross-cultural studies. Nowadays, we readily recognize that, as little boys and little girls, we were pressured to behave in expected ways. The aggressive and spunky girl has to learn to be demure, and the sensitive, artistic boy has to work at being macho. Despite individual differences, socialization forces girls and boys into prefabricated molds. In the process, some aspects of our being get lost or, at least, pushed into the shadows. Later, these traits may reassert themselves and request their due place in our lives. Thus, being masculine and feminine becomes critical to our social development and to our hidden mental life. The tension between the animus and anima in each of us becomes central to our personal integration. We have to harmonize our stereotypically "masculine" and "feminine" sides.

Jung speaks of that reduction of tension and harmonization as "reconciliation of the opposites." Through this reconciliation, we restore balance to

our one-sided inclination. Thus, Jung's reconciliation of the opposites is another version of Freud's treatment of the defense mechanisms, though at a
more abstract level, and the implications for personal and spiritual growth
are the same: a balanced psyche allows the spirit to flow more freely. Consideration of one other pair of Jungian opposites will take the discussion
deeper.

Another constant in human living is the difference between our external
presentation and our inner selves. In fact, to some degree or another, we all
play roles. Different circumstances call for different aspects of our person.
The teacher is also the tennis player, the wife, the mother, the politician, and
the friend. Each situation requires a different presentation, although the
acting person is one and the same. Jung called a person's public presentation the *persona*—the Greek word from which the English *person* comes but
which originally meant the mask that actors wore to indicate their character in a play.

In tension with the persona are hidden, inner qualities, which Jung called
the "shadow." The term *shadow* indicates darkness and suggests that our
deeper qualities are often hidden even from ourselves, and, moreover, they
are often considered threatening and even bad: they are part of our dark
side. In the case of anger, vengeance, jealousy, or lust, it is clear why these
qualities might be considered bad. But although in themselves they are obviously positive traits, a boy's sensitivity or a girl's sharp intelligence might
also be unwelcome and be painted as threatening and bad and be pushed
into the shadow.

Once again, the challenge of the persona and the shadow is to eventually
unveil and harmonize all the aspects of oneself, to reconcile inner and
outer, to become one's full self, or, as the U.S. Army phrased the matter in
an un-Jungian appeal to hypermasculinity, to be all that you can be. Personal integration, putting all the pieces together—or individuation, in
Jung's terminology—is ever the goal, both psychological and spiritual.

The ambiguity in the notion *shadow* calls for special attention. The
shadow could include things that really are bad, truly evil, as well as things
that are merely considered bad in the sense of nasty, unsavory, or socially
inappropriate. Destructive, manipulative, sadistic urges—which could lead
to true violations of the transcendental precepts—are quite a different thing
compared with a boy's sensitivity or a girl's intelligence or a teenager's pu-
bescent "temptations" or a gay person's sexual desires or a wife's wanting
more independence. The latter are hardly wrong or bad. They are just—in
*our* society—challenging characteristics that do need to be uncovered,
owned, and then integrated into one's being.

But things that are truly evil fall into a different category altogether. They
cannot be accepted and integrated. By definition, they debilitate, destroy,
and undo a person and our shared world.

Nonetheless, when Jung spoke of reconciliation of the opposites, he did not make that distinction. Among the supposed opposites of the psyche were "good and evil"—as if these two could ever be reconciled.

Of course, we do need to admit and come to grips with our darker inclinations. We need to make peace between the devil and angel within us. But here, *devil* and *angel* are used symbolically. The one refers to aggressive, risqué, or lustful inclinations, which are a normal part of every person, and the other refers to puritanical, goody-goody, or self-righteous inclinations, which are also quite normal. To make peace between the two is to stop living in the unreal extremes of heaven and hell and to take up life on this earth, here and now.

Even further, it is also useful to explore our truly wicked, vile, destructive, and evil inclinations—not that we might act on them but that we might understand and diffuse them. We need to be open to all the bizarre and peculiar that is in us if we are to find human wholeness. The fascination of vampire novels legitimately plays on shady preoccupations in our souls. But we certainly do not want to become bloodsucking vampires and genuine evildoers.

Sorting out the difference between psyche and spirit highlights the important difference between the socially "bad" and the truly evil, the difference between taboo and wrong. The taboo is a shadow part of the psyche that needs to be integrated into the whole. Wrong or evil is opposed to the spirit and cannot be integrated.

Of course, the spirit works in and through the psyche. The two are inseparable in practice. As in my LSD experience, the spirit gently guides the process of personal integration, peeling off layer after layer of the psyche and reorganizing it. But Jung, like other psychologists, never sorted out psyche and spirit. And Jung's psychology is a favorite of spiritual questers, and it is open to serious misunderstanding.

Jungian psychology is likely to support the erroneous postmodern claims that there is no right and wrong, that evil is merely a shifting cultural category, that good and evil can be reconciled, and that the truly spiritual person needs to delve into the demonic and taste true evil to become completely liberated. Such dangerous claims are the makings of Satan worship and demonic cults, and these are of a kind with fanatical religions. Though demonic cults and fanatical religion lie at polar opposites, they both promise some fantasy liberation in return for unquestioning surrender, that is, for the mere price of one's soul. Neither extreme is realistic, although the pious rhetoric of the religious extreme makes it seem tolerable. But surely, demonism is not to be indulged. Actually going over to the Dark Side is a far cry from the healthy exploration of one's shadow. But Jung and much contemporary spirituality with him are not always clear on this point, and it is crucial: one is not to engage in evil. My point is important enough to deserve this long exposition of Jungian psychology. If my point has not come through, dear reader, please, reread this section.

## THE MECHANISMS OF SPIRITUAL GROWTH

The process of personal—and, thus, spiritual—integration involves the shifting interaction of the psyche and the spirit. The *theoretical key* to understanding spirituality is the human spirit. Explicate the spirit and, as in this book, an explanation of spirituality easily falls into place. But to actually achieve spiritual growth is another matter. The *practical key* to fostering spirituality is the psyche. The psyche both supports and constrains the dynamism of the human spirit, so fostering spiritual sensitivity is a matter of restructuring the psyche.

Ever and always, of course, the human spirit orchestrates inner movement. The spirit seeks unity, wholeness, and open-ended, cosmic integration. The spirit would embrace the universe. Geared toward that goal, the spirit "knows" what leads toward it. And of itself the spirit works toward that goal. The spirit needs no outside impetus. The spirit is the very force of life asserting itself within human consciousness. The spirit needs only to be given space, and it will do its thing.

Therefore, to deliberately facilitate the integration of the spirit requires tinkering with the psyche. Like soil readied for new growth, the psyche must be softened so that the tentacles of the spirit can spring up through it and reach toward the heavens. By getting free of defense mechanisms, reconciling the psychological opposites, undoing warped childhood formation, making use of self-help materials, working through grief and loss, getting into psychological counseling—in these ways the psyche shifts, counterproductive patterns fall away, inner walls break down, and the spontaneous dynamism of the human spirit is freed to take the lead. Spiritual growth proceeds hand in hand with psychological healing. Harmonization of the whole being—body, psyche, and spirit—crystal clear through and through, is the ultimate goal of personal and spiritual growth.

## RELIGIOUS PRACTICES TOWARD A COMMON SPIRITUALITY

Without that explicit understanding, over the centuries the religions have hit upon that process. Religious rituals and spiritual practices tend to prod and shake and massage and remold the psyche. They stir it up so there is room for the spirit to slip in.

Music elicits emotions, and sung words portray images and stir up memories. Annual celebrations bring out tears of loss or smiles of confident stability. Repetitious chants soothe the restlessness of the mind so that other inner forces can assert themselves. Embroidered vestments and filigree ornaments duplicate the cavernous underground of the psyche and, thus, provoke its eruption. Perfumes and incense commandeer the powerful sense of smell and take the mind to new places. Gently flickering candles elicit enduring hope amidst the darkness. Winding processions in long flowing robes trigger archetypes of passage and solemnity. Colored windows, rhythmic chimes, and pounding drums entrain firing patterns in the brain and, seizure-like, provoke freewheeling mental productions. Fasts disrupt body chemistry and induce visions. Night vigils and interrupted sleep expose uncensored dreams to the conscious mind. A host of religious practices engage the mechanisms of the psyche.

An appreciation for the psychological effect of religious practices puts the intellectual content of religion on a back seat. If the ritual is working, the doctrines and official beliefs can be easily overlooked—by believers and by outsiders, as well: no need to make an issue over differing credos. The rituals serve their purpose if they provide occasions to facilitate psychic shifts, which will, in turn, support good living. Once the shift is induced, the natural functioning of the mind effects the required inner transformation, and spiritual sensitivity advances one small step at a time. From this psychological point of view, what ultimately matters in religious practices is not so much what is actually believed, but the psychic process triggered in the context of belief and commitment.

Thus, from a whole other perspective, we arrive again at my repeated conclusion: religious beliefs, especially of the otherworldly kind, become a moot point. Emphasis on the psyche suggests that intellectual matters are hardly the heart of good religion. Personal transformation—but, of course, along a line of open-ended growth—is the substance of valid religion. The religious myths and metaphysical doctrines, whatever they are, project a coherent realm of security and peace into which the believer can periodically enter and within which needed personal transformation can safely occur.

Moments of deep prayer, flashes of religious experience, and wisps of engaging ritual are important even though they are intermittent and passing. No doubt, we lose the sense of transcendence when we turn from spiritual exercises to our everyday world, and the spiritual experience might then seem unreal or irrelevant. Only the spiritual giants could sustain a sense of the spiritual in the midst of mundane chores. Nonetheless, it is important that we surrender ourselves to such moments when they happen to occur— whether within or outside of religion—and without the fear that such surrender is escapism or delusion. Repeated exposure to such passing moments gradually transforms the mind—and we can explain why.

Periodic activation of higher functions within the brain has a top-down effect. It sets up neurological pathways that make it easier for the same experience to occur again, and it entrains lower brain processes into the flow of the higher ones. More simply, this same transformative process can be explained apart from neurology: repeated experiences become habitual and occur more and more easily. This principle is true for everyday activities as well as for spiritual experiences. Said still another way, there are ways to make patterns of experience change; adjustments to the psyche allow the self-transcending human spirit to have more freeflowing influence. Thus, from a number of different perspectives, explanations point to the same conclusion: we are able to transform the very structures of our experience; we can become more and more open to the self-transcending influence of the human spirit within us. We are built to grow spiritually.

Meditation is a particularly powerful technique for psychic transformation. Meditative practice is typical of Buddhism, but meditation has also been a traditional part of other Eastern religions and of the religions in the West, as well. Happily, from sources in both East and West, meditation is again becoming a common practice. All around the globe, people are meditating.

The transformative mechanism of regular meditation is similar to what I just explained regarding other moments of transcendent experience. The transformation is a matter of stilling the restlessness of the mind and, thus, making room for the human spirit to assert itself. Repeated practice makes this effect occur more and more readily as the spirit gradually restructures the underlying psyche and makes spiritual awareness habitual. I discuss this process in detail in *Meditation without Myth*.

What a hopeful occurrence! People from different religions and various cultures around the globe are using the same meditative practices to foster spiritual awareness. By gradually restructuring our psyches, these practices free our minds from the anxieties, fears, competitiveness, and acquisitiveness that might have been programmed into us during our malleable and innocent childhoods and might be reinforced by our spiritually bankrupt and materialistic, dog-eat-dog society. Thus, these practices make us more receptive to the gentle but persistent urgings of our outward moving spirits. We are rendered more able to be open, insightful, honest, and loving, more able to let the built-in urging of the transcendental precepts guide our living. We are initiated ever more deeply into the generative core of spirituality that is common to all humanity.

The process of spiritual growth affects the very structures of our human makeup. This process is independent of the particularities of religious belief and cultural preference. From this perspective on spiritual practice, religious beliefs become irrelevant. In fact, meditative techniques require that during the meditative exercise one let go of all thoughts, all beliefs, all intellectual musings. The very intent of meditation is to get beneath conceptual constructs—and emotion, images, and memories, as well—and to dwell in the purified and content-free source of all human creations: the human spirit. From that source, at that center, people around the globe can experience their spiritual nature and recognize a commonality shared with the whole human race. Healing of the human psyche can release our common human spirit and secure a basis for our global community.

## CONCLUSION

Recalling the tightly knit neighborhood of my childhood, my topic has been the meanings and values, the ideas and ideals, that are at the core of religion and that structure human community. These are spiritual; they are the products of the human spirit. In the form of doctrines and dogmas and of morals and ethics, these also tend to be the focus of religion. Accordingly, I spent a number of chapters analyzing religious beliefs and arguing that those metaphysical superstructures must be optional in a global community.

This chapter has taken a different tack. Rather than focusing on spiritual matters per se, this chapter addressed the human psyche, which underpins the human spirit. Here, the suggestion has been that distortions within the psyche lie behind unbudging insistence on differing religious beliefs. Psychological needs—neurotic defensiveness, anxious self-protectiveness—are the cause of dogmatic rigidity. In fact, as I have argued, metaphysical beliefs carry little legitimacy in themselves; they cannot be shown to be absolutely correct or necessarily mistaken. We insist on them because we need them to shore up our precarious lives.

Because we are fragmented and torn internally, in conflict with our very selves, we are unable to face the mystery of life that comes with unknowing and uncertainty. Healing our psyches, rendering ourselves centered and internally more secure, would free us from our need for dogmatism in the face of the great unknowns. If, psychically whole, we were more attuned to the open-ended dynamism of our spirits, we would find beauty and comfort, marvel and awe, in the very mystery of existence. More at peace with ourselves, we would recognize our fellow human beings in ourselves and easily overlook the nonessential differences among us, our cultures, and our religions.

Attention to the psyche is a *major* requirement in the development of a global community. This chapter has highlighted the matter and given some pointers for understanding and dealing with it. On the foundations laid thus far, the following chapter will sketch what such a global community might actually look like.

# 8

## Our Global Community

Nostalgically I remember my childhood, and I muse about a world at peace. I do not think my dream is childish fantasy. Having experienced true community, I know it can be real. Having tasted true community, I am unwilling to settle for less.

My neighborhood in South Side Pittsburgh held together because the people shared common beliefs and held common values. A common religion and common culture made community a natural. Today the older generation has passed on, and the world is changing fast. Yet I still find basic goodness among the people who grew up there. The ties of religion are dissolved. The younger generation hardly attends church any more, but these people remain golden—kind, honest, generous, supportive. They are living off the moral capital generated during that earlier time of religious commitment. But what will happen when that spiritual inheritance runs out?

The challenge of community today is greater than it used to be. Life was simpler then. The task then was to get along with people much like ourselves. Today we must get along with people who are different from us. We must respect and reverence—not just tolerate—others who are strange to us. We must find common beliefs and common values to hold us together, and they cannot be religious or cultural. The only option I see is that they be grounded in our very humanity. In search of such grounding, I have highlighted a dimension of humanity that is universal—not our bodies, not our psyches, but our human spirits.

Diversity arises from differences in place and time. These affect our bodies and psyches. But the spirit transcends space and time, and it is the same in everyone. It is what makes us human. Accordingly, the beliefs and values that can hold us together must be those that naturally emerge from the

139

human spirit itself. Not ancestors, not culture, not religion, not revelation, not even "God," but only a set of ideas and ideals common to all humanity could structure our global community.

That idea sounds great, but what would it mean in practice? How realistic is it? What will it look like in the concrete?

I have spoken about common meanings and values—beliefs and ethics, visions and virtues, understandings and commitments. These are the expressions of the human spirit. Everyone lives by some set of them. Our problem arises when we hold differing sets and especially when we grant our own set divine authority and try to impose it on others. The challenge of structuring our global community is to find a set of beliefs and ethics by which everybody could live.

## THE SOCIETAL DANGER IN ABSOLUTIZED RELIGIOUS BELIEFS

In chapters 4, 5, and 6, I have shown how we could purify religious beliefs and ethics by requiring that they respect the criteria of valid knowing and loving that are built into the human spirit. It followed that the metaphysical dimension of religion—which pertains to other worlds, to God and other spiritual entities, and to times outside of time—must be kept to the sidelines.

Otherworldly beliefs can be neither proved nor disproved; there is no way to determine their validity. Therefore, to insist on them absolutely is irresponsible. More to the point, to make a public issue of these fictive absolutes and to berate nonbelievers in light of them is simply and egregiously wrong. Such a conversion campaign impugns the honesty of others and discredits their goodwill. In so doing, it undermines the very foundation of the spiritual. To confront others with one's personal religious outlook—street corner preaching, door-to-door solicitation, postings on roadside billboards, advertisements on radio and television and in newspapers and movie theaters—is intrusive. It violates personal privacy. It is abusive, assaultive, and offensive. Many Europeans and Canadians I know have chuckled at the religious intensity of American society and the intrusion of religion in American public life—from the Scopes trial, to the multibuckled Bible Belt, to scandals over sexual foibles, to divinely chosen leaders. Yet, today, all nations are dodging volleys of religious proselytizing. In our, oh, so wishy-washy, pseudotolerant postmodern world with its exaggerated political correctness that grants equal hearing to any foolishness and allows any rationalization to pass as an opinion equal to any other, the obvious begs to be stated: public religious campaigning needs to stop.

Public demonstrations of religion can foster social fragmentation. This realization surfaces worldwide. The French government—committed to "liberty, equality, fraternity"—outlawed distinctive religious garb in the public schools because all French schools are officially nonreligious. The religionists, of course, raised protests of intolerance and discrimination—and rightly so since the ban did not apply equally to the religious symbols of all religions—but that government initiative was on target. Similarly, recognizing the seriousness of the issue—namely, "the transformation of Québec into a pluralist society, fragmented in terms of values, beliefs and ways of life"—this Canadian province developed an elaborated policy: "Religious Pluralism in Québec: A Social and Ethical Challenge." The document acknowledges outright that the Canadian Charters of Human Rights and Freedoms, "*like the religions, propose a value system.*" The values at stake are "broad social consensus," "the basic rules of public life," "social contract," "collective will," "the will to live together," and the "duty to accommodate [others who differ]." At stake is "to decide what place . . . to give religion in public secular life." The concerted Canadian effort to forge a coherent pluralistic society is explicit in this realization: to grant public right to any religion is always to deny the right of another religion. The British government, likewise, explored setting limits on public expressions of religion. And American law has drawn restrictive boundaries around religious preaching and solicitation in public places.

Tolerance cannot be tolerated when its practical effect is to foster intolerance. Undeniably, the flaunting of religious distinctiveness contributes to this very effect. A billboard on the main road leading into my university town reads "Jesus is Lord over Carrollton." What, I wonder, do my Jewish, Muslim, and Buddhist friends there feel when they pass that same way? If the common human decency of religious groups is insufficient to temper their aggression, just as stalking is illegal—because it is abusive—much religious proselytizing of our day ought also to be forbidden. Frequently, it amounts to hawking science-fiction versions of life. To this extent, it sustains illusions, and, like false advertising, it is a menace to society. Making absolute what can in no way be so is simply dishonest. Confronting others with personal and even demeaning pieties is abusive. And religious motivation does not excuse dishonesty or make offense right.

Per se—by definition!—metaphysical beliefs are disconnected from our world. They pertain to some other intuited or imagined realm. Nonetheless, because people hold them, they do have effects in this world.

When metaphysical beliefs are compatible with wholesome living or even advance it, they are valuable assets. They provide a comprehensive picture in which all facets of life hold together, and in light of that big picture, they encourage people to live their lives well. For example, talk at a funeral about reunion in heaven not only provides consolation but also helps people to deal with loss and to return to daily life. Or concern about accruing bad karma—what goes around comes around—can induce people, if for no better motive, to treat others decently.

But metaphysical commitments should never be allowed to become the occasion for dispute—like the outlandish claims that God bequeathed certain lands to certain people or that God established cultural patterns (women's dress, men's prerogatives, sexual taboos, health practices) to be maintained forever and always. In this case, metaphysical commitments betray wholesome living, which alone would legitimate holding them. Such religion ought to be outright derided, publicly ridiculed—not only by stand-up comics and late night television hosts but also by religious leaders and public officials. Such metaphysical commitments make no contribution; they could not be of God. Tolerating them only supports intolerance. Goodwill in their case undermines goodwill.

Even worse, when metaphysical commitments are actually incoherent or actually run counter to our best understanding of things—for example, that intense belief can make anything happen, that truth is just a name for majority opinion, that creationism is a scientific theory, that an embryo is actually a human person, that virginity is a supreme virtue, that any nonheterosexuality is inherently pathological, that only fear keeps people virtuous, that women are constitutionally inferior and ought to be subordinate to men, that evil is only in the eye of the beholder—these commitments need to be discouraged, debunked, and publicly rejected. Like poetry, novels, science fiction, and good movies, religious beliefs can provide a welcome distraction from the burdens of life. Well-done fiction broadens our horizons and helps to keep our hearts light, our minds open, and our emotions flowing. But when people take fiction for reality and live in a life-demeaning way, not only are their personal lives shallow, but their lasting contribution to others is ultimately also diminished. They spend their days studying esoteric topics, they heatedly debate questions that are of no consequence, and they invest in meetings and conventions on ultimately irrelevant topics. They reenact that fictional medieval pastime, discussion about how many angels could dance on the head of a pin. They end up as extras in the drama of life when they could be playing major roles. Or worse, energized by religious fanaticism, they actually win major roles and then begin to rewrite everybody's script. We all lose when people make fantasy into religious reality.

## THE CRITERIA OF TRUTH AND GOODNESS

But how does one know what is actually true?

I have proposed criteria for determining the truth, those built into the human spirit and, therefore, those alone that could govern valid human knowing. The criteria for knowing constitute the first three of the transcendental precepts: be attentive, be intelligent, be reasonable.

To be sure, these precepts confirm empiricism as *the* human way of knowing. But the empiricism in question is not narrow or materialistic. Here empiricism simply means reliance on appropriate evidence. Whatever belief lacks supporting evidence is a public intruder. Whatever evidence bears on any question is a welcome contribution. Indeed, I am actually advocating *spirituality* on the basis of empiricism!

To be sure, again, what I am advancing is Western science, but following Lonergan, I propose it as human, not Western, and I take "science" in a broad sense. I presume that science is simply the channeled inclination of the human spirit's quest for understanding. Indeed, the word *science* comes from the Latin *scientia*, which simply means knowledge. Science is accurate understanding, correct knowing.

To finally understand the process of human knowing—as I believe Lonergan has allowed us to do—is to ground the thrust of Western science in the very structures of the human mind. The scientific method is hardly arbitrary and culture-bound. It is not the modern Western bogeyman. If Western science has played into human disasters—like the overmechanization of life, development of weapons of mass destruction, and damage to the environment—*it is not science itself, but the version and use of it that are at fault.* Like learning, science is a self-correcting process. To reject it outright is to lose our only hope of ever getting things right.

I challenge those who oppose a generalized empirical approach to knowledge—politically incorrect in many circles at this time—to suggest another option, and I wonder how they would defend their suggestion without appeal to relevant evidence, that is, apart from some version of "Western" "science." I will certainly not credit as legitimate defense mere assertion, popular opinion, personal belief, gut feeling, vague qualms and reservations, or individual intuition. When called "revelation" and "inspiration," these supposed sources of "knowledge" obviously belong to another era. They betray us in the present moment. In the face of an emerging global community, there is no overcoming arbitrary and divisive religious beliefs and personal preferences by appeal to secular versions of the same thing. My reservation about "gut feelings," "inspiration," and "intuition" is not to completely discredit them. They are often expressions of important insight and the source of important breakthroughs. My only insistence is that they be tested against the evidence before anyone accepts them as true, begins touting them in public, and rushes off to take action on them.

Three transcendental precepts regard correct knowing; the fourth pertains to values, ethics, ideals, commitments: be responsible. Of course, values were already at stake in the discussion of knowledge in the above paragraphs. My point there was that a generalized empirical method is the appropriate means of arriving at the truth in every instance. I placed value on that method: to follow it is to be responsible.

It should be no surprise that values get mixed with knowledge. In chapter 4, I already spoke of the interaction of the four dimensions of the human spirit. They function in collaboration. They influence and control one another. Therefore, no discussion of knowledge can be value-free. Still, in the above paragraphs I tried to speak specifically of knowledge, and here my discussion focuses specifically on virtues and ethics.

According to Lonergan's portrayal of the human spirit, responsibility is the prime virtue. It characterizes correct choice; it describes authentic actuation of the human spirit operating on its fourth level.

Let it be clear that in this context *responsibility* is not meant to suggest demands made on a person from outside—as if being responsible meant doing what you're told to do, fulfilling your duties, accepting social requirements, being a "good little boy" or a "nice little girl," and the like. Rather, responsibility is the attitude of a person who lives in harmony with his or her own being, and since this being is outgoing, living in harmony with it means living in harmony with other people and with all of reality. Responsibility means fostering life, advancing the positive, investing in a long-term future, or—in the traditional formula—doing good and avoiding evil. The supposition is that such behavior flows spontaneously from the integrated person. One is responsible because one is simply being one's authentically human self. One is acting in accord with one's nature, and this nature inclines us self-aware creatures toward deliberate choices for wholesome and ongoing life.

Shinto, the traditional religion of Japan, has a striking feature that makes my point. Shinto has no ethical teaching. Its only ethical tenet is this: Anybody who needs ethical codes and moral rules in order to be able to live rightly is a corrupt person. Good living flows naturally from a genuine human being. Nobody should have to tell us how to live well.

## VIRTUES TO LIVE BY

The transcendental precepts propose four virtues as fundamental: attentiveness, intelligence, reasonableness, and responsibility—or, in my popular formulation: openness, inquisitiveness, honesty, and love. In contrast, Western and Eastern traditions have proposed lists of other virtues.

The Greeks suggested four that have subsequently been called the cardinal—that is, "hinge" or primary—virtues: justice, temperance, courage, and prudence. Judaism proposed the Ten Commandments, which express an array of virtues: reverence, honor, respect, honesty, fairness, chastity. Christianity added three "theological" virtues: faith, hope, and charity; and Christianity also emphasized humility, that is, honesty about oneself and one's talents in both positive and negative regards. Building on a parable of Jesus recorded in Matthew 25, Christianity also proposed a list of good works: to feed the hungry, to give drink to the thirsty, to clothe the naked, to shelter the homeless, to care for the sick, to visit the imprisoned, and to bury the dead. Though not strictly virtues, these practices express virtuousness. Similarly, Buddhism's Noble Eightfold Path proposes requirements for good living: right faith, right resolve, right speech, right action, right livelihood, right effort, right thought, and right concentration. And akin to love in the West, the consummate virtue in the Eastern traditions is compassion.

In light of the richness of the ancient religious traditions, are the mere four transcendental precepts sufficient? As a common starting point, yes.

The importance of the transcendental precepts is that they ground core virtues in the structure of the human spirit itself. Thus, insistence on them gives virtuousness a new depth. It is no longer merely the inspired teaching of historic prophetic figures or the supposed moralistic preoccupation of goody-goody people. Virtuousness is the very requirement of human health and wholeness. This is the paramount point I have been making all along.

But of course, those four precepts do not contain the richness that the religious traditions do. Nonetheless, those four certainly open onto and support the religious elaborations. I see the religious formulations as teasing out the implications of the four transcendental precepts. The transcendental precepts are abstract; they are theoretical formulations. They are not expected to express all the richness and nuance of more practical, ethical statements.

Moreover, there is no conflict whatsoever between the transcendental precepts and traditional religious ethics at their best. As I have been arguing, those precepts are part of the spiritual core common to all religion. In no way is my insistence on this spirituality for our global community a put-down of traditional religions. Spirituality and religion—both rightly understood—go hand in hand.

What is more, there is amazing consistency among the traditional ethical teachings. Many scholars of religion have pointed out, for example, that "the Golden Rule"—do unto others as you would have them do unto you—occurs in various forms in virtually all the religions of the world. So my claim of a common spirituality built into the human heart and expressed in various religions appears to be sound. Lonergan's epic articulation of the human spirit is a long-awaited contribution and constitutes an incalculable breakthrough. A common spirituality provides a basis for our global community.

## BELIEFS TO LIVE BY

Beyond concern for virtues and ethics, what common *beliefs* would a global spirituality include? Fundamentally and uncompromisingly: belief in the very process of knowing and loving that I am advancing here. That is, the common beliefs would entail commitment to the authentic functioning of the human spirit.

In this book I propose an understanding of spirituality. This understanding constitutes a belief system. So I am proposing a belief system, and I am inviting people to accept it, to believe.

But inviting belief, I am not proposing a new religion. I am proposing a spirituality, a peculiar spirituality. Unlike others invested in themselves, this spirituality is self-effacing. Its concern is not itself, but truth, reality, goodness, life. It would gladly surrender itself if surrender were what truth and goodness required, for as a spirituality, it is simply an attempt to state what leads to truth and goodness.

Moreover, unlike the spiritualities attached to various religions, this spirituality is common to all religions, and it could be accepted apart from any religion. Its basis is the human mind.

Furthermore, unlike other belief systems, this set of beliefs is grounded in empirical evidence and critical thinking. I did not just dream up these ideas but derived them from Lonergan's analysis of human consciousness, and anyone who wishes can reenact that analysis by attending to the functioning of his or her own mind. So I am using the word *belief* in a sense that overlaps with *knowledge*: I am speaking of *understanding* grounded in *data*. I am not asking you to take what I say on faith. I am asking you to examine your own inner experience and in this way to determine whether or not to accept my position as true, whether or not to "believe."

Additionally, my proposal appears as a belief because many do not accept it implicitly or explicitly. It is a sad and disturbing fact of the new millennium that faith in science is giving way to superstition. To be sure, the remarkable achievements of science in the twentieth century dismantled the easy certainty that Newton's mechanistic universe provided. The smug self-assurance of modernity gave way to the open-ended quest of post modernity. Yet science itself plods on as deliberately as ever. Although to understand reality is not as simple as originally believed, scientists have not abandoned the pursuit of grounded understanding. It now appears "merely" to be more complex and subtle than expected. Indeed, with more marvel and enthusiasm than ever, commitment to cumulative explanation still drives postmodern science.

Nonetheless, mostly in defense of their cherished religious beliefs, some want to turn back the clock. They would repeat the religion-versus-science debates of the seventeenth and eighteenth centuries and emerge with a different conclusion. They want to oust science so they can freely hold their own worldviews—such as "creationism." This trend is blatant in my own field, the psychology of religion (but almost exclusively in the religiously preoccupied United States). Supposedly, the "knowledge" derived from religion and that of science are on a par because—such credulity boggles the mind—the theories, mathematical formulae, and explanations of science are as merely suggestive as the myths, symbols, and creeds of religion. Supposedly, there can be no accurate understanding of human experience and behavior unless God is an explicit factor in the explanation because God is ever intervening miraculously. These are professional opinions published at the highest levels by psychologists speaking as psychologists in secular psychological arenas! Along with these professionals marches a motley movement of New-Age-type believers who trust in crystals, intuitions, misunderstood quantum physics, and esoteric beliefs and practices from ancient sources. Once again as in primitive societies, many people will not accept that appropriate evidence is needed to confirm an opinion. People freely reject science—except, perhaps, when they have a toothache! They conceive the world in terms of earth, air, fire, and water rather than the periodic table of elements. They prefer herbs and folk wisdom to contemporary medicine.

Not everyone accepts the understanding of knowledge that I am proposing and especially in matters religious. Many insist on a different belief. They will not be tied down by the need for evidence. That is say—and this is the point—they will not accept their own selves and the structure of their minds as they are. In the sometimes pitiable poignancy of the human struggle, they choose to prefer some fictitious center of certainty. Hence, what I propose here appears to be faith. Its acceptance requires that we choose to believe in ourselves.

Finally, in a usage common in religious circles, my use of the term *belief* also includes commitment, which, strictly speaking, pertains to virtue, not to knowledge. All these peculiarities of this spirituality result because it rests on the most peculiar reality of all, the human spirit, which is the basis of all knowing and loving.

Simply said, I am proposing a religious-like faith, but one that is nonreligious. Rather than religion, I am proposing a spirituality, indeed, the mother of all spiritualities. So, fundamentally and uncompromisingly, the beliefs included in this spirituality for our global community are those that constitute this spirituality itself. I am advocating *belief and trust in the human spirit and commitment to it prior to belief in anything else.* Said otherwise, I am fostering commitment to authentic personal integrity as the foundation of all spirituality, religion, personal fulfillment, community, human progress, and ultimate fulfillment.

My "proposing" may sometimes sound like "imposing" and especially when I question uncritical universal tolerance and challenge the supposed nobility of every deeply held opinion. My suggested solution for a frag-mented world may sound like a creed that I would force upon everybody. Is this suggestion just another version of imperialistic and fundamentalistic religion? Is my solution just another ideology? Not at all.

The "creed" that I advocate is a set of open-ended principles. It is not a set of dogmas or claimed revelations. It is not a fixed list of supposedly already-known answers. It would require only that people be open, insightful, hon-est, and goodwilled in addressing any issue. What the eventual answers would be in any particular case would always remain to be seen. This creed would require allegiance to no predetermined reform program; this creed would im-ply the worship of no one's god. According to this creed, there are no ready-made answers—except that valid answers cannot emerge unless we are com-mitted to the transcendental precepts. My suggestion is commitment to a process, not to a preset agenda. My suggestion is to engage in open and hon-est questioning and goodwilled dialogue even as the very structure of our be-ing seems to require.

If the request to live in honesty and goodwill is perceived as an imposi-tion, have we not already moved beyond all possibility of redemption? Have we not committed what Jesus called the sin "against the Holy Spirit," which will not be forgiven—indeed, *cannot* be forgiven because the very na-ture of this sin is the bull-headed rejection of the very possibility of reform, hope, and new life?

My proposal is radical. There is no question about that. I am actually in-sisting that belief in the human spirit must come before even belief in God. In chapters 5 and 6, I argued that the requirements of the human spirit limit what could legitimately be said about God. But note well: in saying so, I am not saying that the human spirit or anything else comes before God ab-solutely. Rather, I am saying that belief in the human spirit must come be-fore *belief* in God—because God in Godself and people's beliefs about God are not one and the same. Although God is first and foremost, prior to and beyond all other reality, belief in God must be subordinate to sane think-ing. God may be ultimate, and the affirmation of God may be legitimate, but the nature of God remains impenetrable mystery. Appeal to God is al-ways the expression of someone's best guess, never guaranteed truth. There-fore, people's beliefs in God cannot be ultimate because they are merely hu-man and they may well all differ. *Belief and trust in the human spirit and commitment to it must take priority over belief in anything else,* including belief in God.

Heated debate has arisen over attempts to place monuments to the Ten Commandments in government buildings in the United States. People are insisting that their allegiance to God comes before their allegiance to the law, government, and country. On first hearing, this insistence sounds no-ble, but a little thought shows it is misguided.

People miss the difference between God and their personal beliefs about God. People do not recognize that, although God may be supreme, the Ten Commandments only represent a particular religious expression of commitment to God. Therefore, to insist on the Ten Commandments is to insist on placing one's personal religious beliefs above anybody else's.

In fact, in defending the Ten Commandments, people are not defending God but their own chosen way of expressing belief in God. Of course, the Ten Commandments have been fundamental to Western society since its earliest beginnings, so to Westerners they seem obvious, natural, and universal. Besides, much of what they require is simply basic human decency, justice, and goodwill, so there truly should be no opposition to their intent. Nevertheless, in themselves, the Ten Commandments are the particular formula of only one religious tradition, and the fact is that Judaism and Christianity and even different denominations of Christianity list and understand "the Ten Commandments" differently. So they or any version of them cannot be given privileged status in a pluralistic society. To stand for the Ten Commandments is not to stand simply for "God," but to stand for some particular religion's formulas about God.

Not even belief in God can supersede commitment to the human spirit—for that belief is always and merely a particular understanding about God. Belief in the human spirit is the fundamental belief of a spirituality for our global community.

More specifically, what can be said of shared beliefs in our global community? What particular beliefs are in question? What exactly should everyone in our global community believe?

The only beliefs that absolutely everyone could hold are those that respect everyone's humanity. Such beliefs would be nothing other than the best available opinion of the day. That is to say, people would believe what, as best we are able, we have determined to be so—attentively, intelligently, and reasonably: scientifically. For questions amenable to empirical research—How has the universe developed? What is the basis of biological life? What is healthy and unhealthy?—people would give up the answers of speculative religion, folklore, and tradition and accept the hard-won conclusions of the experts in their respective fields. There would be no quibbling and conflict over matters that have discernible explanations—and now, including even spirituality, as being elaborated here. Open-minded, insightful, honest, and goodwilled collaborative investigation would provide the only acceptable understanding of things, that is, the only understanding that any honest person of goodwill could, should, and would accept.

In fact, for many questions we do know or can find reasonable answers. It is striking, for example, that no Biblical Fundamentalists insist that the

Earth is flat although this is precisely the understanding contained in the Bible and commonly held throughout the ancient Near East. In contrast, however, Biblical Fundamentalists continue to deny the theory of evolution and credulously suggest that God planted fossils to test our faith. Such resistance to solid science is downright wicked—if for no other reason, because it corrupts education and deprives youth of sound knowledge and critical-thinking skills: it undermines the very workings of the self-transcending human spirit itself.

Brash insistence on pet beliefs also leads to outright conflict, so we can no longer afford to respect such beliefs. Once, for example, in a public lecture—on a prestigious university campus, no less—I foolishly tried to defend evolutionary theory by appeal to religious authority. I recalled that Pope John Paul II commended evolution as now "more than a theory" because it is so solidly grounded in evidence. To my comment about the pope there came taunts from the hall: "Antichrist! Antichrist!" Are we to respect such bigoted religion? A pluralistic society simply cannot countenance such hostility.

Sometimes the "hard sciences" still provoke controversy, as in the case of evolution. No wonder, then, that the human sciences—biology, medicine, psychology, sociology, anthropology, economics—involve even hotter topics: abortion, stem cell research, the determination of death, sexual variations, child-rearing practices, feminism, homelessness, joblessness, drug use and abuse, medical care, malnutrition, famine, environmental concerns, energy consumption, Third World debt. However, on all these topics, let it be noted well, honest and goodwilled research could easily point to a required conclusion.

The retort that science itself lacks consensus is a red herring. Even on difficult topics, honest and goodwilled research, self-correcting by nature, could certainly propose an answer in due order. In the meantime, responsible action should be tolerant, compassionate, and conservative. That is, when we are still unsure, we should be committed to erring on the side of safety and life. For example, in the current debate over global warming, we should be committed to saving the environment, not to fueling the economy and protecting the profits of air-and-water-polluting industries. To use the supposed uncertainty of science as an excuse for doing what is, in all likelihood, deadly is simply stupid. Perforce, it is unethical. Yet current official policy in the United States—supported by alteration and falsification of reports from the Environmental Protection Agency—continues to run down this path to self-destruction. Such practice is blatantly evil.

This call to achieve consensus by reliance on science is not novel. How else does the international community agree on matters that affect the health of our global village? The World Organization for Animal Health, for example, in conjunction with the Secretariat of the International Plant Protection Convention, regularly establishes *"science-based* sanitary and phytosanitary standards" that govern safe trade in agricultural products. Likewise, international concern about the spread of "mad cow disease" and "bird flu" as well as about lead in paints has been well publicized. Cooperation in all these cases depends on knowledge that all can trust and on shared commitment to global health. Science provides that knowledge, and basic common sense provides the commitment.

Even on many social issues, the overwhelming bulk of scientific evidence already points clearly in one direction. A case in point is homosexuality. There is simply no credible evidence supporting choice or change of sexual orientation, nor is there evidence for anything destructive or harmful in same-sex relationships, but just the opposite. Only prejudiced—that is, prejudged—opinion continues to rail against homosexuality while lesbian and gay teenagers continue, at a rate triple that of other teens, to commit suicide because of induced, needless guilt.

But in a secular society without a moral compass, interminable discussion of such topics is allowed. For crassly political and financial gain, such discussion merely permits delay of responsible action. There can be no societal advance if "democratic debate" is the mere airing of self-serving opinions, complete with "spin" from exorbitantly paid publicity agencies. Current staged versions of universally tolerant and open discussion make a charade of the search for the truth. When every opinion must be respected as much as any other, what sense do notions such as *true, correct, sane,* and *healthy* have? There is no intelligent reason that blatantly false opinion should enjoy an equal hearing. I challenge the supposition, so popular with the "free press," that such "democratic" practice is the best way to counter misinformation. Supposedly, the error will become apparent. In a society where everyday issues have become mind-bogglingly complex, where the intellectual level of the mass media is geared to the lowest common denominator, and, disgusting to say, where the deliberate manipulation of information has become a specialized, lucrative industry, to rely on this quaint notion from a former era is naive, at best. People see through this charade, and they withdraw allegiance from "democratic process." The end result is the undermining of society rather than its upbuilding.

As far as I know, only honest science offers documented understanding open to public scrutiny and meriting common acceptance. Accordingly, science should determine the beliefs structuring a global society. I see no room for question in the matter. As an expression of the transcendental precepts in action, science is our best hope for the future. Indeed, Lonergan has viewed his epistemological achievement as a highpoint in the long history of humankind's attempt to understand the nature of human knowing. Commitment to science, in the broad sense I explained, is a natural expression of the spiritual component of humanity.

## CAN THAT IDEAL BE LIVED?

That picture of scientific consensus within a global society appears idealistic. I do not deny the fact. Indeed, that picture reminds me of the religionless but high-minded universe of *Star Trek*. How could anyone be truly human in such a universe? Must we all become a Mr. Spock?

My immediate, theoretical response is this: "How could anyone be truly human apart from such a universe?" But that troubling question was not about theory; it was about practicality. Is my picture of a global society realistic? Can it be actualized? Responding at the practical level, I would share something of my own spiritual journey. Making myself a case in point, I would suggest that my vision is neither unrealistic nor unique.

I teach Human Sexuality each semester at the University of West Georgia. Attempting to foster openness in my students, I am as open about myself as I can responsibly be. About two-thirds of the way through that course one semester, as I was un-self-consciously talking about my life, an observant student made the comment, "Wow, you certainly have come a long way!"

Come to think of it, indeed, I have. I believe that in my own lifespan my thinking has progressed from the medieval through the modern to the postmodern era of Western history.

In chapter 1, I described the close-knit, conservative, mill-working, Polish, Catholic community of South Side Pittsburgh, in which I was raised. There, sexuality was not to be mentioned, yet today I am known as a spokesperson for an extremely liberal and well-argued position on sexuality—and, in fact, I comfortably walk my talk. But sexuality is a minor example in this story. I have made similar strides regarding the "big questions" of life. My intrepid grappling with them should be evident from what I have written in this book.

At an immature seventeen years of age, I entered a Catholic seminary. From my protective neighborhood in Pittsburgh, I moved into a still more circumscribed and more religiously structured environment. In those days we seminarians were hardly ever even to leave seminary grounds and certainly never without explicit permission. Sincerely and naively, for eight years I submitted to that discipline, and I absorbed Catholic teaching, which covers every aspect of life. By the time I was ordained and had been educated at the Pontifical Gregorian University in Rome, thinking I had received one of the best possible educations in the world, I had bought totally into the Catholic worldview, and as a priest, I embodied it, preached it, and taught it to others.

Once out of seminary and into everyday life, however, the cocoon of my Catholic world began to break open. The need for intimacy confronted me, and sexuality became an issue for this celibate priest. The administrative cruelty of company-men hierarchs disillusioned me, and I questioned the divine institution of popes and bishops. The pressing needs of real people weighed upon me, and I began rethinking official ethics and policy. College-level and adult-education courses fell my way, and I began to translate doctrine into humanistic wisdom. Then, having left parish ministry for a career as a seminary professor, I did doctoral studies in theology and realized that my "best possible" Catholic schooling had been indoctrination, not education. For the first time the real questions shook me, and my budding crisis of faith became official. Study with Bernard Lonergan gave me the intellectual tools to deal with it.

Historical issues pushed me further along—feminism, Vietnam, gay liberation, conservative John Paul II, dashed hopes of the Second Vatican Council, the rise of Biblical Fundamentalism, economic globalization, increasing materialism and unbridled capitalism, 9/11, the emergence of radical Islamism, Enron, WorldCom, and George W. Bush's vendetta against Iraq. I began taking note of public affairs and world events, and I realized that I am a part of them. I recognized my emerging personal views as relevant to our global situation, and I began to express them. More and more firmly, my thinking shifted from the theological to the psychological. I had made the transition from religion to spiritual humanism.

However, my religious upbringing and priestly formation were too intense and my acceptance of them was too sincere to allow me ever to simply throw off all religion. I had to forge a postmodern revision, and it had to be moderate. If I increasingly questioned my inherited Catholicism, I was also respectfully reshaping it in my heart and mind. I knew that the religious questions are real and cannot just be ignored. A new set of answers was needed, not a rejection of the questions.

So, resigned from the priesthood—at least on my part: in its characteristic administrative perversity, the Vatican has never accepted my resignation, but I take this fact to mean that they are allowing me to continue to represent them—I still attend weekly Mass. But I choose my congregation carefully. I need a service that nourishes my soul. Rote ritual or feel-good religion will not do, nor, of course, would fire-and-brimstone preaching or institutional propaganda. I am what disgruntled conservatives call a "cafeteria Catholic." As they say in twelve-step programs, I take what is useful and leave the rest. I am absolutely convinced that much of Catholic teaching and policy is humanly destructive and, thus, surely, not true to the Spirit of Jesus. In *The Transcended Christian* I elaborate my current understanding of Christianity as a player in the global spiritual quest.

I am comfortable worshipping as a Catholic—and equally comfortable in other Christian churches and also in non-Christian gatherings. I use ritual to sustain my spiritual growth. I need to be reminded regularly of higher things. I feel genuine in acknowledging the Mystery behind the existence of reality. I benefit from being challenged to rethink the meaning of life. I appreciate being moved to tears or provoked to laughter over matters of the spirit. I am inspired by praying with others who I believe share spiritual commitments similar to mine. Understanding the Lord's Prayer, for example, to express longing for a reign of peace and justice on earth—*Thy* kingdom come, *Thy* will be done—I am deeply moved to join hands with fellow worshipers and speak those words out loud. I use my Catholicism to nurture my spiritual life, and I remain grateful to the priests—many of whom are my classmates, colleagues, and friends—who are somehow able to remain in the Catholic priesthood and offer genuine spiritual leadership.

Having long given up the obligatory, rote, daily prayers of the priest—the Office of Hours or the Breviary—I developed instead a practice of regular meditation. It remains the mainstay of my spiritual life. *Meditation without Myth* tells my story in this regard.

But I also consider my work—study, teaching, writing, counseling, lecturing—to be a spiritual practice. I continue a "ministry" by advancing the secular cause of truth and love in our world, and I am not alone in this effort and understanding: many people take their work, menial or lofty, to be a sacred charge. Of course, I consider myself particularly blessed—or lucky: the point is the same. I have found my niche. I have had a long and expensive education that allows me to sift through the most difficult of questions. I had a stable and loving upbringing that left me emotionally capable of engaging adventure. And I have had the luxury of years of psychotherapy, which helped me cope with the changing contours of my life.

In my own way, I have moved from a sheltered, denominational religious life into a transreligious, spiritual quest. In their ways, many others have done the same. In my peregrinations across religious lines, I encounter countless fellow pilgrims.

I delight, for example, in periodic phone calls from a remarkable acquaintance on the West Coast. Virtually living on the street and burdened with mental illness, he survives by doing odd jobs, and, intelligent and well disciplined, he spends much time in spiritual pursuit—Buddhist workshops, Muslim practices, Greek Orthodox liturgies, Episcopal lectures, Methodist socials, Unitarian services, academic conferences, relentless reading, study, and thought. His commitment is to a world of justice and peace—a world, I will say, in which people like him, and all others, would be respected, protected, and loved.

A friend in New York City, for example, recently shared an experience. He was astonished to go to a Buddhist center and find over a hundred people there for meditation—on a Tuesday evening!

That friend on the East Coast and my friend on the West Coast and all those in between represent the new wave of spirituality that is rolling around the globe. Respectful of diverse religions and cultures and gaining strength from them, this wave wells up from the human spirit common to us all.

With more or less emphasis on belief in God, many other books today are echoing these same themes—for example, the Dalai Lama's *Ethics for the New Millennium*, Robert Emmons's *The Psychology of Ultimate Concerns*, Robert Kane's *Through the Moral Maze*, Richard Holloway's *Godless Morality*, Hans Küng and Helmut Schmidt's *A Global Ethic and Global Responsibility*, and Elena Mustakova-Poussardt's *Critical Consciousness*. Similarly, Kirk J. Schneider, author of *Rediscovery of Awe*, writes of "enchanted agnosticism" and portrays a vision strikingly similar to what I am suggesting. He foresees

> a time when enchanted agnosticism is echoed in schools and temples, in board-rooms and in embassies, in bedrooms and in alley ways—in every human sphere . . . when churches throw open their doors to mosques, and mosques to synagogues; when Buddhist priests can perform sacred chanting rites before Hindu congregants; and when Jewish temples sanction Protestant services. . . . when every major denomination would regularly . . . host every other major de-nomination and yet maintain their respective identities. . . . when . . . awe-based living . . . is practiced in business and diplomatic circles; when politicians and mediators and entrepreneurs *model* the actions they expect of others. . . . when diplomatic and trade meetings are attended not only by policymakers, but also by ethical philosophers, spiritual leaders, and organizational psychologists; when, for example, attendees participate in professionally facilitated process groups and promote frank exchanges of feeling; and when the input from sci-entists and philosophers matches that from legislators and generals.

In *Beyond Religion* David Elkins expresses a similar vision:

> Perhaps the day will come when the validity of one's spirituality will be judged not by the correctness of one's theology but by the authenticity of one's spiri-tual life. . . . And there may even come a time, perhaps centuries from now, when religion itself will fade away, leaving only the universal wisdom that has proven effective in the development of our spiritual nature.

To the same effect, Elkins cites the famous French sociologist of religion Emile Durkheim: "There is something eternal in religion which is destined to survive all the particular symbols in which religious thought has suc-cessfully enveloped itself."

The spirituality for our global community that I propose may seem like science fiction, but it is becoming a reality. Numerous individuals inside and outside religion are actualizing it in their own lives. Commonly, peo-ple are talking and writing about it. To become more widespread, this spir-itual movement now requires the active participation of our religious and secular institutions.

## THE CLUMSY "SEPARATION OF CHURCH AND STATE"

The greatest obstacles to global community are governments, business, and the religions themselves. In the terms of American politics, the problem is the clumsiness of "separation of church and state" thus far.

In traditional societies, like the one in which I grew up, religion and government are of a piece. The values of religion permeate society at large, so a lofty vision guides all activities.

But secularization severs secular institutions from religion, and with religion needed values get shunted aside. Then secular institutions are free to go their merry way. Any real concern for ethics can be dismissed as a religious preoccupation, "inappropriate for secular society." Then even the term *ethics* loses its genuine meaning, and minimalist codes of conduct—professional "ethics"— replace heartfelt commitment to the good. *Ethical* gets equated with *legal*— which, as recent history has abundantly shown, might hardly serve the common good at all. Then society at large is left without a moral compass, but this state of affairs is advantageous to unscrupulous people of power and wealth, so they perpetuate it.

Fundamentalists of every stripe are aware of that problem. They know that without a spiritual base a society is doomed. Indeed, with secularization and globalization, modernization runs roughshod over indigenous cultures and religious traditions, and the spiritual and mental anguish of the trampled populations is profound. The movie *Whale Rider*, based on the book by Witi Ihimaera, offers a beautiful and sensitive portrayal of the breakdown of an indigenous culture as it confronts modern technology. The movie *The Last Samurai* offers another example, this time more blatantly political and disturbingly bloody but still powerfully inspiring—a lofty tribute to the values of a traditional society, although couched in terms of the rugged individualism that sells to contemporary America.

Thus, the goal of the fundamentalists is to restore religion to society and to recreate the integral communities of premodern times. But fundamentalists do not appreciate the depth of the problem, and they have no viable solution for it. Overly strict religious commitment limits their vision. Believing they already possess the truth, they fail to seek understanding of the problem. So in the United States, Biblical Fundamentalists—I will not call them Christians— proselytize aggressively and aim at turning the nation into a theocracy. Islamic fundamentalists wage terrorist war against "godless" Western ways. (Such, I believe, was part of the far-reaching rationale behind the 9/11 attacks, not the suggested inanity of petty jealousy over American freedoms. As Stephen Zunes astutely phrased the matter, "We are not hated because of our freedom and democracy but because our policies in the Middle East have little to do with freedom and democracy.") Jewish fundamentalists attempt to secure a religious enclave in territory supposedly bequeathed to them by God.

And all fundamentalists ostentatiously wear their religious amulets, dress in distinctive religious garb, and publicize their religiousness. But the return to traditional religion is no solution to today's problems.

In the clumsy "separation of church and state," institutional religions also gain this-worldly advantage. They inherit their own arenas of power, money, and influence, and they go on conveniently shielded from much of the scrutiny of society's legal organs. The child-abuse scandals in the House of God Church in Atlanta, the Roman Catholic sex-abuse scandals, and the Mormon wife/slave scandals offer interesting cases in point.

In secularized society, the assigned role of religion is to attend to people's "spiritual needs," but secularization supposes that spiritual needs are idiosyncratic and variable, particular to the religions and people in question and irrelevant to public life. Accordingly, to maintain their congregations in this secular situation, almost as in marketing, the religions must sharpen their distinctive identities. Catholics are focused on sex and abortion and long-standing, monolithic tradition; Southern Baptists, heterosexuality and the subservient role of women and children; Lutherans, Presbyterians, and Methodists, religious fellowship; Episcopalians, rituals as elaborate as the Catholic: "all of the church with half of the guilt"; Mormons, family life; Jews and Muslims, cultural survival; Native Americans, the environment; Buddhists, meditation.

Conceived in this way, the now splintered religions have no institutionalized mode for collectively addressing the issues facing society. The agencies of spirituality have become mere ornaments to public life: clergy is allowed to offer an "invocation" at an event of state.

This state of affairs effectively short-circuits spiritual concerns on every front. On the one hand, it turns the religions themselves into mere brands and flavors, and, on the other hand, it guts them of any immediate public relevance. Although religion is supposed to foster spirituality, although genuine spirituality should be common to all religions, and although spirituality is crucial to the wholesome functioning of society at large, spiritual concerns have gotten lost in the "democratic," capitalist, and consumerist shuffle.

I have proposed a spiritual vision suited for our global community. This spirituality arises from the recent realization that religion and spirituality are not the same thing. Moreover, this spirituality is grounded in the human spirit. Thus, it is not particular to any one religion, culture, or people, yet it should be relevant across religions and across cultures.

Outcroppings of such global spirituality are already emerging among enterprising individuals within, outside of, and across religions. But for such a spirituality to actually inform our global community, more than isolated individual effort is needed. The religions, the secular institutions, and their relationship need to be reconceived. Public agencies need to explicitly include public room for spiritual concerns.

## SPIRITUALIZATION OF THE RELIGIONS

What would that global spirituality require of the religions? Above all, the religions must begin to emphasize their commonalities and to downplay their unique features. They must stop huckstering their wares by emphasizing traits of brand recognition. As is their primary role, they must invest their greatest resources—each in their own way—in authentic generic spirituality.

This is not the time for religions to be staking out turf, touting distinctive doctrines, and offering formulas that pit the saved against the damned and one religion against another. Such maneuvers are precisely the problem with religions today. If the religions lack the spiritual wisdom to recognize this problem, they discredit themselves before the eyes of all who are able to see; they show themselves fully unworthy of allegiance and respect. Far from speaking for God, they are diabolical: they do evil in the name of good.

At this point in history, whether they act knowingly or unknowingly, the religions must be held accountable—because their specific charge is to guide people toward truth and goodness. Failing in this task, perhaps unaware even of what this task means, they are the corrupt, hireling shepherds whom Jesus condemned; they are the devious spiritual leaders to whom Jesus said, "Woe unto you!"

The Vatican's 2000 document about Christ as sole savior of the world, *Dominus Iesus*, is a case in point. Instead of emphasizing the uniqueness of Christian belief about Jesus, the Vatican could easily and helpfully have emphasized Jesus's teachings as profound instruction on good living for the entire world. And why not? That all can be saved is, in fact, official Catholic teaching. Catholicism is lucid on this point: one need not be Catholic, one need not be Christian, one need not even believe in God; one need only be a person of sincere goodwill to be saved. So, except to self-servingly shore up the sagging church itself, there was no need for the Vatican to push the esoteric belief that Christianity supersedes every other creed. All the less was there need for Pope Benedict XVI to reiterate the point, inverting the emphasis of the teaching of the Second Vatican Council, in his immediately notorious 2007 *motu proprio* (a statement from the pope's own office "on his own initiative"). Besides, of what use is such a claim when other religions routinely make it, as well? If Vatican officials understood what that Christian belief means in practice—namely, that the attitude of Jesus (basic human goodness, core spirituality) is the only stance that is saving—they would have spoken otherwise.

Similarly, the screeching preaching of the Biblical Fundamentalists—I live in the Bible Belt—is another instance that falls to the same analysis and merits the same response. Adulation of Jesus, rather than commitment to what he stood and died for, is a betrayal of Jesus.

In the same way, the hard-line positions of Judaism and Islam are not helpful. Their concern is not so much doctrinal belief—as with Christianity—but cultural inheritance. So Judaism and Islam become blatant examples of how religion and culture can overlap and be identified. Jewish scholars, for example, routinely point out that it is impossible to say whether Judaism is a religion or a culture. In fact, it is both, and the two are interwoven. Similarly, Muslims insist that their religion is not something that can be detached from a particular way of life. These religions are tightly tied to specific cultural practices, to precise geographical locations—"holy land"—and even to privileged languages—Hebrew and Arabic. In themselves, these religions have all the makings of particular, self-contained cultures.

But of course! These religions developed in conjunction with particular ancient societies, and these religions emerged to serve the needs of those particular ancient societies. At the origins of these religions, religion and society, faith and culture, were one. Therefore, to a large extent, fidelity to these religions means maintaining cultural traditions, and these traditions are beyond discussion: they are believed to have been revealed and required by God Almighty. The branching of Judaism into Orthodox, Reform, Conservative, and Reconstructionist strains resulted precisely from attempts to loosen the spiritual core of Judaism from its cultural wrappings. The frightening difference between fundamentalist and moderate Islam expresses similar attempts. But when those cultural wrappings are thought to have been required by God, it becomes very difficult for Judaism and Islam to move into the third millennium.

Needed is the shocking realization—hammered away at in this book—that it is simply impossible to reconcile such culturally entangled faiths with the contemporary world if maintaining faith means tenaciously dragging along cultural baggage from the distant past. The fact is that we are in a new era. The fact is that the religious solutions from the past cannot meet the spiritual needs of the present. In principle, the matter is a simple as that—but in practice, it is not always easy for people to admit the obvious, especially when religion is at stake, and it is always painful for people to loosen their grip on their cultural heritage. I know the pain; I have made the transition.

Jewish history holds an important lesson in this regard. When the Romans destroyed the Jewish temple at Jerusalem in 70 CE, Judaism lost its central focus of identity. Jews wondered how they could go on. They could not conceive of Jewish life without the temple. Besides, if the Romans destroyed God's temple, it would seem that the Roman gods were stronger than the Jewish God. Rabbis agonized over this state of affairs and could make no sense of it. The eventual rabbinical consensus was simply that "we have to get on with life." So, centered on the synagogue, study, and prayer—now a religion without animal sacrifice as its standard form of worship—Judaism morphed into a new form and survived in this form for two millennia.

The pluralism and globalization of our own day have precipitated a crisis equal in magnitude to the destruction of the Jewish temple. However, since no physical structure has been destroyed but only a worldview, the religions can go on pretending that nothing has changed; people can isolate their consciousness and continue to live in their ghettoized minds and worlds. More spiritually sensitive souls, however, will recognize the crisis—and again find a creative way to adjust.

The history of Islam also contains instances of radical change precipitated by historical circumstances. In fact, Islam thrives in many different cultures, from East Africa to Malaysia. This fact shows that Islam's core commitment to God's will and a just society is, indeed, relevant to a pluralistic global community, and there do exist movements within Islam that are struggling to reconcile Muslim belief with the contemporary world. However, this task is particularly challenging for Islam. Judaism and Christianity have spent centuries moving from a medieval to a postmodern worldview and still have a long way to go. Yet history is requiring Islam to make the same transition within a generation or two—and despite the bungled, manipulative, and self-serving political policies of Western powers. Thus, unfortunately, conservative religious and political forces predominate in the Islamic world, and radical militarist groups have hijacked Islamic tradition to advance their own agendas. As a result, one must hesitate to make any comments about Islam. People who offer criticism get murdered—which fact must, in itself, say something about the supposed divine origins of such religious fanaticism.

Refusing to let society advance with the times, strong forces within Judaism and Islam rigidly require ancient cultural practices that are clearly incompatible with the needs of our global community—and, it goes without saying, unjust to the adherents of these religions as well, most blatantly, the women. Indisputably, however, there is a profound sense of the spiritual at the core of Judaism and Islam. Loosened from claims of naively conceived, eternally binding, divine revelation, that spiritual core—not its dated husks—needs to be emphasized.

Surely, attention to that spiritual core would allow these religions to legitimately evolve and, responding realistically to the needs of the times, become major contributors to a global spiritual community. The end result would be a society that was secular but nonetheless spiritual, a society committed to no particular religion but nonetheless grounded in a spirituality common to all religion. The clumsy Western version of "separation of church and state" would be redressed, and the guiding vision of Judaism and Islam—that spiritual commitments permeate every aspect of life—would, indeed, be realized. A universalistic and ecumenical perspective is, in fact, a part of both Judaism and Islam in their very beginnings. This perspective needs to be highlighted, and insistence on cultural specifics, toned down.

Because they claim absolute knowledge of the truth and have a developed doctrine of revelation, the "religions of the book"—Judaism, Christianity, and Islam, and the more recent arrival, Mormonism, as well—present the biggest challenge to our global community. These religions are the most likely to be self-righteously competitive. In contrast, Eastern religions tend to be less hegemonic.

Hinduism believes that many different paths lead to the same spiritual mountaintop. This tolerant belief leaves ample room for a plurality of religions, and in a global community this result is to the good. However, this same belief sometimes appears relativistic, suggesting that there is no truth or falsehood, no absolute right or wrong, no ultimate validity to things in this world of space and time. This suggestion is antagonistic to a this-worldly spirituality.

Nonetheless, in contrast, Hindu practice often belies such aspects of its doctrine. While seeming to deny the validity of life in this passing world, Hinduism does lead its believers to live heartwarmingly good lives here. With its unending religious festivals and its array of gods and goddesses, all expressing facets of the one Absolute, Hinduism has found rich and variegated ways to convey profound spirituality to people of different temperaments and sensitivities.

On the other hand, other aspects of Hindu practice—such as the caste system, which is grounded in metaphysical speculation about karma and reincarnation—need to be rethought so that the spiritual dignity of every person in this present life is respected and protected. It would be useful, then, for Hindu teachers to clarify and emphasize their commitment to the good in this world and, rather than projecting the good into another world or another lifetime, to name the commitment to good in this world as itself an expression of the Absolute. Otherwise, like the Western "separation of church and state," Hindu religious tolerance, based on the separation of this world and some supposed other world, plays into spiritual amorphousness. Because anything does not go, unqualified tolerance eventually does a disservice to the pluralism of a global community.

Of all the religions I know, Buddhism is most compatible with the spirituality I am outlining here. With no belief in God and with emphasis on meditative practice, Buddhism fosters that very cultivation of the human spirit—"Buddha nature"—that grounds all spirituality. The delightfully uplifting presence of the Dalai Lama exemplifies the power of Buddhism, and his work toward the development of a global ethics is one with the thrust of this book. Only Buddhist metaphysics—which, like Hinduism's, downplays the validity of this world in theory while stunningly supporting it in practice—poses potential problems. Yet, from what I know of Buddhist teaching, speculative doctrine is not its concern. Buddhism has already learned to hold only lightly to its metaphysical superstructure, so its profound understanding of spiritual practice would be compatible with any religion.

Indeed, the nontheist spirituality that I am proposing might be a Western version of Buddhism. The Buddhist emphasis dovetails with the long-standing Catholic outlook that sees nature as the all-important foundation on which grace builds. This conception lies at the heart of the vision I am proposing in this book. In fact, my retreats at the Tibetan Buddhist meditation center Karma Chöling, in Vermont, have significantly influenced my thinking.

I deliberately propose a generic spirituality that could be and should be at the core of every religion. What I advocate is surely compatible with all religion at its best. After all, I did not pull these ideas out of thin air. They are circulating in spiritual communities around the globe. So *without losing their distinctiveness in their in-house dealings,* publicly and in consort, the religions could fully endorse this core spirituality. In *The Transcended Christian* I suggest in detail how such a feat might play out in Christianity.

If only the religions would begin publicly advocating this generic spirituality instead of pushing their distinctive beliefs and values! Then they would not only advance the spiritual understanding of their adherents—something that religious leaders should surely desire. But speaking with one voice, through their public insistence and through the civic influence of their adherents, the religions would also foster the spiritual sensitivity needed in our secular institutions. *To revitalize secular society with a nonsectarian spiritual infusion would be the most outstanding religious contribution of the third millennium.*

## SPIRITUALIZATION OF SECULAR INSTITUTIONS

The ultimate thrust of my pragmatic agenda must already be clear. It is to transform secular society and ground our global community by introducing a common spirituality as an essential human dimension of every individual and institution. It is to do, through a generic spirituality in our global community, what particular religions used to do in their specific, isolated communities. It is to establish on a global scale the coherence of shared meanings and values that I knew in my childhood neighborhood of Catholic South Side Pittsburgh.

Critical to this enterprise is the recognition that spirituality is not a restrictedly religious affair, but an essentially human one. Spirituality is necessarily an aspect of every individual life—as well as a dimension of all collective life. Spirituality is not optional. To be sure, secular society must be neutral in the face of particular religions, but it cannot be neutral regarding matters of the human spirit: its very survival and advance depend on them.

There is no avoiding the matter of meanings and values. To reject one set is to choose another. Even to choose not to choose is to make a choice: pretended neutrality offers no escape from the human responsibility for shaping our world. Such is the human condition. There is no avoiding the poignant human burden of sorting out true spirituality from false. Blandly, neutrally, and "democratically" praising every opinion that claims the name "religious" contributes to the leveling of all values. The only sane response in our current situation is, as best we can, to advocate the meanings and values that foster positive growth. As argued here, that set of meanings and values is the heart of core spirituality. The agenda must be to establish this spirituality in the global, secular society at large.

The greatest challenge to this agenda will be precisely to introduce universally shared values into secular institutions. If this same project is already challenging enough in the case of the religions, with the religions success is at least probable. After all, although much of religion does not actually practice what it preaches, religion at least preaches loftily, so religion is liable to the charge of hypocrisy when it does not follow through, and embarrassment, if nothing else, might pressure religion to get with the program. But freed of religious influence, secular institutions make no pretense of fostering lofty and noble goals. Efficiency, affluence, comfort, national defense, competitiveness, the financial bottom line—these are the only de facto creed of the secular institutions. They will surely resist tooth and nail changes that hold them to higher standards.

Sad to say, the common good is hardly ever the prime concern of politicians and business men and women. I make this statement well aware that it has echoed through the centuries since Plato in the West and Confucius in the East. In the United States alone, the wealthiest nation ever to exist, for example, it is outrageous that people live on the streets, children suffer malnutrition, people lack adequate health care, education is ineffective, support for the arts is scarce, drug abuse is rampant, and imprisonment substitutes for rehabilitation. Politicians may propose ingenious rationalizations as to why these glaring social problems cannot be solved, but ultimately, the reason is greed. Honest and loving attention to these problems could surely resolve them. The challenge is to make honesty and love the guiding priorities, rather than materialistic competitiveness.

Strange that no one has noticed: economic prosperity does not bring personal fulfillment. While the standard of living has continued to rise for much of the American population, measures of personal happiness show a steady decline—consistently since the 1950s. Since 1960, the rate of depression in the United States has steadily increased, and suicide rates among adolescents have tripled.

Material goods and opulent wealth cannot fill the emptiness of the human soul. Thomas Lewis, Fari Amini, and Richard Lannon, three MDs proposing *A General Theory of Love*, make the following comment regarding social ills: "The real battle our country fights" is against emotional pain—"isolation, sorrow, bitterness, anxiety, loneliness, and despair." Unless secular institutions attend to essential human needs and help heal the human heart—even as traditional religions and communities used to do in their own way—acquisitiveness, competitiveness, greed, and selfishness will continue to control our world.

In fact, we do have resources enough for everyone. There is no justification for even one death by starvation in today's world, yet one in seven human beings on this planet suffers from malnutrition, and some fifty-three thousand people die of starvation every day, among them one infant every five seconds. More than sufficient resources for all could be available—if only people were at peace in their own hearts and felt bonded to one another. Then people would be content with adequate comforts and modest means. Then the beauty of nature, the inspiration of art and music, and the support of caring companions would fill life's long moments. If, as a baseline, everyone were guaranteed the basics of life, there would be no absolute need for frantic scrambling for advantage. Life could be lived as a gift to celebrate: *l'chaim!* With attention to psychological as well as physical needs, we could easily establish this baseline if we really wanted to.

However, with the guarantee of the basics of life, the counterargument goes, people would lose all motivation; there would be no reason to push forward. Well, I have yet to be convinced that all our pushing has gained us any real human advantage. The past technologically dominated century has seen more war and more collective human suffering than any prior era. The opulence of our society in certain quarters has not produced deeply felt happiness or personal fulfillment. Competitive striving for meaningless baubles gets the human race nowhere.

Besides, that counterargument presumes that people are basically lazy. It forgets that such supposed laziness may be related to the superficiality of contemporary society. Why work long hours when, as the inane system currents runs, you and your children might be better off on public assistance than in working a minimum wage full-time job? Why struggle to get ahead when getting ahead in our society is so paper-thin a reward? As social critic Urvashi Vaid phrased the matter, why wear yourself out at a job making things nobody else really needs so that you can have money to buy other things you don't really need? Things don't fill the longing of the human heart. Rather, by destroying family and community, the pursuit of things stokes that longing.

If the human spirit is truly a dynamic force within us, far from being lazy we are built to reach out and move forward. As Abraham Maslow argued in proposing his famous hierarchy of human needs, when hunger, safety, and belongingness are satisfied, people attend to higher needs; they soon begin to "self-actualize." Psychologically healthy people freed from the oppressive requirements of sheer survival are likely to turn their attention to truly substantive matters—art, music, philosophy, science, literature, fellowship. These would more than make up for that feared loss of productivity in competitive, materialistic pursuits. True happiness would outweigh the "loss" of consumer society's trinkets.

As is obvious from this point-counterpoint discussion, the spiritualization of secular society would reframe all the questions about societal good. The taken-for-granted starting point of the discussion would be concern for the common good. The commitment in the discussion would be to openness, honesty, and goodwill. Then the counterarguments would have no ground on which to stand. They would make no sense—even as our crazy-making society even today makes no sense to visitors from traditional societies.

The accumulation of wealth in capitalistic society ultimately serves neither the rich nor the poor. All are impoverished when the requirements of the human spirit are neglected. And these requirements, with their demanding psychological prerequisites, cannot be met unless the institutions that control society also champion them.

Policies sensitive to the needs of the human spirit could be gradually put into place if only they were an option on the horizon. Thus, I propose a spirituality for our global community. Expanding commitment to this common vision would put politicians' feet to the fire. As individuals and religions increasingly supported such a spiritual agenda, political and business leaders would have to follow suit. A pervasive culture of solid beliefs and high values—including universal prenatal care, nutrition and education for children, and parenting classes for adults—would form an upcoming generation naturally committed to these beliefs and values. Just as religiously bonded communities used to form people of solid character tolerably well even without current psychological awareness, a spiritually bonded secular society could do the same and, today, even better.

In a just and compassionate world there would be no pressing need for defensiveness, violence, and greed. More attention to psychological health—and less to conformist "law and order"—would naturally support inherently rich living.

To a large extent, we now know how to prevent emotional illness and how to heal the psyche; needed is only the will to do so. To a large extent, we now have available a spirituality suited for our global community; needed is only the willingness to implement it. Here Aristotle's observation ominously applies: "What a society honors will be cultivated." Likewise, the words of Pope Paul VI to the United Nations apply: "If you want peace, work for justice."

## CONCLUSION

I propose no utopia. I merely suggest a sane approach to wholesome living. Inequalities, frustrations, suffering and pain, heartaches, sickness, and death, these are unavoidable—not to mention deliberate wrongdoing: corruption, jealousy, greed, crime, hostility, revenge. There is no getting beyond these ultimately. Yet simply to acknowledge this fact—Western religion calls it our "fallen state" and "human sinfulness," and Buddhism speaks of *dukkha*, pervasive suffering—simply to recognize that human heartache is inevitable supports the program I have outlined. To accept human life as it is provides a baseline from which to move on. We will never make life perfect. Of course, we won't! Even worse, some will have to pay an unfair price for the justice and peace we do achieve. At times, those committed to the common good will need to put personal dreams aside and in self-sacrificing love make up for the evildoing of the selfish and the hateful. Such is the lesson of Jesus's dying "to save the world" and the lesson of the Bodhisattva's delaying personal enlightenment until all beings are enlightened. No, we will never have a perfect world. But standing by one another, we can certainly make life easier. With worldwide cooperation and multiple inputs, we can certainly create a better world.

However, agreeing on what *better* means is the crux of the problem, and the definitions of *good, better,* and *best* are a spiritual matter. The approach I have presented in this book addresses this matter head on—apart from diverse religions, varied beliefs in God, or the particularities of different cultures. Grounded in the very makeup of the human being: body, psyche, and spirit, this approach is suited for the pluralistic society that is emerging on a global scale.

This is a balanced view, a middle path. I neither disparage belief in God and religion nor exalt religious doctrines uncritically. I neither damn secular society nor grant it untrammeled reign. Within society and religion both, I merely highlight the spiritual dimension of our human make-up and sanely ask that we respect it under all circumstances, that we be our genuine selves. Authentic humanity—and the fulfillment it promises—is my sufficient plea.

I make my proposal as a suggestion. I will not insist that it is final. If others find this suggestion flawed, let us correct it, refine it, replace it. But let us at least address the challenge before us. Let us not use the complexity of the challenge as an excuse for avoiding it. We cannot go on avoiding this challenge for long. The movement of history is urgent; it will not forgive our indifference. Somehow we must find a way to structure a global community. Apart from such effort, there could well be left no civilized society to restructure.

After his beating by the L.A. police, Rodney King voiced the perennial plea, "Why can't we all just get along?" In some ways, I have been addressing this fearsome question in this book. I believe I have explained something of what it would take to get along. And I believe I have suggested some ways to move toward that realization. I am aware that what I propose is the task religion has addressed for millennia and with discouragingly limited success. In my secular garb, I am still the idealistic priest trying to bring peace and harmony to the human family.

I take on this task, eyes wide open. Why apologize to secular amorality for a good intention? I remember my upbringing, the people from whom I came, the community that they—poor and uneducated—were able to create. I envisage such a community again. But I know that, if it is ever to exist, it must now function on a global scale.

Honestly, I do not expect to be overwhelmingly successful in my task. I do not expect success where giants before me have consistently failed. And surely, there will be no success when pessimistic naysayers and self-serving manipulators concoct unending excuses for inaction.

Still, I do look for some progress. Today we know more about psychology, medicine, economics, and the like than we ever have. We know what makes people tick and societies function. Today we can realistically expect success where prior efforts failed. Hope burns in my heart. I am not asking for much. I would be grateful for the dawning of just a little new light. Ah, yes, my dear reader, I would be content—and my task advanced—if you would only choose to make this task yours, too.

# Index

Abraham, 28, 94
addiction, and self-debilitated
        humanity, 63
advertising, false, and religious
        proselytizing, 141
afterlife, different beliefs about, 33–34
agnosticism, enchanted, 155
alcoholism, 121–122, 127
All, the, vii, 34, 117, 118
Allah, 29, 76, 101
America:
    and restrictions on religious
        expression,
        141;divisions in, 7–8, 10
American experiment, 10
Amini, Fari, 163
Amish, 103
angels(s)
    and spirit, 43;
    and trust in providence, 103;
    biblical notion of, 106;
    pure spirits, 127;
    symbolic image, 133
anger, in the child, 126
anxiety, and communal support, 35
Aquarius, Age of, 23
Aquinas, Thomas. *See* Thomas Aquinas
archetypes:

and Jung, 131;
anima and animus, 131;
defined, 131;
good and evil, 133–134;
persona and shadow, 132;
structure of the psyche, 131
Aristotle:
    and Plato, 49, 113;
    and social values, 165;
    and wonder, 56
Armstrong, Karen, 27
Army, U.S., and hypermasculinity, 132
atheism:
    ambiguous meaning of, 30–31, 77;
    and critique of beliefs about God,
        77;
    and honest theism, xiv, 30, 80, 91,
        98, 103.
    *See also* theism
atman, 22, 111–112, 115
Augustine of Hippo, Saint, 107;
    and human participation in the
        divine mind, 110
Aum Shinrikyo, 28, 75
Aumism, 28
authenticity, human:
    and responsibility, 144;
    definition of, 71;

# About the Author

Daniel Helminiak was born and raised—with an older sister, a younger brother, and a massive extended family—in Pittsburgh, Pennsylvania. Studying at the Pontifical Gregorian University, he was ordained a Catholic priest in Rome and ministered for four years in a suburban Pittsburgh parish. Preparing for an educational ministry, he received a Ph.D. in systematic theology at Andover Newton Theological School and Boston College, where he was teaching assistant to Prof. Bernard Lonergan, SJ, the "Thomas Aquinas of the twentieth century." Daniel taught theology and spirituality at Oblate School of Theology in San Antonio, and pursing his interest in spirituality, completed a Ph.D. in human development at The University of Texas at Austin. Currently, as Professor in the Department of (humanistic and transpersonal) Psychology at the University of West Georgia, near Atlanta, where he lives, he teaches spirituality, human sexuality, neuroscience, and statistics. He is a Fellow of the American Association of Pastoral Counselors and is licensed as a Professional Counselor in Georgia.

As a social scientist, theologian, and psychotherapist, Daniel is concerned to integrate religion and psychology and, thus, to suggest what wholesome human living means in a pluralistic and secularized world. Said otherwise, his specialization is spirituality. Most widely known for the best seller *What the Bible* Really *Says about Homosexuality* (1994, 2000), in addition to scores of technical and popular articles, he has also published *The Same Jesus: A Contemporary Christology* (1986), *Spiritual Development* (1987), *The Human Core of Spirituality* (1996), *Religion and the Human Sciences* (1998), *Meditation without Myth* (2005), *Sex and the Sacred* (2006), and *The Transcended Christian* (2007). He lectures internationally on these topics. Daniel is on the Web at www.visionsofdaniel.net.